No Place Like Home

DIARIES AND LETTERS OF NOVA SCOTIA WOMEN 1771-1938

No Place Like Home

DIARIES AND LETTERS OF NOVA SCOTIA WOMEN 1771-1938

Margaret Conrad, Toni Laidlaw
and Donna Smyth

Formac Publishing Company Limited
1988

Cover art by: Peg Fraser, Applecross Designs

Canadian Cataloguing in PublicationData

No Place Like Home

Main Enty under title:

ISBN 0-88780-066-1

1. Women — Nova Scotia — Diaries. I. Conrad, Margaret.
II. Laidlaw, Toni III. Smyth, Donna

HQ1459.N6N66 1988   305.4'09715   C88-098617-4

Published with the assistance of the Nova Scotia Department of Tourism and Culture

Formac Publishing Company Limited
5502 Atlantic Street
Halifax, Nova Scotia
B3H 1G4

Printed and bound in Canada

CONTENTS

ACKNOWLEDGEMENTS

Those who helped us acquire and interpret the diaries are acknowledged in the text. In addition, we would like to thank the archivists who took time to track down material and answer our queries: Patricia Townsend, Acadia University Archives; Robert Morgan, Beaton Institute, University College of Cape Breton; Charles Armour, Dalhousie University Archives; Margaret Murphy, Legislative Library; Allan Dunlop, Public Archives of Nova Scotia; Helen Hall and Eric Ruff, Yarmouth County Museum. Barbara James and Georgina Chambers offered valuable assistance in the earlier stages of the project and Gillian Thomas proved an indefatigable sleuth in tracking down obscure references during the many years in which we lived with our "recording angels." Alison Prentice, Lorraine McMullen, Eric Hanley and Barry Moody read the entire manuscript at various stages and offered encouragement as well as helpful suggestions. The monumental task of transcribing the diaries — often from wretched script — and entering our manuscript on disks — which had to be done twice, such were the vagaries of computer technology in the 1980s — was shared by three treasured experts: Joy Cavazzi, Eileen Dale and Elizabeth Grigg. We are particularly grateful to Elizabeth Jones and Lynn MacGregor who saw the manuscript through its final stages at Formac.

The costs associated with the project were covered by a grant from the Canadian Research Institute for the Advancement of Women which came to our aid when the Social Sciences and Humanities Research Council turned down our application for funds. Dalhousie and Acadia universities were generous in both the use of their facilities and in providing research grants from various sources, including the Small Universities Fund provided by the SSHRCC.

Margaret Conrad
Toni Laidlaw
Donna Smyth

INTRODUCTION

In 1980, Toni Laidlaw, with the help of several of her graduate students, began collecting evidence relating to the past and present experience of women in the Maritime Provinces of Canada. It soon became apparent that there was a rich untapped source of women's diaries and autobiographical letters chronicling the lives of Maritime women since the mid-eighteenth century. Toni subsequently applied for funding from her university to defray the mounting costs of collecting and transcribing the documents that she found. As the material expanded, Donna Smyth and Margaret Conrad were drawn into the project. Dalhousie and Acadia universities and the Canadian Research Institute for the Advancement of Women were generous in their support. The result of these endeavours is a collection of over one hundred life stories of Maritime women.

Maritime chroniclers were initially an elusive group. It was not unusual in archival collections to find women's papers filed under the name of the male head of the household. When women's papers were included, archival inventories often dismissed them as trivial. Even in cases where families had privately treasured and carefully preserved the writings of their womenfolk, they were frequently surprised that we were interested in this material rather than that of paternal ancestors. This response is a telling comment on the traditional focus of history and what our society considers important to remember about the past.

The perspective that we bring to our material is a feminist one, prompting us to give primary emphasis to the experience of women as they themselves describe it. Given the fact that women's lives have long been obscured by the silence surrounding the so-called private sphere, there is a certain appropriateness in having personal chronicles become the public record. Of course, there are also risks in letting the documents speak for themselves, the most obvious of which is the possibility of losing the reader in a wash of words originally written without thought for style or context. We have decided to take that risk, confident that the rhythm of women's life chronicles have a coherence and compelling quality all of their own. The diaries, where women talk to themselves, describe the detail of daily life, with all its repetition, disorder and incompleteness. The letters, where women talk to each other, reiterate the daily routines of women's lives. It is these routines which become the centre of the story, while the time lapses, events half-told and unidentifiable friends and relatives become less significant, though still intriguing, aspects of the narrative.*

For the purpose of this volume, we have narrowed our Maritime Provinces focus to include only the writing of Nova Scotia women. Even then, the task of selection has not been an easy one. Not only have we collected a large quantity of material from both public archives and private sources, but also that material varies considerably in human and historical interest and readable quality. We have tried to select chronicles in which the woman's story is told in her own unique voice, thus allowing editorial intrusion to be kept to a minimum. We have also endeavoured to preserve the sense and substance of the social context in which the individual narrative is embedded. For this reason, we have chosen to publish long excerpts which convey something of the texture of women's daily lives. Ultimately, we have selected fifteen manuscripts which we feel are the most

---

* Women's personal chronicles, in the words of Dale Spender, "constitute an exciting, expanding — and illuminating — era of women's studies." ("Journal on a Journal," *Women's Studies International Forum*, Vol. 10, No. 1 (1987), p. 1.) Our approach to women's autobiographical writing paralleled that of pioneers in the field, including Estelle Jelinek, ed., *Women's Autobiography: Essays in Criticism* (Bloomington, 1980) and *Her Self: Women's Autobiography from Antiquity to the Present* (Boston, 1986) and Margo Culley, ed., *A Day at a Time: The Diary Literature of American Women from 1764 to the Present* (New York, 1983). See Margaret Conrad, "Recording Angels: The Private Chronicles of Women from the Maritime Provinces of Canada, 1750-1950," CRIAW Paper #4 (Ottawa, 1983), revised and reprinted in *The Neglected Majority*, Vol. 2, ed. Alison Prentice and Susan Mann Trofimenkoff (Toronto, 1985), pp. 41-60.

original and the most revealing about a certain time, place, class or culture.

We make no claims to provincial comprehensiveness in this collection. The focus on written material has eliminated Nova Scotia women who could neither read nor write or whose private chronicles have not survived the ravages of time and poverty. We have, for instance, no records from Indian, Black or Acadian women in the province. At the present time, these cultural groups within Nova Scotia are in the act of retrieving their own history just as we are recovering ours. Indeed, our documents do not even represent the full spectrum of literate white, English-speaking Nova Scotia women. The vast majority of women who "found some consolation in scribbling" came from evangelical backgrounds — Quaker, Lutheran, Baptist, Methodist — where introspection was encouraged for both women and men. "Women on the move" — to new jobs, new places, and so encountering new attitudes and ways of life — were more likely to chronicle their experiences than those who stayed in familiar surroundings.

Although literacy, religion and mobility tend to bias our documents towards middle-class women of evangelical backgrounds, the variety of women's experience is the most obvious feature of our collection. Most Nova Scotia women who tell their stories are working women: missionaries, teachers, office workers, farmers, housekeepers and factory workers. We have women who went to sea with their sea-captain husbands and women who managed the household while waiting for their husbands to return from distant places. We have single women, wives, sisters, mothers and grandmothers. Our evidence would discourage any discussion of a quintessential Nova Scotian woman — or even Nova Scotian woman diarist — for any part of the period covered by these documents.

The history found in these documents does not describe events as they are usually presented in textbooks. Diaries and personal letters turn traditional history inside out. Instead of forming a backdrop to 'great events,' ordinary lives here occupy centre stage. So-called 'important events' are reduced to rumours and abstractions. Wars, revolutions, depressions and elections are sometimes mentioned but are rarely described as directly related to the lives of our chroniclers. In some ways, what we have in these documents is history as it is experienced by most men and women. Yet, there is a particular female eye through which events are viewed and which suggests that women's position in society, their roles and their values in the period chronicled here, give them a unique angle of vision and common preoccupations. This fact was brought home to us when we encountered diaries whose authors could not initially be identified. Most anonymous diarists described the climate, farmyard activities, commercial transactions, community events, even important international happenings. However, with rare exceptions, only women paid attention to what happened inside the house. When details of food preparation, housecleaning and family relationships were included in the daily narrative, we were safe in assuming that "anonymous" was a woman.

We have left our own commentary on the documents to the end of the book. The reader will therefore hear women speak for themselves before we present our analysis of the material. The fifteen diaries are separated into groups of five, representing three distinct periods in the history of Nova Scotia women. Our "gentlewomen" establish the pre-industrial rhythm of women's lives; the "comers and goers" document the forces influencing women's choices during the transition to industrialism; and the "new women" reveal aspects of women's culture in the twentieth century. Each entry is prefaced by a brief introduction and followed by an epilogue explaining, where possible, how the woman's story ended. To the extent that it is feasible, we have rendered the documents in their original form with the grammar and punctuation unchanged, except where meaning is obscured, in which case the correct spelling is provided in brackets. Periods and capitals have been added only when necessary for comprehension and consistency. Any omissions from a diary entry have been acknowledged by ellipses. For the benefit of those who are not familiar with Nova Scotia and its history, we have provided an introductory essay describing the broad outlines of major 'historical' developments and the experience of women generally in the province. Finally, an "Afterword" explains how we as researchers found meaning in the chronicles we chose to publish. Our interpretation, of course, is only that — an interpretation — and we hope that readers will bring their own experience to bear on the words of these Nova Scotia chroniclers.

A NOVA SCOTIA HERITAGE

In 1771 when Anna Green Winslow in Boston sat down to write a journal for her parents back in Cumberland Township, Nova Scotia was poised precariously between its European heritage and North American destiny. Although the frontier colony remained under British control after the American Revolution, it was profoundly influenced by forces emanating from the new United States of America. Indeed, a kind of double colonization characterized the sea-bound province which looked Janus-like toward both European and North American centres of gravity. Waves of immigrants from both of these centres migrated to the colony in the seventeenth and eighteenth centuries. Unlike many of the North American frontiers of European settlement, Nova Scotia did not attract a large population of single males to exploit a resource frontier of fur, fish and timber. Instead, it was settled by successive waves of pre-industrial families, who by a combination of subsistence production and commercial exchange sought to better their material condition. According to the 1767 census, 44% of the colony's population, estimated at a tiny 11,779, consisted of women. By the middle of the nineteenth century the numbers of men and women in a population of over 275,000 were virtually equal.*

The ethnic mix of Nova Scotians in 1851 testified to the complex forces set in motion during the preceding three centuries of North Atlantic migrations. Only slightly over 1,000 Micmac survived as a reminder of the fact that the colony's original inhabitants were Amerindians. Another 10 percent of the population were Acadians, the descendants of settlers of primarily

* Census of Canada, 1665 to 1871, *Statistics of Canada, 1871*, Vol. IV (Ottawa: 1876).

French origin, who came to Acadia in the seventeenth century. Though Acadian families tried to steer a neutral course in the rivalry for control over North America, the British, who held peninsular Nova Scotia after 1713, could never forget that their conquered subjects were a potential 'fifth column' for the French based as near as Louisbourg on Ile Royale (Cape Breton). Imperial policy proved as brutal as it was efficient. Beginning in 1755 the Acadians, numbering over 10,000, were placed on prison ships and scattered along the English colonies of the Atlantic seaboard. After the Seven Years' War (1756-1763) in which the British were victorious, hundreds of refugee Acadians returned to 'Acadie' only to find their farms already occupied. Over 8,000 New England Planters, Yankee families looking for land and ready access to the rich inshore fisheries, had begun moving into western Nova Scotia, following the capture of Louisbourg in 1758. They were soon joined by smaller numbers of Yorkshire English and Ulster Irish who were also attracted by the prospect of available land in a British colony. Thus, the Acadians who made the long trek back to their homeland could not return to their original farms. Instead, they were given grants primarily in southwestern Nova Scotia and on Cape Breton Island. They shared with the German and French-speaking Protestants of Lunenburg and Halifax, recruited from the German states between 1750 and 1753, the distinction of being the largest minorities of non-British origin in Nova Scotia.*

Given the predominantly Yankee roots of Nova Scotia's 20,000 people in 1776, the colony could easily have become the fourteenth state in the newly declared independent United States of America. But this was not to be the case. Geographical factors, the presence of a strong British naval and military base at Halifax and the careful neutrality of most inhabitants combined to keep Nova Scotia within the British Empire. The colony therefore became the destination of some 30,000 American Loyalists, who were forced, or who chose, to leave the United States

* W.S. MacNutt, *The Atlantic Provinces: The Emergence of Colonial Society, 1712-1857* (Toronto, 1965); Naomi Griffiths, *The Acadians: Creation of a People* (Toronto 1973); Jean Diagle, ed., *The Acadians of the Maritimes* (Moncton, 1982); Esther Clark Wright, *Planters and Pioneers* (Windsor, 1978); Winthrop Bell, *The Foreign Protestants and the Settlement of Nova Scotia* (Toronto, 1961).

during and after the revolutionary war. To accommodate their loyal subjects, the British government divided the old colony of Nova Scotia into three parts. In 1784 New Brunswick and Cape Breton became separate colonies, with capitals at Fredericton and Sydney respectively.

The urban origins of many of the Loyalists caused them to cast rather jaundiced eyes at the rough frontier colony in which destiny had dumped them. A high portion of the Loyalists left 'Nova Scarcity' for more promising prospects elsewhere. Many went to the new colony of New Brunswick; others saw greener pastures in Britain. Still others returned to the United States, once the memory of the hated 'Royalists' had time to fade. Black refugees, both slave and free, made up nearly 10 per cent of the Loyalist migration. They found themselves the objects of discrimination from Nova Scotia authorities and fellow immigrants. Not surprisingly, most of the free Black immigrants seized the opportunity in the 1790s to move to the African haven of Sierra Leone. The majority of the over 5,000 Black people recorded in the 1851 Nova Scotia census were members of families who opted to stay in the colony after slavery was abolished at the beginning of the century, or were more recent immigrants, many of whom had won their freedom by fighting for Britain against the United States in the War of 1812.*

In the eighteenth century Nova Scotia was primarily an extension of the North American settlement frontier. In the nineteenth century it was on the front line for thousands of British immigrants who sought to escape the overcrowding, poverty and famine associated with a rapidly industrializing imperial power. Between 1773 and 1860 the eastern end of the Nova Scotia peninsula and the island of Cape Breton (which was again added to Nova Scotia's jurisdiction in 1820) absorbed successive waves of Scottish immigrants, both Highlanders and

---

* James W. St. C. Walker, *The Black Loyalists: The Search for a Promised Land in Nova Scotia and Sierra Leone* (New York, 1976); Robin Winks, *The Blacks in Canada: A History* (New Haven, 1971); Marion Gilroy, *Loyalists and Land Settlement in Nova Scotia* (Halifax, 1937).

Lowlanders. By mid-century, the Scots were the largest ethnic group in Nova Scotia, which at last had a population befitting its seventeenth century name.* Another group seeking a Nova Scotia home were the Irish, who began arriving in significant numbers with the founding of Halifax in 1749. Their presence became more marked after the Napoleonic Wars which ended in 1815, and, in particular, after the Great Famine of the 1840s. Halifax remained the destination of many Irish but the sons and daughters of Erin could be found all over the colony where they moved in their quest for what little empty space was left in an already well-populated colony.**

By 1861 over 90 per cent of the Nova Scotia population was native born, an indication for a pre-industrial colony that the filling-up period had come to an end and that population growth thereafter would come from 'natural increase.' Since half of the people were under 21 years of age in 1861, the potential for growth seemed excellent. Opportunity beckoned everywhere. Located like a great wharf jutting into the Atlantic, Nova Scotia was well situated to play a leading role in the North Atlantic trade network dominated by Britain and the United States. The products of farm, fisheries, forests and mines were in demand all over the world and Nova Scotians were prepared to sail wherever they were called. So international was Nova Scotia's economic outlook in the 1860s that many of its leading citizens were less than enthusiastic about the Confederation of the British North American provinces in 1867. Die-hard anti-Confederates were convinced that the 'scheme' had been perpetrated especially to destroy their prosperity by un-scrupulous provincial politicians, devious 'Upper Canadians' and an unfeeling 'Mother Country.'***

As well as possessing a young population, and a fiercely in-dependent outlook, Nova Scotia at mid-century was a radically

* D. Campbell and R. A. MacLean, *Beyond the Atlantic Roar: A Study of the Nova Scotia Scots* (Toronto, 1975); J. M. Bumsted, "Scottish Emigration to the Maritimes, 1770-1815: A New Look at an Old Theme," *Acadiensis*, Vol. X, No. 2 (Spring, 1981), pp. 65-85.

** Nova Scotia Census, 1861, in *Statistics of Canada, 1871*, Vol. IV, Table III, p. 346.

*** Kenneth Pryke, *Nova Scotia and Confederation,1854-1874* (Toronto, 1979); G. A. Rawlyk, *The Atlantic Provinces and the Problems of Confederation* (St. John's, 1979).

Protestant colony. Nearly 60 per cent of the population professed to being Presbyterian, Baptist, Methodist, Congregational or Lutheran. The Anglican Church, which had made a feeble attempt to become the leading church in the colony, claimed the adherence of less than 15 per cent of Nova Scotians. Slightly more than a quarter of the people — mostly Acadians, Irish or Scots — were Roman Catholics. Since the 1820s, Catholics no longer experienced discriminating laws barring them from full civil rights. Ironically, only women faced a narrowing of their voting privileges in the 'responsibly' governed colony as legislators set out specifically to exclude women from the franchise in 1851.*

Nova Scotia women left no private record of how they felt or even if they were aware of their shrinking political sphere. Given the centrality of the family in pre-industrial societies and the distrust of state intervention, especially among those of evangelical persuasion, the urgency of a female franchise may not have been obvious. Certainly very few women had ever exercised their theoretical right to vote even if they had possessed the requisite property qualifications. Yet the disenfranchisement of women in a period when democracy was a key word on every politician's lips was one of many clues to the enormous changes that would take place in women's lives over the next one hundred years.

In mid-nineteenth century Nova Scotia, as elsewhere, two functions dominated women's lives: production in the home and reproduction of the next generation. But even in these basic areas, all women did not share the same experiences. Observers noted that German women in Lunenburg County were more likely to be seen working in the fields than were their English counterparts, while census figures tell us that women of Scottish origin married later and therefore had fewer children than other women in the province.** In contrast, Acadian women married early and raised large families. Experiences also

*   John Garner, *The Franchise and Politics in British North America,1755-1867* (Toronto, 1969), pp. 155-56.
**   Lorne Tepperman, "Ethnic Variations in Marriage and Fertility: Canada, 1871," *Canadian Review of Anthropology and Sociology*, Vol. 11, No. 4 (November 1974), pp. 324-43; Mather Byles DesBrisay, *History of the County of Lunenburg* (Toronto, 1895), pp. 356, 361.

differed according to class. Upper class women, for example, usually had servants to help them with household chores while women in subsistence farming and fishing villages often had only older daughters or an unmarried sister to help around the house. Those facing real poverty frequently had to hire themselves and their children out simply to survive. The plight of Indian and Black women in Nova Scotia was often particularly difficult. Pushed to the margins of a society which was racist as well as sexist in its values, these women were resourceful in making a living for their families. By the mid-nineteenth century Micmac women were renowned for their quillwork crafts while Black women could be found at the Halifax market where they sold brooms, baskets and other items of home manufacture.*

Despite these important differences in women's circumstances, the quality of productive and reproductive life for all women was about to undergo a dramatic transformation. We can guage the extent of the change by comparing the evidence of our later chroniclers with a description of women's work in the Yankee settlements of the Annapolis Valley, published by two English male observers in 1774.

> The women are industrious housewives, and spin the flax, the growth of their own farms and weave both their linen and woolen cloth; they also bleach their linen and dye their yarns themselves. Though they will not disdain to work out of doors, either in time of hay or harvest, yet they are exceedingly diligent in every domestic employment. The candles, soap and starch, which are used in their families, are of their own manufacturing. They also make their own yeast, and make a kind of liquor, by boiling the branches of the spruce tree, to which they add molasses and cause it to ferment in the manner we do treacle beer in England.**

By the mid-nineteenth century the availability of manufactured cloth and a wide variety of store-bought commodities had

---

*   Ruth Holmes Whitehead, *Micmac Quillwork* (Halifax, 1982); Mrs. William Lawson, *History of the Township of Dartmouth, Preston and Lawrencetown, Halifax County, Nova Scotia* (Halifax 1893), pp. 188-89.

**   John Robinson and Thomas Ripsin, *Journey Through Nova Scotia ....* (York, 1774), reprinted in the *Report of the Public Archives of Nova Scotia, 1944-45* (Halifax, 1945).

reduced the tasks of middle-class women considerably and by the beginning of the twentieth century the more affluent homes had sewing and washing machines to ease the drudgery of women's work. Such luxuries by the end of the century became the dream of all women who leafed through the pages of the Eaton's catalogues that were delivered to rural homes by the increasingly efficient postal system. The goal of owning these labour-saving devices might even be sufficient inducement for a woman to prolong the period she spent in the paid labour force or prompt her to raise a few extra chickens and churn more butter for a commercial market.

Nova Scotia women in the nineteenth century were also experiencing profound changes in their legal status. Although many of the new laws were as much a result of examples set in Britain as they were of local initiative, Nova Scotia women did not lag behind their Canadian sisters in their legal rights. A relatively progressive divorce law was adopted in 1857 and in 1884 the provincial legislature passed the Married Women's Property Act, which gave married women the right to own and control property, to sign contracts and to be legally liable on the same basis as single women and all men. Before the passage of this act, married women were considered mere extensions of their husbands, without status in the eyes of the law. Similar patriarchal views gave fathers in Nova Scotia the custody of children in case of separation or divorce until 1893. In that year the provincial legislature passed a Child Custody Act which authorized the court to award custody to mothers of children up to the age of majority if "the welfare of the infants, the conduct or circumstances of the parents, and the wishes of the mother as well as of the father warranted it."*

Another area where the status of women was being profoundly transformed was the socialization of children. In the eighteenth century most rural children received at best a few rudiments of reading, writing and ciphering; otherwise, both

* Susan Perley, *Women and the Law in Nova Scotia* (Middleton, 1976), pp. 7, 14; Constance Backhouse, "'Pure Patriarchy': Nineteenth Century Canadian Marriage," *McGill Law Journal*, 31 (March 1986); Constance Backhouse, "Shifting Patterns in Nineteenth Century Canadian Custody Law," in *Essays in the History of Canadian Law*, Vol. I, ed., David H. Flaherty (Toronto, 1981), pp. 212-48.

boys and girls were apprenticed for adult life on the family farm and might work for kin or neighbour before setting up their own households. Occasionally, women taught neighbourhood children in their homes. After the passage of public school legislation in the 1860s the role of mothers as educators in the home was diminished and sometimes directly undermined. Though women often served as teachers in the poorly-funded school system — many of our diarists taught school at some point in their lives — their power was limited by the hierarchical system in which they functioned and was often directly related to the number of youthful citizens under their care.*

In the nineteenth century women also had smaller families than were common a century earlier. Figures for Canada as a whole indicate that the fertility of women in the eighteenth century was 8.4; of women born in 1825, 7.8; in 1845, 6.3; in 1867, 4.8; and in 1909, 3.11. Although fertility remained high among certain groups, on a province-wide basis, Nova Scotia had the lowest fertility (3.91) of any province in Canada in 1871. The end of immigration, the low fertility of women of Scottish backgrounds and perhaps the already obvious trend of outmigration of Nova Scotia's young people combined to reduce the size of the average family. By the turn of the century a rapidly industrializing Ontario had a lower birth rate than Nova Scotia, which since 1931 has maintained a birth rate equal to or above the Canadian average. **

The extent to which Nova Scotia women resorted to abortion or artificial methods of birth control to regulate family size is difficult to determine. In 1892 the Canadian government declared contraceptives and abortifacients illegal, thereby shrouding sexual practices in a cloud of secrecy and fear.*** To

---

* Alison Prentice, "The Feminization of Teaching" in *The Neglected Majority*, ed., Susan Mann Trofimenkoff and Alison Prentice (Toronto, 1977), pp. 49-65.

** Jacques Henripin, *Trends and Factors of Fertility in Canada* (Ottawa, 1972), pp. 336-37; Roderic P. Beaujot and Kevin McQuillan, "The Social Effects of Demographic Change: 1851-1981," *Journal of Canadian Studies*, Vol. 21, No. 1(Spring 1986), pp. 57-69; Tepperman, "Ethnic Variations in Marriage and Fertility: Canada,1871," pp. 324-343.

*** Angus McLaren and Arlene Tigar McLaren, *The Bedroom and the State: The Changing Practices and Politics of Contraception and Abortion in Canada, 1880-1980* (Toronto, 1986).

some extent late marriages served as a form of birth control as did prevailing views of the time that sexual activity was fundamentally debilitating. Contrary to commonly held beliefs, women in the last century did not marry earlier than they do today. Though some women married at a young age, the average age of marriage for women in Nova Scotia in 1871 was over 25 years, and varied from a low of under 24 in the western Nova Scotia counties of Lunenburg, Shelburne, Annapolis and Kings to a high of over 28 in the Scottish settled counties of Antigonish and Victoria. In comparison, the average age of marriage for Nova Scotia women since the Second World War has been under 25 and the ethnic variations have narrowed considerably.*

New directions in women's production, reproduction and control over their sexuality were accompanied by reduced infant mortality and death due to childbirth. Though the figures are not available for Nova Scotia, infant mortality generally in colonial British North American in 1851 was 184.1 per 1,000. In other words, nearly one in five children died in infancy. A century later, Nova Scotia's infant mortality rate had declined to less than 40 per thousand, slightly lower than the Canadian average.** Similarly, the likelihood of experiencing death in childbirth diminished for women in the twentieth century as complications due to infections and difficult births were reduced by the trend to smaller families and improved medical practices. The same factors account for the increased life expectancy of Canadian women which rose from 42 years in 1851 to 70 years a century later. The significance of the trend to smaller families and longer life cannot be over-estimated. In the twentieth century motherhood no longer dominated a woman's whole adult life; and marriage, once the only means by which women could reach their productive potential, was now only one of several options open to women.

---

* Douglas F. Campbell and David C. Neice, *Ties that Bind — Structure and Marriage in Nova Scotia* (Port Credit, 1979), pp. 41, 43; Ellen M. Gee, "Marriage in Nineteenth-century Canada," *Canadian Review of Sociology and Anthropology*, Vol, 19, No. 3 (1982), pp. 311-25.

** Beaujot and McQuillan, "The Social Effects of Demographic Change: Canada 1851 - 1981," Table I, p. 59; Daniel Kubat and David Thornton, *A Statistical Profile of Canadian Society* (Toronto, 1974), p. 52.

The tendency to the single life and later marriages among Nova Scotia women and the attractiveness of urban employment to women in their late teens and early twenties became the subjects of public concern by the end of the nineteenth century. Even the Dominion Statistician, George Johnson, remarked in 1891 on the decrease in family size in the Maritime Provinces, attributing it to "the spread of education which enables females to become better wage earners and therefore less interested in marriage."* What Mr. Johnson failed to note was that women's role within the family had become so circumscribed that elder daughters were among the first to leave home to find employment in the very jobs women had hitherto performed in the home: keeping house, teaching children and producing food and clothing. Of course, single women had long found urban centres more congenial than rural areas for earning a living. As early as 1851 the Halifax census recorded a 'surplus' of women. The provincial capital was particularly attractive to spinsters and widows who survived by keeping boarders, operating retail outlets, teaching school and performing various domestic services.

Although Nova Scotia industrialized relatively quickly in the second half of the nineteenth century, much of the new activity was in heavy industry associated with the development of the province's coal resources in north-eastern Nova Scotia and Cape Breton. Job opportunities for women were better in the United States, particularly in Massachusetts, the cradle of industrialization in North America. Thomas Chandler Haliburton, as early as 1849, described this annual spring scene in a province of "comers and goers":

> Loud and hearty cheers, from the noisy throng on the quay, announce that a vessel with the colonial symbol of Spring — a spruce bough at her foretop — has just cast anchor, the first comer, and that another had just hauled into the stream, and the first goer of the season.

* Cited in Alan A. Brookes, "The Golden Age and The Exodus: The Case of Canning, Kings County," *Acadiensis*, Vol.XI, No.1 (Autumn 1981), p. 67.

Apart from this assemblage is a group of comers: many kind words and benedictions are heard, many tears shed, and loving embraces exchanged in this sad and surrounding circle. It is a leave-taking of friends and relations, of some mature females, who are about to seek their fortune in the great republic, where they are to cease being servants, and become factory ladies, and where they will commence their career by being helpers, and hope to terminate it by becoming helpmates.*

It has been estimated that a quarter of a million people, or nearly one in three adults, left the Maritime region in the period between 1860 and 1900; and the exodus continued until the Depression of the 1930s closed the border to job-seeking Canadians.** Nova Scotia women left the province in equal or slightly larger numbers than did men but their migration patterns differed. Men were attracted to frontiers of opportunity throughout North America. Women, especially young, unmarried women, focused their attention on the urban centres of the eastern seaboard. There they found work as domestics, clerks and factory workers and later flooded the emerging female professions of teaching, nursing and office work. One early twentieth-century American observer, Albert Kennedy, remarked that the nursing profession in Massachusetts was dominated by women from "the Provinces" and that "provincial" women were in demand as domestics and clerks. He described them as, on the whole, a superior lot, "physically sturdy, mentally alert and do exceedingly well in their professions." He, too, noted the trend toward the single life:

An appreciable proportion of these women remain in industry permanently. Their incomes are equal or better than those of men whom they know, and they refuse to exchange single competence for the double poverty that must result in marriage. For this rea-

---

* Thomas Chandler Haliburton, *The Old Judge, or, Life in a Colony* (1849; reprint Ottawa, 1978), pp. 304-5.
** Alan A. Brookes, "Out-migration from the Maritime Provinces, 1860-1900: Some Preliminary Considerations," *Acadiensis*, Vol. V, No. 2 (Spring 1976), pp. 26-56; Patricia A. Thornton, "The Problem of Out Migration from Atlantic Canada, 1871-1921: A New Look," *Acadiensis*, Vol. XV, No. 1 (Autumn 1985), pp. 3-34.

son many never marry at all, but live out their lives in single-
ness*....

Kennedy's statement notwithstanding, the majority of Nova
Scotia women eventually opted for marriage, simply extending
the traditional waiting period between schooling and marriage
to accumulate a little money and to contribute to the still largely
subsistence households 'back home.' Most of the migrant
women decided to stay in the United States, often finding Nova
Scotia husbands more easily in exile than in their homeland.
Others worked for a few years and then, like Hannah Richardson in this volume, returned home to childhood sweethearts.
Still others came back to arranged marriages with distant cousins who had inherited a family farm or to take care of aged
parents who refused to give up their patrimony in Nova Scotia
in order to live out their last days in 'the land of hope and glory.'

It is impossible to discuss Nova Scotia women and their
society in the nineteenth century without discussing the colos-
sal influence of the sea. The pre-eminence of provincial fleets in
the world-wide carrying trade meant that the lives of most
people in the coastal towns were defined by the ocean trades. In
addition, many Nova Scotians gained their livelihood primarily
from the fisheries. The sea was a difficult reality for Nova Scotia women. It carried their men away from home for long
periods of time and sometimes forever. Areas dependent upon
the sea often had a surplus of women in successive censuses,
documenting the savage cruelty of the seafaring trades. Most
women did not go to sea. Indeed, in some ports the prevailing
superstition held that pigs and women on a boat were bad
luck.** Nevertheless, the female relatives of sea captains often
accompanied their husbands and fathers on voyages that took
them all over the world. A few women even worked as deck
hands.*** In many cases, women travelled in dank, cramped ca-
bins, swabbed the decks and longed for the day when their ships

---

*   Albert J. Kennedy, "The Provincials," with an Introduction by Alan A.
     Brookes, *Acadiensis*, Vol. IV, No. 2 (Spring 1975), p. 94.
**   Helen Creighton, *Folklore of Lunenburg County, Nova Scotia* (Toronto,
     1976), pp. 15-16.
*** Judith Fingard, *Jack in Port: Sailortowns of Eastern Canada* (Toronto,
     1982), pp. 48, 57-61.

would return home. Other women, especially toward the end of the nineteenth century when vessels became larger, travelled in style with chefs, household pets and a Victorian parlour, equipped with an organ and daintily embroidered samplers.

The continuing domestic responsibilities of *many* women determined the status of *all* women in the late nineteenth century. Women's place, it was argued and many Nova Scotia women agreed, was in the home; only men should earn a 'family wage.' As a result of such views, Nova Scotia women, like women in all industrial societies, experienced discrimination in the workplace.* They were systematically paid lower wages than the men with whom they worked while barriers, both visible and invisible, impeded their advancement to higher paying jobs. The symmetry of the gender-biased industrial order was flawless in its uniformity. In factories, women performed meticulous, repetitive work while men served as bosses and union organizers; in offices, women were hired as secretaries, men as managers; in schools, women taught in the crowded classrooms while men were groomed to be the principals and inspectors; in hospitals women worked as nurses and charwomen, men as doctors and administrators. Given this situation, it is not surprising that women traded their poorly paid jobs for marriage, especially since marriage was the only socially sanctioned institution in which women could bear and raise children.

Single, divorced and widowed women, and the few married women who worked as sole supporters of their families were the first to sense how unfair the system was for women. Wives trapped in violent and unhappy marriages were also aware of the problems posed by their dependent status. When the women's movement swept the western world in the late nineteenth century, it inevitably found support in Nova Scotia. Demands for equal access to work and education, for the right to vote and hold public office, and for recognition of women's

---

* For the larger context see Mary Lynn McDougall, "Working-Class Women During the Industrial Revolution, 1780-1914," and Theresa M. McBride, "The Long Road Home: Women's Work and Industrialization," in Renate Bridenthal and Claudia Koonz, eds., *Becoming Visible: Women in European History* (Boston, 1977) pp. 255-324. In the Canadian context see Alison Prentice *et al, Canadian Women: A History* (Toronto, 1988), pp.113-41.

special needs as mothers and domestic managers challenged the patriarchal foundations of provincial society. Although victories were slow in coming, Nova Scotia women, like their counterparts elsewhere, gradually changed the context of their lives. The forces set in motion at the turn of the century continued to redefine the status of women throughout the twentieth century.

Literacy was an important tool for those women seeking to raise the general level of consciousness concerning women's role and status in society. As early as the 1850s Mary Eliza Herbert, editor and major contributor to the short-lived journal, the *Mayflower*, was writing novels which focused on the "female dilemma."* *Kerchiefs to Hunt Souls*, a novel by Maria Amelia Fytche, published in 1895, addressed the "Woman Question" and advocated education, careers and reformed working conditions for women.** In 1895 Nova Scotia women contributed to a "Woman's Extra" supplement in the Halifax *Herald*. Among the issues raised were higher education for women, civic responsibility and the ubiquitous 'servant problem.'

Even the church, an institution often credited with keeping women in their place, served unwittingly as a vehicle for the ambitions of Nova Scotia women. This was particularly true of the evangelical churches, such as the Baptist and the Methodist, which had a wide following in the province. A glimmer of female discontent can be detected as early as the eighteenth century. The Reverend John Payzant, a Congregationalist preacher, recorded in 1791 that in Cornwallis, Kings County, Lydia Randall publicly denounced the teachings of the church and went on to announce that:

> marriage was from the Divil. That she was determined to live separate from her Husband, for it was as much sin for her to have children by him or any other man and she saith that there [were] many that would follow her in it, that there many young women that were converted, which she had soon see them have children

* "Belles and the Backwoods: Fiction in Nineteenth Century Maritime Periodicals," *Atlantic Provinces Literature Colloquium Papers* (Saint John, 1977), p. 46.
** Carrie MacMillan, "Introduction" to *Kerchiefs to Hunt Souls* (Sackville, 1980), p. xvii.

by an man [than] to Marry ... her new scheme was so right with her that she made her business to propagate it.*

What became of Mrs. Randall and her libertarian views we do not know. Certainly her behaviour was frowned upon by male church leaders. Nevertheless, evangelical pietism appealed especially to women and it was obvious by the second half of the nineteenth century that the evangelical churches were extending in a limited way the rights of women. Drawing upon the New England example, Baptist and Methodist Church 'Fathers' opened the doors of their rural universities to women in the 1870s and 1880s. In so doing, they made Mount Allison University in Sackville, New Brunswick, and Acadia University in Wolfville, Nova Scotia, the first co-educational universities in Canada.** Similarly, Nova Scotia women led the nation in the founding of exclusively female missionary societies designed to sponsor single women in the overseas mission fields.*** This leadership in areas of "evangelical feminism" suggests a particular orientation among Nova Scotia women, whose feminism was defined by their Christian sensibilities.

This evangelical orientation served to encourage middle-class women to become involved in the various reform causes that gained momentum at the end of the nineteenth century. Many women supported the temperance movement which was given strong endorsement by the evangelical churches. In Halifax, Methodist Church women sustained the Jost mission to serve the city's poor.**** Other women, including a few of our diarists, became involved in such secular organizations as the Women's Institute, Victorian Order of Nurses, Red Cross, YWCA, IODE and Local Council of Women. The club move-

* Brian C. Cuthbertson, *The Journal of John Payzant* (Windsor, 1981), p. 44. See also G. A. Rawlyk, *Ravished by the Spirit: Religious Revivals, Baptists and Henry Alline* (Montreal, 1984), Chapter 4.
** Margaret Gillett, *We Walked Very Warily* (Montreal, 1981), pp. 11, 39; John G. Reid, "The Education of Women at Mount Allison, 1854-1914," *Acadiensis*, Vol. XII, No. 2 (Spring 1983), pp. 3-33.
*** Wendy Mitchinson, "Canadian Women and Church Missionary Societies in the Nineteenth Century," *Atlantis*, Vol. 2, No. 2 (Spring, 1977), pp. 57-75; Olive Banks, *The Faces of Feminism* (Oxford, 1981).
**** Ernest R. Forbes, "Prohibition and the Social Gospel in Nova Scotia," *Acadiensis*, Vol. 1, No. 1 (Autumn 1971), pp. 11-36; Christina Simmons, "'Helping the Poorer Sisters': The Women of the Jost Mission, Halifax, 1905-1945," *Acadiensis*, Vol. XVI, No. 1 (Autumn 1984), pp. 3-27.

ment continued unabated after the First World War when women could be found in organizations ranging all the way from various ladies' aid and missionary societies associated with the church to service and professional clubs. It was through such organizations that women were able to express a separate political voice, a voice which became more powerful after women received the vote in Nova Scotia in 1918.

Recent research on the suffrage movement in Nova Scotia has revealed that the province's women were not as quiescent on the issue as it was earlier implied by suffrage historian Catherine Cleverdon.* In 1893 a bill to give Nova Scotia women the vote on the same basis as men passed second reading in the Assembly by two votes. Only a concerted effort on the part of anti-feminist forces prevented its passage into legislation. Thereafter, Nova Scotia suffragists experienced the same problems as other Canadian women in bringing the suffrage campaign to a successful conclusion in 1918. Women's suffrage enthusiasm was temporarily diverted when a disastrous explosion levelled much of the city of Halifax in December 1917. The role of women as crisis managers in this instance was particularly visible since so many of the province's men were fighting the First World War in Europe.

Women's general contribution to the war effort has yet to be fully documented. While a minority of principled women expressed a pacifist opposition to war generally, most women seem to have participated eagerly on the home front and the more adventuresome volunteered for overseas service as nurses and clerical staff. Pictou County native Margaret C. MacDonald was Matron-in-Chief of Canada's Nursing Service during the war. Others, like Bessie Hall in this volume, worked in the Volunteer Army Division whenever their services were needed.

* Catherine Cleverdon, *The Woman Suffrage Movement in Canada* (Toronto 1950). For a critique of Cleverdon's analysis see, Ernest R. Forbes, "In Search of a Post-Confederation Historiography, 1900-1967," *Acadiensis*, Vol. VII, No. 1 (Autumn 1978), pp. 3-21; See also Ernest R. Forbes, "The Ideas of Carol Bacchi and the Suffragists of Halifax," *Atlantis*, Vol. 10, No. 2 (Spring 1985), pp. 119-26; and his unpublished "Edith Archibald and the Feminist Movement in Halifax, Nova Scotia."

Many socially prominent women used their organizational skills gained in the club movement to mobilize women's energies in knitting socks, wrapping bandages and raising money for 'the boys overseas.'*

In 1919 the provincial government, endeavouring perhaps to capture the 'women's vote,' established a Royal Commission to investigate women's working conditions and to recommend on the desirability of implementing mothers' allowances.** A limited women's minimum wage bill was passed the following year but it was not until 1972 that laws were passed to require equal pay for equal work. In 1930 mothers' allowances, for those who met a commission's strict guidelines of eligibility, became available in the province. Federal legislation for universal mothers' allowances was passed in 1944 and universal old age pensions followed in 1951. Although a few women ran for public office, none did so successfully until Gladys Porter won a Kings County riding in 1960.***

While a handful of Nova Scotia women went to sea or to the overseas mission fields and a great many more spent at least a year or two working in the United States, the majority of Nova Scotia women, until the Second World War, lived in rural villages and followed the seasons in their productive labour. But even for these women their world of kin and community was changing, just as their responsibilities and expectations were gradually being altered. Increased literacy, spatial mobility and new family strategies for survival combined to transform the life course of most women by the first half of the twentieth century. Women, who had hitherto gone from their father's home to that of their husband, stretched the time between leaving school and marrying to include a few years of paid labour in a school, shop or office, or in someone else's home. This experience enabled a woman to bring a stronger sense of personal

* M. Stuart Hunt, *Nova Scotia's Part in the Great War* (Halifax, 1920); Mary Tingley, "Women and the War in Wolfville," MA Thesis, Acadia University, 1983.
** *Journals and Proceedings of the House of Assembly of the Province of Nova Scotia*, 1920, Appendix No. 33; 1921, Appendix No. 34.
*** Shirley B. Elliott, ed., *The Legislative Assembly of Nova Scotia, 1758-1983* (Halifax, 1984), pp. 177-78. Bertha Donaldson (Labour, Pictou) and Grace McLeod Rogers (Conservative, Cumberland) ran in the provincial election of 1920, the first Nova Scotia women to do so.

accomplishment as well as a financial contribution to her marriage. It may also have helped her to adjust more easily to the challenge of widowhood. Even if widowhood did not mean poverty, which it often did, it usually meant new responsibilities. Mary MacQuarrie, mother of 12, writing in 1929 had this to say about her life after the death of her husband during the years of the First World War:

> We were left, the younger girls and I, fairly comfortable. However, when the war was over the three girls were married, thus leaving my old mother and me to face the world. The prospect was not very bright in Glace Bay and I had nobody belonging to me there; I sold all my property and bought a home in Sydney, because I had to make a home for my mother while she lived. When she died four years ago I rented my house, sold all my things and started to visit my scattered family. I sometimes wish I had kept my old home, but if I were by myself I wouldn't be able to stand the loneliness after always having a full house, and it would be more than I could bear to have to sit at a lonely table and not have people coming in at night. So here I am at the age of 74, going from place to place. I have been with Ethel in Baltimore, three winters and one summer; and with Flora in Buffalo and Syracuse; and with Alice in Montreal. I hope to be for a while with Flora in Sydney where she is going to live for the next five years.*

Statements such as this make us realize that to see the period between 1850 and 1950 as one where self-sufficient families sheltered women from the forces of change is to fly in the face of evidence, both statistical and qualitative.

All of the women in this volume were born before or soon after the turn of the twentieth century. Each story is unique and perhaps in some way untypical of the general trends for the period. Nevertheless they add flesh and blood to the dry bones of statistical evidence and raise questions about the quality of women's lives in this period that cannot be answered by punching the keys of a computer terminal. Many of our diarists and letter writers would be surprised to find that their daily activities were of interest to modern readers and a few might be horrified to think that their awkward prose was actually com-

---

* Memoir of Mary Killian MacQuarrie, typescript, Beaton Institute, University College of Cape Breton.

mitted to the printed page. We recall the lives of these Nova Scotia women not to pry or even to judge. Rather they serve as a reminder of an earlier era when women's lives were in some ways vastly different from our own, even if the challenges they faced sometimes seem hauntingly familiar.

GENTLEWOMEN

ANNA GREEN WINSLOW

ANNA GREEN
WINSLOW
1759-1779

Anna Green Winslow was born in 1759 in Cumberland. The township straddled the wind-swept Isthmus of Chignecto connecting what is now the province of Nova Scotia to the mainland of North America. Her parents, Anna Green and Joshua Winslow, were members of prominent Boston families and belonged to the Old South Congregational Church. After taking part in the siege of Louisbourg in 1745, Joshua Winslow was appointed commissary general of the British forces in Nova Scotia. In this capacity he participated in the British occupation of the Chignecto area and served at Fort Beausejour after its capture from the French in 1755. The expulsion of the Acadians and the second capture of Louisbourg in 1758 consolidated British control over the Maritime region. Career soldiers such as Joshua Winslow were in a good position to take advantage of Governor Lawrence's generous offer of free land to willing settlers. In January 1758 he married his cousin Anna Green and the couple moved to Cumberland which by the early 1760s was attracting settlers from New England.*

Joshua Winslow played a prominent role in the organization of the new township and briefly served as the area's member in the provincial assembly. At least two of the Winslow's four children were born in Cumberland, Anna Green and her brother John Henry. Education was highly prized among people of the Winslow's class and culture. Young ladies were to be taught the

* W. G. Godfrey, "Joshua Winslow," *Dictionary of Canadian Biography*, Vol. V, 1801-1820.

accomplishments — sewing, dancing and writing — and were also formally initiated into adult social life. Since the rude frontier colony had little in the way of educational institutions or high society, Anna was sent at the age of ten to live with her "Aunt Deming" in Boston. Here she could be properly 'finished' under the watchful eye of Sarah Deming, Joshua Winslow's sister, who earned her living taking in young lady boarders attending some of Boston's many private schools.

Anna's diary, encouraged by her elders as a means of communicating with her parents and as an exercise in penmanship, reveals a spirited, affectionate twelve-year-old girl evolving into a sophisticated young woman. "Aunt says I am a whimsical child," writes Anna who confessed to being subject to "egregious fits of laughterre." At the same time she was learning the distinction between Whigs and Tories and participating in the boycott of British textiles by wearing homespun. Boston in the early 1770s was the centre of colonial resistance to British imperial policy. This resistance would ultimately lead to the Declaration of Independence by thirteen of Britain's North American colonies in 1776. Young women like Anna were expected to be "daughters of liberty" in their refusal to purchase British imports such as textiles and tea. Anna comments on the presence of British troops in the city, which was a particular source of tension for the civilian population.

In the diary, childish delight in jokes and pranks alternates with a young woman's concern over clothes and appearance. Conscious of her frontier background, Anna was anxious to "get it right." When she finally makes a grand appearance in "my yellow coat, black bib and apron, my pompedore shoes, the cap my aunt Storer sometime since presented me (blue ribbon on it) and a very handsome loket in the shape of a heart she gave me ...," Anna crows to her absent parents: "And I would tell you, that *for the first time they all lik'd my dress very much.*" The elaborate headgear fashionable in the 1770s prompts a humorous description of the "Hedus roll" which, although it "makes my head itch, and ach and burn like anything," was proudly worn by our young diarist as the emblem of beauty.

Anna also testifies to her New England Congregational heritage in her preoccupation with religious matters. She carefully paraphrased sermons and conversations on theological questions, some of which clearly show attempts by the church to divert young ladies from too great a preoccupation with physical appearance. Anna quotes John Bacon (the Mr. Beacon of the diary), the new minister of the Old South Church as saying: "My dear young friends, you are pleased with beauty, and like to be tho't beautifull — but let me tell ye, you'l never be truly beautifull till you are like the King's daughter, all glorious within ...."

Daughters in New England were also taught housewifery, practical skills required by young "ladies," who in adult life would be expected to maintain an efficient and harmonious household. Anna describes making "pyes," sewing shirts and shifts, spinning yarn and knitting socks. She practised the social graces at a series of little parties called "constitutions." Boys were excluded from these affairs where Lucinda, the black maid, often played the flute while the elegantly dressed young ladies danced the minuet together. In contrast to this decorous world is the story of Bet Smith, who stole, cavorted with soldiers and eventually got her 'comeuppance' at the whipping post and gallows. Anna seems more amused than shocked at Bet's antics and, reflecting the attitudes of her seniors, shows little compassion for this unlady-like, lower class woman.

Anna's diary offers an unusually candid description of the experiences of a privileged young girl coming of age in the late eighteenth century. Although Anna was writing in Boston, the social values of her circle of relatives and friends were typical of those held by the elite among Planters and Loyalists who constituted the first major groups of English-speaking settlers to Nova Scotia. Anna's preoccupation with both inner and outer beauty, practical as well as ornamental accomplishments, was reflected in the lives of many New England women who migrated to Nova Scotia. While the pioneering experience wrought havoc with external beauty and ornamental refinements, these immigrant women planted their values concerning family, religion, education, gender roles, material well-being — and diary writing — firmly in Nova Scotia's rocky soil.

ANNA GREEN WINSLOW DIARY
1771-1772*

[nd] … I guess I shall have but little time for journalising Till after thanksgiving. My aunt Deming says I shall make one pye myself at least. I hope somebody beside myself will like to eat a bit of my Boston pye thou' my papa and you did not (I remember) chuse to partake of my Cumberland performance. I think I have been writing my own Praises this morning. Poor Job was forced to praise himself when no man would do him that justice. I am not as he was. I have made two shirts for unkle since I finish'd mamma's shifts.

Nov 18th, 1771
Mr. Beacons text yesterday was Psalm cxlix. 4. For the Lord taketh pleasure in his people; he will beautify the meek with salvation. His Doctrine was something like this, viz: That the Salvation of Gods people mainly consists in Holiness. The name Jesus signifies Savior. Jesus saves his people from their Sins. He renews them in the spirit of their minds - writes his Law in their hearts. Mr. Beacon ask'd a question. What is beauty — or, wherein does true beauty consist? He answer'd, in holiness — and said a great deal about it that I can't remember, & as aunt says she hant leisure now to help me any further — so I may just tell you a little that I remember without her assistance, and that I repeated to her yesterday at Tea — He said he would lastly address himself to the young people: My dear young friends, you are pleased with beauty, & like to be tho't beautifull — but let me tell ye, you'l never be truly beautifull till you are like the King's daughter, all glorious within, all the orniments you can put on while your souls are unholy make you the more like white sepulchres garnish'd without, but full of deformyty within. You think me very unpolite no doubt to address you in this manner, but I must go a little further and tell you, how cource soever it may sound to your delicacy, that while you are without holiness, your beauty is deformity — you are all over

---

*   Alice Morse Earle, ed., *Diary of Anna Green Winslow: A Boston School Girl of 1771* (Boston, 1894).

black & defil'd, ugly and loathsome to all holy beings, the wrath
of th' great God lie's upon you & if you die in this condition,
you will be turn'd into hell, with ugly devils, to eternity.

Nov. 27th
We are very glad to see Mr. Gannett, because of him "we hear
of your affairs & how you do" — as the apostle Paul once wrote.
My unkle & aunt however, say they are sorry he is to be absent,
so long as this whole winter, I think. I long now to have you
come up — I want to see papa, mama & brother, all most, for I
cannot make any distinction which most — I should like to see
Harry too. Mr. Gannett tells me he keeps a journal — I do want
to see that — especially as Mr. Gannett has given me some speci-
mens, as I may say of his "I and Aunt" etc ....

November the 29th
My aunt Deming gives her love to you and says it is this morning 12 years since she had the pleasure of congratulating papa
and you on the birth of your scribling daughter. She hopes if I
live 12 years longer that I shall write and do everything better
than can be expected in the *past* 12. I should be obliged to you,
you will dismiss me for company.

30th Nov.
My company yesterday were
Miss Polly Deming,
Miss Polly Glover,
Miss Betty Draper,
Miss Bessy Winslow,
Miss Nancy Glover,
Miss Sally Winslow,
Miss Polly Atwood,
Miss Han Soley.

Miss Attwood as well as Miss Winslow are of this family. And
Miss N. Glover did me honor by her presence, for she is older
than cousin Sally and of her aquaintance. We made four couple
at country dansing; danceing I mean. In the evening young Mr.
Waters hearing of my assembly, put his flute in his pocket and

played several minuets and other tunes, to which we danced mighty cleverly. But Lucinda was our principal piper. Miss Church and Miss Chaloner would have been here if sickness — and the Miss Sheafs, if the death of their father had not prevented. The black Hatt I gratefully receive as your present, but if Captain Jarvise had arrived here with it about the time he sail'd from this place for Cumberland it would have been of more service to me, for I have been oblig'd to borrow. I wore Miss Griswold's Bonnet on my journey to Portsmouth, & my cousin Sallys Hatt ever since I came home, & now I am to leave off my black ribbins tomorrow, & am to put on my red cloak & black hatt with the red Dominie - for the people will ask me what I have got to sell as I go along street if I do, or, how the folk at New guinie do? Dear mamma, you dont know the fation here — I beg to look like other folk. You dont know what a stir would be made in sudbury street, were I to make my appearance there in my red Dominie & black Hatt. But the old cloak & bonnett together will make me a decent bonnett for common ocation (I like that) aunt says, its a pitty some of the ribbins you sent wont do for the Bonnet. — I must now close up this Journal ….

N.B. My aunt Deming dont approve of my English & has not the fear that you will think her concernd in the Diction.

Dec 14th
The weather and walking have been very winter like since the above hotch-potch, pothooks & trammels. I went to Mrs. Whitwell's last wednessday — you taught me to spell the 4 day of the week, but my aunt says that it should be spelt wednesday. My aunt also says, that till I come out of an egregious fit of laughterre that is apt to sieze me & the violence of which I am at this present under, neither English sense, nor anything rational may be expected of me. I ment to say, that, I went to Mrs. Whitwell's to see Mad^m Storers funeral, the walking was very bad except on the sides of the street which was the reason I did not make a part of the procession. I should have dined with Mrs. Whitwell on thursday if a grand storm had not prevented, As she invited me. I saw Miss Caty Vans at lecture last evening. I

had a visit this morning from Mrs Dixon of Horton & Miss Polly Huston. Mrs Dixon is dissipointed at not finding her sister here.

Dec 24th.
Elder Whitwell told my aunt, that this winter began as did the Winter of 1740. How that was I dont remember but this I know, that to-day is by far the coldest we have had since I have been in New England. (N. B. All run that are abroad.) Last sabbath being rainy I went to & from meeting in Mr. Soley's chaise. I dined at unkle Winslow's, the walking being so bad I rode there & back to meeting. Every drop that fell froze, so that from yesterday morning to this time the appearance has been similar to the discription I sent you last winter. The walking is so slippery & the air so cold, that aunt chuses to have me for her scoller these two days. And as tomorrow will be a holiday, so the pope and his associates have ordained, my aunt thinks not to trouble Mrs Smith with me this week. I began a shift at home yesterday for myself, it is pretty forward. Last saturday was seven-night my aunt Suky was delivered of a pretty little son, who was baptiz'd by Dr. Cooper the next day by the name of Charles. I knew nothing of it till noonday, when I went there a visiting. Last Thursday I din'd & spent the afternoon at unkle Joshua's I should have gone to lecture with my aunt & heard our Mr Hunt preach, but she would not wait till I came from writing school. Miss Atwood, the last of our boarders, went off the same day. Miss Griswold & Miss Meriam, having departed some time agone, I forget whether I mention'd the recept of Nancy's present. I am oblig'd to her for it. The Dolphin is still whole. And like to remain so.

Dec 27th
This day, the extremity of the cold is somewhat abated. I keept Christmas at home this year, & did a very good day's work, aunt says so. How notable I have been this week I shall tell you by & by. I spent the most part of Tuesday evening with my favorite, Miss Soley, & as she is confined by a cold & the weather still so severe that I cannot git farther, I am to visit her again before I sleep, & consult with her (or rather she with me) upon a perticular matter, which you shall know in its place. How strangely industrious I have been this week, I will inform you with my

own hand — at present, I am so dilligent, that I am oblig'd to use the hand & pen of my old friend, who being near by is better than a brother far off. I dont forgit dear little John Henry so pray mamma, dont mistake me.

Dec 28th
Last evening a little after 5 o'clock I finished my shift. I spent the evening at Mr. Soley's. I began my shift at 12 o'clock last monday, have read my bible every day this week & wrote every day save one.

Dec 30th
I return'd to my sewing school after a weeks absence, I have also paid my compliments to Master Holbrook.* Yesterday between meetings my aunt was call'd to Mrs. Water's & about 8 in the evening Dr. Lloyd brought little master to town (N.B. As a memorandum for myself. My aunt stuck a white sattan pincushin for Mrs Waters. On one side is a planthorn with flowers, on the reverse, just under the border are, on one side stuck these words, Josiah Waters, then follows on the end, Dec 1771, on the next side & end are the words, Welcome little Stranger.)** Unkle has just come in & bro't one from me. I mean, unkle is just come in with a letter from Papa in his hand (& none for me) by way of Newbury. I am glad to hear that all was well the 26 Nov ult. I am told my Papa has not mention'd me in this Letter. Out of sight, out of mind. My aunt gives her love to papa, & says that she will make the necessary enquieries for my brother and send you via Halifax what directions and wormseed she can collect.

1st Jan 1772
I wish my Papa, Mama, brother John Henry, & cousin Avery & all the rest of my acquaintance at Cumberland, Fortlaurence, Barronsfield, Greenland, Amherst &c. a Happy New Year, I have bestow'd no new year's gift, as yet.*** But have received one

* Samuel Holbrook, Anna's writing master, was one of a highly honoured family of Boston writing teachers.
** A pincushion was a conventional gift to a mother with a young baby.
*** Although Christmas gifts were not exchanged in this Congregational family, New Year's gifts apparently were.

very handsome one, viz. the History of Joseph Andrews abreviated. In nice Guilt and flowers covers. This afternoon being a holiday I am going to pay my compliments in Sudbury Street.

Jan 4th

I was dress'd in my yellow coat, my black bib & apron, my pompedore shoes,* the cap my aunt Storer sometime since presented me with (blue ribbins on it) & a very handsome loket in the shape of a hart she gave me — the past pin my Hon^d Papa presented me with in my cap, My new cloak & bonnet on, my pompedore gloves, &c, &c. And I would tell you, that *for the first time, they all lik'd my dress very much*. My cloak & bonnett are really very handsome, & so they had need be. For they cost an amasing sight of money, not quite £45 tho' Aunt Suky said, that she suppos'd Aunt Deming would be frighted out of her Wits at the money it cost. I have got one covering, by the cost, that is genteel, & I like it much myself. On thursday I attended my aunt to Lecture & heard Dr Chauncey preach a third sermon from Acts ii. 42. They continued stedfastly — in breaking of bread. I din'd & spent the afternoon at Mr. Whitwell's. Miss Caty Vans was one of our company. Dr. Pemberton & Dr. Cooper had on gowns, In the form of the Episcopal cassock we hear, the Doct^s design to distinguish themselves from the inferior clergy by these strange habits. N. B. I dont know whether one sleeve would make a full trimm'd negligee as the fashion is at present, tho' I cant say but it might make one of the frugal sort, with but scant triming. Unkle says, that all have popes in their bellys. Contrary to I. Peter v. 2. 3. Aunt says, when she saw Dr P. roll up the pulpit stairs, the figure of Parson Trulliber, recorded by Mr Fielding occur'd to her mind & she was really sorry a congregational divine, should, by any instance whatever, give her so unpleasing an idea.**

---

* A reference to fashion made popular by the Marquise de Pompadour (1721-64), mistress of Louis XV of France.
** Congregationalists had a traditional antipathy toward the Anglican Church and the episcopal airs exhibited by its clergy. Congregrational ministers who attempted to bring Anglican practices into their churches were often strongly criticized by their membership.

Feb 9th

My honored Mamma will be so good as to excuse my useing the pen of my old friend just here, because I am disabled by a whitloe on my fourth finger & something like one on my middle finger, from using my own pen; but altho' my right hand is in bondage, my left is free; & my aunt says, it will be a nice oppertunity if I do but improve it, to perfect myself in learning to spin flax. I am pleased with the proposal & am at this present, exerting myself for this purpose. I hope, when two or at most three months are past, to give occular demonstration of my proficiency in this art, as well as several others. My fingers are not the only part of me that has suffer'd with sores within this fortnight, for I have had an ugly great boil upon my right hip & about a dozen small ones — I am at present swath'd hip & thigh, as Samson smote the Philistines, but my soreness is near over. My aunt thought it highly proper to give me some cooling physick, so last tuesday I took 1-2 oz. Globe Salt (a disagreeable potion) & kept chamber. Since which, there has been no new erruption, & a great alteration for the better in those I had before.

I have read my bible to my aunt this morning (as is the daily custom) & sometimes I read other books to her. So you may perceive, *I have the use of my tongue* & I tell her it is a good thing to have the use of my tongue. Unkle Ned called here just now — all well — by the way he is come to live in Boston again, & till he can be better accomodated, is at housekeeping where Mad^m Storer lately lived, he is looking for a less house. I tell my Aunt I feel a disposician to be a good girl, & she pleases herself that she shall have much comfort of me to-day, which as cousin Sally is ironing we expect to have to ourselves.

Feb 10th

This day I paid my respects to Master Holbrook, after a week's absence, my finger is still in limbo as you may see by the writeing. I have not paid my compliments to Madam Smith, for, altho' I can drive the goos quill a bit, I cannot so well manage the needle. So I will lay my hand to the distaff, as the virtuous women did of old — Yesterday was very bad weather, neither aunt, nor niece at publick worship.

Valentine day
My cousin Sally reeled off a 10 knot skane of yarn today. My valentine was an old country plow-joger.* The yarn was of my spinning. Aunt says it will do for filling. Aunt also says niece is a whimsical child.

Feb 18th
Another ten knot skane of my yarn was reel'd off today. Aunt says it is very good. My boils & whitloes are growing well apace, so that I can knit a little in the evening.

Feb 21
...last Thursday I purchas'd with my aunt Deming's leave, a very beautiful white feather hat, that is, the out side, which is a bit of white hollond** with the feathers sew'd on in a most curious manner white & unsullyed as the falling snow, this hat I have long been saving my money to procure for which I have let your kind allowance, Papa, lay in my aunt's hands till this hat which I spoke for was brought home. As I am (as we say) a daughter of liberty I chuse to wear as much of our own manu-factory as pocible. But my aunt says, I have wrote this account very badly. I will go on to save my money for a chip & a lineing &c ....

Feb 22
... It has been a very sickly time here, not one person that I know of but has been under heavy colds — (all laid up at unkle Storer's) in general got abroad again. Aunt Suky had not been down stairs since her lying in, when I last saw her, but I hear she is got down. She has had a broken breast. I have spun 30 knots of linning yarn, and (partly) new footed a pair of stockings for Lucinda, read a part of the pilgrim's progress, coppied part of my text journal (that if I live a few years longer, I may be able to understand it, for aunt sais, that to her, the contents as I first mark'd them, were an impenetrable secret) play'd some, tuck'd

---

*　A reference to the custom that on Valentine's day the first person of the opposite sex seen that morning was the observer's valentine. Apparently the first person Anna saw was a farm labourer.

**　Cotton cloth treated to produce an opaque finish.

a great deal (Aunt Deming says it is very true) laugh'd enough, & I tell aunt it is all human nature, if not human reason. And now, I wish my honored mamma a very good night.

Monday noon, Feb 25th

I have been to writing school this morning and Sewing. The day being very pleasant, very little wind stirring. Jemima called to see me last evening. She lives at Master Jimmy Lovel's. Dear mamma, I suppose that you would be glad to hear that Betty Smith who has given you so much trouble, is well & behaves herself well & I should be glad if I could write you so. But the truth is, no sooner was the 29th Regiment encamp'd upon the common but miss Betty took herself among them (as the Irish say) & there she stay'd with Bill Pinchion & awhile. The next news of her was, that she was got into gaol for stealing: from whence she was taken to the publick whipping post. The next adventure was to the Castle, after the soldier's were remov'd there, for the murder of the 5th March last. When they turn'd her away from there, she came up to town again, and soon got into the workhouse for new misdemeanours, she soon ran away from there and sit up her old trade of pilfering again, for which she was put a second time into gaol, there she still remains. About two months agone (as well as I can remember) she & a number of her wretched companions set the gaol on fire, in order to get out, but the first was timely discovered & extinguished, & there, as I said she still remains till this day, in order to be tried for her crimes. I heard somebody say that as she has some connections with the army no doubt but she would be cleared, and perhaps, have a pension into the bargain. Mr. Henry says the way of sin is down hill, when persons get into that way they are not easily stopped.

Feb 27

This day being too stormy for me to go to any school, and nothing as yet having happen'd that is worth your notice, my aunt gives me leave to communicate to you something that much pleas'd her when she heard of it, & which I hope will please you my Papa and Mamma. I believe I may have inform'd you that since I have been Boston, Dr. Byles* has pretty frequently preached & sometimes administer'd the sacrament, when our Candidates have preached to the O.S. Church, because they are not tho't qualified to administer Gospel Ordinance, till they be settled Pastours.... My aunt Deming gives her love to you mamma, and bids me tell you, as a matter you will be very glad to know, that Dr Byles & his lady & family, have enjoy'd a good share of health & perfect harmony for several years past....

March 17
Yesterday, I went to see aunt Polly, & finding her going out, I spent the afternoon with aunt Hannah. While I was out, a snow storm overtook me. This being a fine sun shine (tho' cold) day I have been to writing school, & wrote two pieces, one I presented to aunt Deming, and the other I design for my Honor'd Papa, I hope he will approve of it. I sent a piece of my writing to you Honor'd Mamma last fall, which I hope you receiv'd. When my aunt Deming was a little girl my Grandmamma Sargent told her the following story viz. One Mr. Calf who had three times enjoy'd the Mayorality of the city of London, had after his decease, a monoment erected to his memory with the following inscription on it.

Here lies buried the body of
Sir Richard Calf,
Thrice Lord Mayor of London.
Honor, Honor, Honor.

A drol gentleman passing by with a bit of chalk in his hand underwrote thus —

O cruel death! more subtle than a Fox
That would not let this Calf become an Ox,
That he might browze among the briers & thorns
And with his brethren wear,
Horns. Horns. Horns.

My aunt told me the foregoing some time since & today I ask'd her leave to insert it in my journal. My aunt gives her love

---

* See the introduction to Rebecca Byles for background on the Byles family.

to you & directs me to tell you that she tho't my piece of linnin would have made me a dozen of shifts but she could cut no more than ten out of it. There is some left, but not enough for another. Nine of them are finish'd wash'd & iron'd; & the other would have been long since done if my fingers had not been sore. My cousin Sally made three of them for me, but then I made two shirts & part of another for unkle to help her. I believe unless something remarkable should happen, such as a warm day, my mamma will consent that I dedicate a few of my next essays to papa. I think the second thing I said to aunt this morning was, that I intended to be very good all day. To make this out,

"Next unto God, dear Parents I address
"Myself to you in humble Thankfulness,
"For all your Care & Charge on me bestow'd;
"The means of Learning unto me allow'd.
"Go on I pray, & let me still pursue
"Those Golden ARTS the Vulgar never knew."

Yr Dutifull Daughter
ANNA GREEN WINSLOW.

The poetry I transcrib'd from my Copy Book.

April 14th
I went a visiting yesterday to Col. Gridley's with my aunt. After tea Miss Becky Gridley sung a minuet. Miss Polly Deming & I danced to her musick, which when perform'd was approv'd of by Mrs Gridley, Mrs Deming, Mrs Thompson, Mrs Avery, Miss Sally Hill, Miss Becky Gridley, Miss Polly Gridley & Miss Sally Winslow. Col Gridley went o' of the room. Col brought in the talk of Whigs & Tories & taught me the difference between them
....

May 16
Last Wednesday Bet Smith was set upon the gallows. She behav'd with great impudence. Thursday I danc'd a minuet & country dances at school, after which I drank tea with Aunt Storer. To day I am somewhat out of sorts, a little sick at my stomach.

May 25

… Whenever I have omited a school my aunt has directed me to sit down here, so when you dont see a memorandum of that kind, you may conclude that I have paid my compliments to mess Holbrook & Turner (to the former you see to very little purpose) & mrs Smith as usual. The Miss Waldow's I mentioned in a former are Mr. Danl Waldo's daughters (very pretty misses) their mamma was Miss Becca Salisbury. After making a short visit with my Aunt at Mrs Green's, over the way, yesterday towards evening, I took a walk with cousin Sally to see the good folks in Sudbury Street, & found them all well. I had my HEDDUS roll on, aunt Storer said it ought to be made less, Aunt Deming said it ought not to be made at all. It makes my head itch, & ach, & burn like anything Mamma. This famous roll is not made wholly of a red Cow Tail, but is a mixture of that, & horsehair (very course) & a little human hair of yellow hue, that I suppose was taken out of the back part of an old wig. But D___ made it (our head) all carded together and twisted up. When it first came home, aunt put it on, & my new cap on it, she then took up her apron & mesur'd me, & from the roots of my hair on my forehead to the top of my notions, I mesur'd above an inch longer than I did downwards from the roots of my hair to the end of my chin. Nothing renders a young person more amiable than virtue & modesty without the help of fals hair, red Cow tail, or D_____ (the barber). Now all this mamma, I have just been reading over to my aunt. She is pleas'd with my whimsical description & grave (half grave) improvement, & hopes a little fals English will not spoil the whole with Mamma. Rome was not built in a day.

EPILOGUE: ANNA GREEN WINSLOW

Anna's early death in 1779 at Marshfield, Massachusetts, is a matter of family tradition. There is no public record or known grave. This lack of documentation probably reflected the turmoil that engulfed the Winslows and other Loyalist families once the revolutionary war began.

On 18 April 1772 Anna recorded that her parents were "preparing to quit (their) habitation" at Cumberland and return to their home in Marshfield. Their timing could not have been worse. Joshua Winslow's Tory sympathies forced him to flee back to Nova Scotia. Although he was evenutally rewarded for his loyalty with administrative positions in Quebec, he remained separated from the family during much of the war. Meanwhile, Mrs Winslow continued to live in Marshfield, where Anna, her last surviving child, died of consumption at the age of 19. When the war ended Mrs. Winslow joined her husband in Quebec but when he died in 1801 she returned to her beloved New England to live out the remaining fifteen years of her life.

REBECCA BYLES
1762-1853

Rebecca Byles belonged to the younger generation of Loyalists who, during the American Revolution, fled to Nova Scotia for asylum. The Boston Byles were a well-known clerical and literary family. Rebecca's grandfather, the Reverend Mather Byles (1705-1788), was a Harvard graduate, a writer, humorist and pastor of the Hollis Street Congregationalist Church, Boston, for some forty years. In 1776 he was dismissed from his church and threatened with deportation because of his Loyalist sympathies. Ultimately, he was allowed to remain in Boston where he lived, in comparative poverty, with his two daughters, Mary (Polly) and Catherine (Kitty), the aunts to whom Rebecca writes.

Rebecca's father, the Reverend Mather Byles Junior (1734-1814), was also a Harvard graduate. He began his career as a Congregational pastor but was later ordained in England as a priest of the Anglican Church. In 1776, he left for Halifax with his family and was there appointed chaplain to the garrison. Rebecca's mother, Rebecca Walter, died in 1775 at the age of 37, leaving behind five children, the oldest of whom was Rebecca. She had a brother, Mather, and three sisters: Elizabeth (Betsy or Eliza), Anna (Nancy) and Sarah (Sally). In 1777, Mather Byles, Jr. married Rebecca's "second mother," Sarah Lyde, who died in 1787. There were two surviving children of the second marriage, Louisa and Belcher. In 1788, Rebecca's father married for the last time. Susanna Reid, herself a widow, survived her husband and there were no children by the marriage.

During the Revolution, mail between Nova Scotia and the new republic was subject to official perusal. Therefore, Rebecca's letters were politically discreet. The distress of separation from family and settling in a new home in a frontier province were mostly implied. Despite the pain of political exile, Rebecca's youthful correspondence suggests that she adjusted reasonably easily to Halifax where social norms for young ladies did not differ significantly from those of the city of her birth. Originally tutored at home and in private schools much like those attended by Anna Winslow, she continued her education at Mrs. Cottnam's Female Academy in Halifax. As Gwendolyn Davies has pointed out, the refugee Loyalists were quick to recreate their educational and literary institutions as a "consolation to distress."* Rebecca was familiar with the work of John Locke, as well as the popular English poets and she herself wrote poetry. The neo-classical revival of the period is evident in her reading of Alexander Pope's "Homer" and the Latin plays of Terence translated into French.

During the eighteenth century, the novel emerged as a popular literary form. Rebecca, like many educated young women, enjoyed novels and was familiar with Samuel Richardson's *Pamela*(1740), as well as Fanny Burney's *Evelina*(1778) and *Cecilia*(1782). Although such books were often frowned upon by puritan divines and later critics for their preoccupation with "sensibility and suffering," they offer the modern reader a guide to the emotional and imaginative world of literate women like Rebecca Byles. Plots focused on domestic dilemmas of love and friendship and featured fictional paragons of virtue and correct behaviour for young women to emulate.**

Rebecca's open questioning of gender roles is a reminder that the status of women was among the issues raised in the 'age of reason.' While the young Rebecca was prepared to see women "fill the most important offices in Church and State," she gradually became more critical of literary women, such as the prominent British historian and feminist Catherine

---

*   Gwendolyn Davies, "Consolation To Distress: Loyalist Literary Activity in the Maritimes," *Acadiensis*, Vol. XVI, No.2 (Spring 1987), pp. 51-68.
** John Butt, *English Literature in the Mid-Eighteenth Century*, edited and completed by Geoffrey Carnall (Oxford, 1979), p. 449; Lorraine McMullen, *An Odd Attempt in a Woman: The Literary Life of Frances Brooke* (Vancouver, 1983), p. 58.

Macaulay(1731-1791),* who wrote for the "public eye." Her growing conservatism reflected not only personal changes as she groomed herself for her approaching marriage but also the general climate of opinion which was becoming increasingly reactionary. While preparing for marriage, Rebecca was much influenced by advice books, including Dr. John Gregory's *A Father's Legacy to His Daughters* (1775). His view that women were morally superior to men but inhabited a private domestic sphere separate from the public world of men gained wide currency among the upper classes in the late eighteenth century and was cheerfully adopted by Rebecca Byles as she prepared to embrace the noble bonds of marriage and motherhood.**

Rebecca remained a faithful correspondent with her aunts for over 50 years. Her letters not only document how a Loyalist family survived and thrived in colonial British North America (for Rebecca is ever scrupulous in describing the fate of her vast family network), they also chronicle the growth of an adolescent girl into a mature woman, the matriarch of a large and powerful Nova Scotia family. Because the Byles correspondence is so extensive, it is impossible to let Rebecca tell all of her story in this forum. Only a selection of her earliest letters, written between 1777 and 1785, when Rebecca was adjusting to her new home and blossoming into young womanhood, are reproduced here. They show a Rebecca who was often playful and always affectionate, a dutiful adolescent who masked anxiety over money and family problems so as not to worry her aunts and grandfather who were living under virtual house arrest in Boston during the war years. They also provide a glimpse of the lively intellectual and social world of Loyalist Halifax where the "rage for matrimony" prevailed among the uprooted exiles and where the young Doctor Almon wooed and eventually won Rebecca's heart.

---

*   Dale Spender, *Women of Ideas* (London, 1983), pp. 127-37.
**   Nancy F. Cott, *The Bonds of Womanhood: Woman's Sphere in New England, 1780-1835* (New Haven, 1977), p. 128.

REBECCA BYLES LETTERS
1777 - 1785*

8 November 1777

I received your agreable Letter very safe. It gives me great pleasure to hear that you are alive, and well, which is all I can know in the present state of affairs; we are impatient to get Letters from our Friends, and when we do, we know very little more than we did before. I hope with you that the unhappy Barrier will soon be removed, and we shall meet again, but we must not Repine. I know it will give you pleasure to hear how happily we are situated in this Time of Universal Confusion. We enjoy a large share of the Comforts of Life, and the greatest uneasiness is the Situation of our Country. Mrs. Cottnam is in Town at the Head of a Female Academy. My sisters and myself go to her, they to plain sewing & Reading, & I to Writing, learning French (parley vous Francais Mademoiselle) and Dancing, which employs good Part of my Time. We have enjoyed our Health better since we came down here than ever we did before in our Lifes, and have a great deal to be Thankful for. My Brother and Sisters join me in Duty to Grandpappa Aunt Polly and you....

1 October 1778

.... Mamma was Brought to Bed of a Daughter, the 5th of last August, who was Christen'd about a Fortnight after by the Name of Louisa. She was nurs'd by Mrs. Manjoy, a Sister of Mrs Drapers, who Informed me her Sister and Family were in England, and lived very Comfortably on the Pension allow'd them by the Crown. Mrs. Tailor lives very near us, and follows her Old Occupation of keeping Boarders, by which I believe she gets a Comfortable Subsistence. One of her Daughters was married some time ago to a *Doctor Clark*, Nephew to Doctor *Billy* Clark that lived at the North End of Boston. The *Miss Cummings* are well, and always high in your Praises. Mrs and Miss Cottnam

---

* Rebecca Byles's letters to her aunts are found in the Public Archives of Nova Scotia, MG 1, Vol. 163. Most of the letters are addressed specifically to Catherine Byles (Aunt Kitty) but occasionally she addresses both Aunts.

go on the same tract. Betsy has been learning to Write and work a Sampler there this Summer. The first of last May was the beginning of her taking a Pen in Hand, and for the Time has made I think very great Improvement. Her first attempt in the Letter way is to be made to you. I think I have Punctually Obey'd you in writing a very tedious Epistle, but Remember it was your own Desire. But as I have several other Letters to write I will soon Releive you and hasten to a Period. I Distributed your Kisses as you desired tho' Miss Betsy made some Objections that she was too much of a Woman. Sally has been very unwell but is on the Recovery. They all beg to be included, with me, in Duty to grandpappa, Aunt Polly & you ....

6 January 1779
... I have now I think discuss'd the usual Topicks in telling you we are alive and well and have not forgot you & what more shall I say? Why if I Remember right, you told me my most trivial Transactions would give you pleasure. Well then, since I wrote last some part of the Time has been imploy'd in translating a very long Sermon for Doctor Breynton from French into English, and in reading Pamela and Terences Plays in French, some part in hearing Pope's Homer & the rest divided between Writing, Working & the various Employments of the Family. Thus I have endeav'd to shew you how I employ my *Time*. Time which is so peculiarly precious at my Age & I know it is my Dear Aunts Prayer that I should improve as I ought the invaluable Moments.

27 December 1779
Tho' we had but about half an Hour's Notice of a Cartel's sailing for Boston, my Pappa had taken up his Pen to write to you a few lines, when he was call'd of[f] to a perticular friend, Dying of an Apoplexy, on whom he was oblig'd to attend directly. He therefore disired me to take his Place, & inform you that we are all well and that there has been no material Alteration amongst us since we last wrote, which was in September by Mr Tidmarsh who took Charge of a Packet consisting of seven Letters for you, my Grandmamma & Miss Patten, which we suppose you receiv'd & which we impatiently wait the return of the Flag to have them acknowledged. *When*, my Dear Aunt will this stupid in-

tercourse of saying nothing be put a stop to; for my part I am heartily tired of it, & I am sometimes determin'd I will not write again, till I can write & speak with freedom. But upon second thoughts, that is an imprudent determination; we will therefore go on in the same track and mutually pray that it may be put a speedy end to. I thought much of you and Sally Patten on Christmas Day when we used to be generally together. Louisa is to be enoculated for the Small Pox this week, which I wish was well over. Your friends the Miss Cumming's are well. Our Family all join me in tenderest Affection and Duty to our ever Dear Grandpappa and you, whose situation I sincerely Sympathize with, & heartily wish it was in my power to alleviate. But how ever my Dear Aunts keep up your Spirits and follow the old Maxim, "that whatever is is right." I will now put me close to my Letter, with sending you compliments of the Season ....

16 August 1780
Tho' you are, let me see, one, two, three, four & I believe five Letters in my Debt, & I have rack'd my invention in vain to find something to write about, I cannot forbear indulging the scribling Humour I find myself in, and the disire I have of assureing you of my unalterable Duty & Affection, which believe me Time has not diminish'd: how much, how earnestly do I long to see you, to do every Thing in my Power to soften & alleviate all your Distresses, & divide with you all my Pleasures. But since the divine disposer of all Things has seen fit to seperate us, it becomes us chearfully to submit, nor even allow ourselves in one anxious wish, one murmurring Thought.

We, I think, seem to be settled here. We have bought a large, convenient House, with a very good Garden, Yard, & every other convenience, & what I exceedingly value, live exactly opposite our Friends Mrs. and Miss Cottnam, with whom I spend a good deal of my Time very happily. They both disire to be remember'd. The Widow Taylor this Spring married her second Daughter to a Captain Ross, & her third, my Namesake, is soon, I hear, to follow her example, so that she will have but one left with her. Mr. Domett & Wife went from New York to England some time ago, and I hear has return'd to the same Place with an employment under Government. Mrs. Lovell & her

Daughters are well & often speak of you. Her two Youngest Daughters are soon to be married to a couple of Hessian Officers. The Miss Cuming's are well. You see my Dear Aunt I write you an account of all your Friends, pray do the same by me, perticularly of my Grandmamma Walter, my Aunt Otis, my Cousins Abbot & Hesilrige to whom present my Duty and best Regards. Tell my Grandmamma that I have wrote her three times, & would have wrote now, if I had had Time. Let me know also whether Sally Patten is Dead or Alive. Your Packet by the way of Penobscot has not reach'd us, nor do I think it ever will: I therefore beg you will send Duplicates by the return of the Flag, as we are all impatient, especially Nancy, who is quite discourag'd at waiting so long for an answer to the first Letter that ever she wrote. Louisa desires me to tell her Aunts she loves them Dearly. My Brother & Sisters beg leave to present with mine their Duty to our much esteem'd Grandpappa, Aunt Polly and you, but I fancy I hear you say, I am very Sorry Becca your Scribling Humor, as you call it, came on when you were writeing to me. Have Patience, my Dear Aunt, & I will conclude with assuring you, etc ....

10 September 1782
And now My Dear Aunt, I must write you in Rhyme
Tho' unluckily blest with nor Genius or Time.
My Duty Affection & Love to rehearse.
I can scarce do it in Prose. 'Twill sound worse in Verse;
However to send you the best I am able
I'm seated Pen, Paper and Ink on the Table;
Have call'd on Apollo, and all the Nine Muses,
And see with their *Aid* what my Paper produces.
The Aid of the Muses I hear you reply;
While you Glance o'er the Lines with a critical Eye;
The Absence, Contempt & Disdain of the Nine;
Are seen in the Nonsence of every dull Line;
Forbear my dear Becca, pray throw by your Pen,
And never attempt to *write Verses* again.
Have Patience one Minute, my Aunt till I tell,
That our Family, Friends, & Connexions are well;
That we all wish to see you, the sooner the better:

As vastly more pleasing than writing by Letter.
The *Cake* placed with Care on my Pillow was laid,
But for want of three Pins, or Time 'lapsed since t'was made;
It produc'd no Effect nor created a Dream.
Which tho' I cant help it defeated your Scheme.
I now will conclude with disires for a Peace
And believe me yours truly Affectionate Niece.
"Rebecca Byles's Composition"
"Be sure it is no Imposition."

24 March 1784
Yours my best of Aunts of Febry 13th. hath laid me under Fresh obligations....

Cecilia I have read, & am much obliged to you for your Anecdotes respecting the accomplished Authoress; they were quite new to me. I never found it so difficult to beleive any thing, as that such a work could be the product of a Female Pen. To support with Humour & Spirit through the whole, such a great variety of Characters both in the highest & lowest Scenes of Life, seems to me to require a more extensive Knowledge of the World, than could possibly come under a Ladys Observation; I am not sure that I give Cecilia the preference, perhaps it is because the Aimable Characters of Evelina struck me more forcibly, particularly Mr. Villers & Lord Orvilles; Cecilia I acknowledge is more the World we live in. Harrells Character is the best supported of any I ever saw. To the Credit of the Female Sex be it said, that it ranks the first of modern Novels. The English Nation at present abounds with Female writers; Miss Aikins I dare say you have read, as a Poetess she ranks very high. Her Poems I have read several times with renew'd Pleasure, & there are many others whose worlds will long be preserv'd; Miss Mores Essays I am now reading. If they pursue the same plan of Education in England that they do here, I am not in the least surprised Polite Literature should be the Province of the Ladys. Our Boys are all intended for the Army or Navy, or some Post under Government, where neither Knowledge or Honesty are required. Indeed they retard a Persons advancement; to Dance, make a Genteel Bow, fill up a *printed*

Message Card, & sign a receipt for their Pay, Compleat their Education, & they step forth *accomplished Gentleman*: with the Girls some how or other, we think different. They have the best Education the place affords, and the accomplishment of their *Minds* is attended to, as well as the adorning of their Persons. In a few Years I expect to see Women fill the most important Offices Church and *State* ... Betsy wrote you about a Month since. Nancy & Sally are thinking about it. Mathers determinations I know not. Louisa & Belcher disire their Duty. Belcher is one of the finest Boys I ever saw, Manly, Sensible, & Handsome. My most Affectionate Duty await my Grand-Father, & my new elected *Grand-Mother*. Two or three ways she has Threatend to be related to me, it is hard if some dont succeed; the Hour of the Day, the want of Paper, and a reason which Belcher thinks of much more Consequence, the necessity of immediately going into the Kitchen to tye up a Pudding (NB Sally's Week) Obliges me much against my inclination, to deprive you of the Pleasure of reading any more, and in Haste to Subscribe myself, Your Affectionate Neice

18 Jan 1785
Having dismiss'd my Company, regaled on some Apple pie that forcibly call'd you to my memory, ship'd off my Beau, I am retired for the sole purpose of fullfilling the promise I made to my Aunt Polly. Our last Packet to you was favor'd by Capt Fullerton and has I hope long ere this reached you, and that the welcome answers are dancing on their Passage; would a Vessel from England & Boston arrive with the interesting accounts of the Health of those whose Happiness I strongly feel is my own, methinks I should not have a wish ungratified; our last Letters from my beloved Parent were dated on the 23d of October, but contain little more than accounts of his Health and pleasing situation, the Specimen I sent you the other Day, will hold good now. He has removed his Lodgings from Pimlico to Soho Square, where he says, he lives in Stile. The only publick News is a confirmation of Doctor Silvester Gardiners being on the point of Marriage with Miss Katy Goldthaiwth, or properly spelt, Goldthwait. My own time this Winter has passed very agreeably. Our weather has been beautiful, beyond what I could

have form'd any idea of here, our Family compleatly Healthy, and we have this some time increased the size of it, by a Young Physician* who came recommended to my Brother, and is one of those *soft, pleasing, agreeable* Characters, that steal insensibly on your good opinion, and without knowing which way, you find on reflexion he *possesses* it. Our Breakfasts generally introduce some useful subject, and our Evenings in agreable insinnuating Chit chat, thus many a dull Hour is enliven'd which would otherwise pass over in unnoticed langour. My acquaintance tho' not very numerous are *select* and for the most part conversible; and I see myself indulged with the Friendship of several whom I highly *Love, Esteem & Value.* Among the first in this list, I place my excellent maternal Mrs. Cottnam. In her indulgent Bosom I repose every thought of my soul. She is the unreserved Mistress of my most secret thoughts. The Friendship she warmly professed for my angelised Mother, has diffused itself through our Family, and her goodness has indulged your happy Neice with a peculiar share. To describe her Character I cannot. I will not attempt yet she possesses every thing, that is excellent in Woman, and her advise will allways regulate the most important concerns of my Life. My Grissey also holds a distinguished place in my Heart, and in their united company I pass those Hours, which leave the most pleasing impression on my Mind. Forgive me beloved Aunt this digression. I flatter myself you will be pleas'd at knowing what so nearly concerns your Beccas happiness, and if the pleasing attention of a Gentleman, who is high in my Opinion will add to the group, I think I may say I possess them; our Betsy's Letter will inform you of many social parties, I have this gay Season been engaged in, where ceremony was banished "and Friendship, universal Friendship reign'd." I am just now reading a Book, I am much pleased with; did you ever see it? More's travells through France, Germany and Italy. He is a pleasing elegant writer, a vein of delicate humor runs through the whole, which is highly interesting, without entering into a dry detail of the political customs, and National Character of the People. He by many descriptive and pertinent anecdotes, clearly conveys them to your imagination; the amiable Character of the Emperor of Germans, engages my

*   A reference to her future husband, James William Almon.

Affections, while the great one of the King [of] Prussia excites my astonishment; what Powers of mind must that Man possess; how indefatigable his attention to Business; how perfect the discipline of his Army; yet when I see how shocking to humanity that discipline is obtain'd, that Men are merely considered as mechanical machines, only to breathe and move at the command of his Officers, I feel a rebellious Spirit arise, and congratulate myself that I was born in a land of freedom, where the rights of the subjects are more on an equality. I am very partial to the genevans, sensible, humane, hospitable, Generous, disinterested, with minds universally cultivated. I join the Author in thinking it a desirable retreat for those who are contented with moderate calm enjoyments, and who wish in a certain degree to retire from the Battle of the World to narrower & calmer & consequently happier Scenes. I think were I to recommend a course of reading to a Young Mind it should be History in preferance to any other. It tends to enlarge their ideas, extend their Humanity, increase their knowledge of the World, and I think has a tendency to mend the Heart, by painting those Virtues, & Vices on Paper, which in an intercourse with Life, might pass unnoticed. I have felt my Passions more interested, and my attention more engaged in an affecting trait of History than in the most work'd up Novel, I ever saw; but whither am I rambling, I wish I could oftenner recollect that I am engrossing time of yours, which might, and Which would, be spent to much more valuable purpose, but I have apologised so often I will not attempt it any more, but recommend it to you to support it with as much Philosophy as you can; one of those necessary evills with which Life abounds ...

15 April 1785
... Since my last I have been engaged in a course of Studies which will make you *Smile*: "the Dutchess de Craie on the importance of the female Sex, a Lady of Quality's advice to her children, Dr. Gregory's Legacy to his Daughters, and Letters of advice to New married Women. My Brain is quite confused with different Systems, and I have some thought of collecting the Beauties of all in a Volume of my own writing. You subscribe so liberally to Mathers Publication. You will certainly do some-

thing for me. The two first are I think just worth reading. There are a good many clever things amidst a great many trite Observations, and useless disquisitions. Dr. Gregory is beautiful; *short*, comprehensive & delicate. The thousand little decorums, and niceties of a female Character it appears allmost impossible for a Man to comprehend; but if they can I should suppose a work of this kind would be of more universal utility wrote by them than by one of the other Sex, because we may imagine that in his own, he spoke the language, *the real Sentiments* of the worthy part of his own Species, while a Woman can only judge by prejudiced experience. Am I right? I am not clear that I have made myself perfectly intelligible. Will you endeavor to Comprehend me? The last is by a Lady and except what relates to the Education of Children is *"Gregory diffused."* The Sentiments are just, the Language elegant, and the Stile Affectionate. It was recommended me, by my friend Mrs. C. & fully deserves the encomiums she bestowed, & I would strongly advise the perusal to every one, who has the prospect of wanting it. The Family are all well, and let the thousand *blots* & *incorrections* of this Letter convince you they are *in Spirits*. My Letter being instantly call'd for, prevents my enlarging any further....

1 June 1785

... I should have liked excessively to have made one at your Tea table with *Mrs Macauley*; I am not prejudiced in her favor. I think the qualities necessary to form a female Historian, must be at the expence of some of the most distinguish'd traits of the female Character; indeed I acknowledge myself by no means an advocate for a Womans ever exposing her Writings to the publick Eye. To debar them from committing to Paper the effusions of a correct Taste, or lively imagination, can only be the idea of *narrow* and *little* Minds, but I think a Woman would never wish them to go beyond the circle of her intimate connexions, that modest reserve, that retiring delicacy which is generally thought a distinguishing Characteristick of an amiable Female, & which recoils at the idea of having her Person constantly exposed to the publick, would I should imagine have the same effect on her writings. The free censures, the ill natur'd criticisms of one sex, the envy & jealousy of the other, would I think give Birth to many disagreable sensations, but perhaps I am wrong - it may be a peice of false delicacy. I do not know that I ever said so much on the subject before tho' I have allways thought it - the province of the two sexes are so very different, and when blended together, form so happy an union, that I have an amazing aversion that either should encroach on the privilege of the other. An account of my belov'd Parents arrival, you have in a Letter of an older date, which accompanys this, & which was intended by a Sloop which left us unfortunately before I could get it on board; could Mather have staid with us I should have been happy, but Alas a few Days only saw us all *pleased* round the *Parental Board* and I feel a kind of presentment it will be the last;* I feel with more than a Sisters tenderness the loss of his endearing Company; some of the most pleasing moments of my Life have been spent with him, and let my future lot in Life be what it will, they will always be reflected upon with renew'd Affection....

[Your letter of] April 29th [is] an abominable peice of Yankee twistification, and I shall show my contempt, by passing it over in silence, only telling you that your advice has had so good an effect upon me; that it has opend my Eyes to a design of the Doctors, to rob me of one of my Teeth, which I have with a good deal of address eluded ... should he attempt to *steal* any thing else, I should certainly inform you, out of Gratitude for the *hint*....

2 July 1785

The warm expressions of tenderness with which your Letters abound & the tender concern you profess to take for my welfare, induced me to take your Letter, wherein you appear'd so alarmed at the Doctors dishonesty, into my serious consideration; and after nicely inspecting that, & his behavior, will you not call me ingenuous when I tell you I found the strongest reason to suspect him; a thousand little circumstances, which my own unsuspecting Character made me overlook, now presented themselves to my Mind, my Thimble was lost, my Thread case met with the same fate. In short I was so alarm'd that I began to think of Barricading the House, & even should matters come to

---

* Rebecca's brother Mather had decided to move to New Brunswick "to turn Farmer & Cultivate Land." Anne Byles to Aunt Kitty and Polly, 30 May 1785.

an extremity, of laying a trap for him; fortunately for him, while I was sitting one delightful Moon light Evening, setling my arrangements, and wondering at your penetration, he entered! whether he perceived that I was alarmd! & wish'd to reinstate himself in my good Opinion, I know not, but he abruptly introduced the subject, and in a short time in *language* & *Sentiments* that "struck in unison with my Soul" convinced me that an exchange is no robbery, & I found that for value received, I had long been in possession of ample payment; but as Young People are apt to be deceived, I was determin'd to act cautiously & defer'd giving him an answer in his favor, till'd I had call'd in the advice of my Friends, and was not disagreably surprised, to find them already from his long intimacy, prepared in his favor, & that every thing depended on myself — need I explain myself further, & tell you the result; forgive my not enlarging further. I have stole a few moments to write thus far; when I shall be able to again I know not. Present my most Dutiful regards to my revered Grand Parent, emplore his Prayers, his Blessing, on his happy *Grandaughter* & now my beloved Aunts how greatly would it add to my pleasure to have you with me, to hear you approve my choice. His Picture which was sent much against my inclination, *I asure you*, you have; but the valuable Original even our Betsy who I ever thought was partial to him is not Qualified to give you a part descrption of. Some time hence, when I hope you will believe me, I will do it. He has just come in, and disired me to present his *best respects* which having done, I hasten to conclude my beloved Aunts, warmly & steadily attached Neice ....

EPILOGUE: REBECCA BYLES

In August 1785, Rebecca married James William Almon to whom she discreetly referred in her letters. Once married, Rebecca became absorbed in her life as a wife and mother. Of their six children, four survived infancy. She and her husband, whom she referred to as "the dear partner of her Heart," were happily married, and his death, in 1817, was hard for her to bear. However, unlike many widows, she was left "the means for frugal independence." As she grew older, Rebecca became noticeably more conservative in her views. She mocked her cousin Mrs. Crocker for writing her *Rights of Women* and described her as being "certainly crack." She was even more distressed by the growth of the Baptist Church in Nova Scotia. When her daughter, Amelia, and her husband James W. Johnston became converts, she wrote: "It has given me a great deal of Pain to have my Child removed from the faith in which she was educated." In a letter written on 4 August 1827, she noted that Baptists "appear to me to aim at a Spirituality not to be attained by Mortality, to give a glomy view of Religion, and with a view to magnify the Grace of Christ to make a Man completely a Machine to be worked upon .... " Clinging firmly to Church of England faith, she was bewildered and upset by the changes in the world around her. She died at the age of 91, a Loyalist to the last.

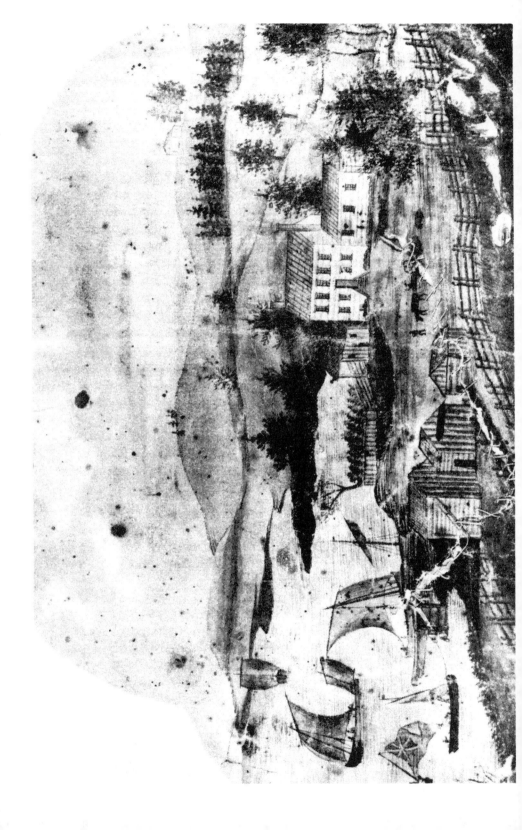

LOUISA COLLINS
1797-1869

Louisa Collins was the second of at least eight daughters born to Stephen and Phoebe Collins of Colin Grove, near Cole Harbour.* It is likely that her mother was the daughter of Reuben Coffin, a Nantucket Quaker, who lived in nearby Dartmouth. Little is known about Louisa's early life. References in her diary to Anglican prelates indicate that the Collins family were Anglicans, but church attendance seems not to have been an important aspect of family life. Like our earlier chroniclers, Louisa came from a diary-writing family. Both her father and grandfather kept logs containing brief entries about the weather and crops.** Louisa's entries are more forthcoming than those of her male relatives but her diary survives only for the brief period between August 1815 and January 1816. Nevertheless, from it we can gather something of the daily rhythm of farm activities and the rich social life experienced by rural families in the early nineteenth century. Paths in the woods led to nearby farms owned by the Allens and Brinleys, while Louisa's beau, Thomas Ott Beamish, as well as many others mentioned in the diary, crossed the harbour by boat regularly.

Louisa's diary shows us a world where women made most of the family clothing, worried about the hay crop and hurled curses at Napoleon "Bonnyparts." Between mundane duties in the dairy and the spinning room there were romantic trysts in the bower and jokes about "Yankee bundling." Such an unself-

* We would like to thank genealogist Marion D. Oldershaw, for her help in tracing the identity of the writer of this diary which was originally attributed to Phoebe Collins, and Mr. Dale McClure, whose vast knowledge of the Collins family and their early nineteenth century world was of great value to us in interpreting this diary.
** Public Archives of Nova Scotia, MG 1, Vol. 1846.

conscious acceptance of courtship practices might well have shocked Rebecca Byles who, if we can believe her letters, seems to have followed more circumscribed courtship rituals. Louisa's matter-of-fact description of her weekly chores cannot help but impress the modern reader with the exhausting nature of women's work in pre-industrial society. Her duties included haymaking, churning butter, spinning, reeling and weaving, sewing, cooking, washing, gathering berries, and "our ushal saterdays work," house-cleaning. That she had both time and energy left for three mile walks, social calls, "rural hops," and "ropery romps" is testimony to the fact that women were anything but the fragile flowers so often depicted in nineteenth century novels. We also sense that there is a division of duties in the Collins household. While Louisa was literally the 'spinster' in the family, she did not engage in commercial transactions. "Mama is Know tying up her readishes and turnips for market tomorrow morning; as that don't belong to my part of the work I have left her to herself .... " Louisa reports in her first diary entry printed here.

Scattered references to Blacks and Indians in the text are a reminder that Nova Scotia had a racially diverse population. That Louisa felt some ambivalence toward those unlike herself is clear. She makes reference to an unpleasant boat trip "crowded with blacks" and an alarming chance encounter with "a drunking Indian." At the same time she tells us (in a later diary entry not recorded here) that "this morning I have bin out to see an old black man, our old nabour Colly. He is very sick. I administered sum mint tea, and a warm broth." This latter activity suggests not only the philanthropic visits to the poor and sick obligatory for middle class women throughout the nineteenth century, but also the role women generally played in maintaining community well-being in the days before professional services and the welfare state appropriated these functions.

The importance of female companionship is apparent in Louisa's journal. Even before her marriage, Louisa regularly visited Thomas's mother and sister Harriet, who would soon be part of her extended family network. Indeed, Louisa's relationship with Harriet seems as vital and intense as that with "Mr.

Beamish." Since Harriet lived across the harbour in Halifax, the two young women were often separated. The exchange of notes therefore became an important part of Louisa's routine, the women typically being the ones who maintained the lines of communication. Louisa's sisters were also close companions. Louisa mourns the loss of her bed companion, sister Phoebe, when she goes on an overnight visit. Eliza, Charlotte and Louisa spend a morning "sitting in the haycart in the barn," an ideal location to share secrets and plot domestic strategies.

A network of female friends and relatives was not only a convenience; it was an essential feature of Louisa Collins rural world. When the wife is resident, Louisa refers to the homestead by her name; for example, "Mrs Pott's." She only uses a man's name if his wife is dead or absent from the home. Such practices, also followed by Louisa's grandfather, locate the woman at the heart of the household, the basic unit of production and social intercourse in pre-industrial society. Given the importance of 'home' in this period of Nova Scotia's history, it is easy to understand why women placed such emphasis on marriage. Only by this route could they establish their own households and take leadership in the important areas of production and reproduction which were centred in the home.

Reading "novils" and writing poetry were also important features of Louisa's life. It is likely that she was educated at home and therefore lacked the 'finished' literary tastes of Anna Winslow or Rebecca Byles. She was also a generation removed from these women and her propensity for poetic outbursts suggest the shift in sensibility that marked the transition between the 'rational' eighteenth and 'romantic' nineteenth centuries. Popular novels reflecting the Romantic Movement in literature encouraged self-dramatization and romantic trysts in secluded bowers, even if those bowers were surrounded by Canadian bush. Much of the fiction at this time, such as Barbara Hofland's *Patience and Perseverance*, was targeted at a female audience with the result that reading fiction was increasingly regarded as a frivolous pastime. Louisa hinted as much in her entry for 12 October when she describes her father reading a newspaper while her mother reads a novel: " … when mothers lead the way it is know wonder if daughters gos a stray." These New World domestic scenes would have delighted Jane Austen whose novels captured the nuances of similar situations in Old World settings.

Eighteen-year-old Louisa drifted between the factual rendering of daily events and bursts of rhetoric expressing her romantic inclinations. Her spelling and punctuation have been kept virtually as they were transcribed from the difficult script in the original text. Half the fun of reading Louisa's diary is discovering exactly how she pronounced the words she wrote in 1815.

LOUISA COLLINS DIARY
1815*

August the 15th

The dairy as ushal thakes up most of my morning on Tuesdays and after finishing there I picked a baskit of black currents for Miss Beamish — in the afternoon I sowed a littel while and then went out and raked hay, I wrote a note to my friend Harriet this evening — Aunt Cliffords girl and her sister have bin over all day picking Currents — Mama is know tying up her readishes and turnips for market to morrow morning; as that don't belong to my part of the work I have left her to her self — we have had a fine day to day, I shall retire early to night for I feel quite tired after my days work and call for neaturs sweet restorer, balmy sleep, how refreshing are thy downey pinnions to the toiling laborer who lays him down in peace, where know greedy fantom haunts his brain of sum black and guilty deeds.

August the 16

I have bin all the morning making hay — in the afternoon Mrs Beamish came over with papa and brough her black girl — I have bin out walking about with Mrs Beamish; it is a long time since she was here and every thing is much altered — she is know sitting talking with mama about old affairs — I recived a note from Harriet by papa — I have bin little disappointed to day for I expected a friend this afternoon — we have had a beautiful day.

August 17th

I am very buisy all the morning with house work — in the afternoon I went with Mrs Beamish and picked sum berrys — when we returned home we found Mrs Allen here, after tea the evening was so beautiful I walked home with her; we met Mrs Brinley and we all went up then with her .... we then went and took a walk ... as we returned we stoped in at Mrs Poots's [Potts] and I tapped at her window wch gave a little alarm; we had a

---

*   Public Archives of Nova Scotia, MG 1, Vol. 1463, C.B. Ferguson typescript. Corrections and annotations have been generously provided by Dale McClure.

good rap with her and then left her. Mrs Brinley and Sally came part the way home with C and me as we had know bow; we were to give the signal to each other when out of danger by a loud scream, wich we did. It has bin very warm to day but not very clear; the evening is remarkable pleasant with a beautiful fool moon.

August the 25
I have returned from town* to day with Mr Beamish. I have bin spending a week with his mother and sisters. Never did I spend a pleasenter week, all tho the weather was so unpleasant as to prevent me from going out, but murth and good humer ran'd [reigned] with in which maid up for every other difishency. It never was known to rain harder than it did for two days and since we have never bin free from fog: it is soon a week since we have had a fine day, I am afraid there will be much hay spoilt. Papa has got a great dele down since I have cum hom I have bin picking peas with mama — there is nothing knue in town; at present everything is very dul.

August the 26
I have bin carding and spinning this morning, and in the afternoon I went with the girls and pick'd sum baberys — Papa has bin to town to day but has brot know knus — I stoped at my littel bower this afternoon but it looked so dul I cold not stay long, and the weather being very dul hurried me from the spot where I have spent many happy moments — I have not seen any one since I came home, and time passes heavely on — night has thrown on her sable mantle, and I know prepare for bead.

August the 27
My morning was mainly taking up in the citchin geting dinner … after dinner … I was quite alone, till Mr. Beamish came; we went to the orchard and pick'd sum currents and then we took a walk to Mr Russals lake; when we returned tea was ready. The fog came in very thick and Mr Beamish stade all night — George

* Halifax

came up with Beatsy, and Mr B and he has taking my bead — I hear them snorring famously, and I shall folo there example.

August the 28
I have bin picking currents from nine this morning til fore this afternoon. We have got a large washingtub ful for wine — since, I have bin raking hay till nerely night — Mr Beamish and George left here very early this morning. I did — not see them — while I was picking currents my thoughts were imployed with how I should be and what I should be doing this day twelve months.

August the 30th
As it was quite late last night when I came home I had not time to write down yesterdays work — I was very bussy making wine neare all day, and butter — in the afternoon I pickd sum berrys, and then went to Mrs Allens to tea — I meet Mrs Brinly coming over to see me, but she insisted on my going with her — in the evening we went over to Mrs Poots's and had a ropery romp. Sally was dressed as a little dutch man and introduced as Mr P-bow ... To day I have bin buisy making hay till I was very tired — after dinner Aunt Elizabeth came up and Mr Beamish — mama and aunt were picking currents all the afternoon and Mr B and me took care of Jenny — I have worked a small piece of triming to day beside making hay — Mr Beamish brought me a note from Harriet — and I wrote a short one to her. I hope my friend Thomas is near his journys end for the night looks very dark. How often do I wish there was a bridge across the harbour that I might see my friends with out any danger — papa has bin to town today. It gros late and I feel moore inclined to sleep than write — I know here the ferry horn blowing and the night is very dark which makes it sound quite melencholy — heven grant that my friend may git over safe.

August 31st
This morning I was sowing as it was so unpleasant I cold not go out — I worked a peace of triming and allterd two frocks — this afternoon the Miss Prescott's and Aunt Sally came and spent the evening and there brother — I was very buisy sowing when tha came, for we did not expect cumpenny the weather was so un-

pleasant, tha have jest gon and I think tha will have a mudy walk and the night is very dark — I hope that loving brother of theres will not leve them in the mud.

September the 1
This has bin a very rainy day, and I have bin sowing all day till a bout five oclock when it left of raining and mama and me went and pick'd sum pease and beans — I have bin allterring a frock and working sum triming — it has rainned very hard to day and I fear much of our hay is spoilt. I sincerly hope to morrow may be fine — it is so cold this evening that I have bin sitting by the fire — winter approches fast and we have had very little warm weather.

September the 2
This has bin a very busy day with me and all — we had our house to clean all over after the rain, and since ten oclock I have bin makin hay till quite dark — Papa has bin to town to day. He brought me a note from Harriet and the muslin I sent for — I am to tired to write and bead I think will be the best place — the weather has bin very fine to day.

September the 3
To day has bin a dul day — in the morning I took a walk to my Bower and pickd sum baabers on my way, the afternoon it raind hard. I wrote a note to Harriet — there has bin know one here to day — our old man has gon to take a walk and has not returned — I went out to milk — it is a stormy night it thunders and lightens — our milk boy will have a bad time home — I have sent my note by him.

September the 4
I have not dun much of anything to day, in the morning I made hay a little while, and since I have bin sowing — Charlotte came home from Dartmouth this morning — Mrs Macy and her daughter have cum from Nantucket tha arived on Sunday last — there is nuse of Bonnyparts bing taking — I hope it is true,

there is know punnishment two grate fer sich a rech — homenny lives has bin sacrefised for his ambition.*

September the 5
After I had finished making my buter this morning I went to spinning. Mrs Brinly sent for sum of us to go to Miss Farquarson. I declined going and none went but Betsy — in the afternoon mama and the girls went to pick berrys and I was left a lone, except little Joanne who was a sleep — last night the frost was so greate as to kill all the cucumber, and it has bin very cold all day.

September the 6
I have bin carding and spinning all day, it has bin an unpleasant day and rained so as to prevent Papa from going to town — I have bin sowing a little this evening on a cap which bothers me to make it fit — nothing has happened to day worthy of notice — it know rains very hard and I shall retire early.

September the 7
We have had a very large wash to day which keep me very buisy — in the afternoon Mrs Brinly came over to tea; we went and took a walk and got sum berrys we did not git home till tea time, we got in deep conversation about old times. Edward came for her in the evening. Tha have jest gone and it is quite late and very cold.

September the 8
After my ushal work in my dairy I went to hay making and worked nearly all day, I took a walk to Dansvil grove and passed a solitary hour in my favourite spot; the beauty of Neatur are beginning to fade, and chill winter will soon spread his heavy mantil — then fare well you rural walks and shady groves — I received a note from my friend this evening, and I have jest answered it — it growes late and I feel very fatiged after my days work.

* A reference to Napoleon Bonaparte, Emperor of France, 1804-1815.

September the 9
After my ushel Saturdays work, I went out and made hay till night. Papa was in town this morning; he brote me a note from Harriet. She has not bin very well: Captain Osburn has returned from New York. While we were all out making hay this afternoon Uncle Coleman and Eliza came; tha came out and worked with us till we finished; when it began to rain. We have bin sitting by the kitchen fire warming ourselves the weather is so cold.

September the 10
We were sitting in the hay cart in the barn all the morning — Eliza and Charlotte and me — after dinner George Coleman and Edward and John Allen came over for the girls to go over there. E and C went to tea — Mr Beamish came up in the afternoon. We went to the orchard to pick sum Currents; we then returned to the barn and sit in the hay till tea. After tea Betsy and Maryann went over to join the party — I expect Eliza will return with them — I think we shall have a real Yanky bundal* for Mr B dus not go home to night. I know hear him and the two old people talking a bout old times — and I must join them.

September the 11
Mr Beamish did not go home till after breakfast this morning as it was a rainy morning — Eliza and me sit down to sowing all the morning. In the afternoon we took a walk round the rode to Mrs E Allens. Eliza and Charlotte got mashured for a pare of boots, on our way we went to Mrs Frostes but I did not go in. When we got home tea was ready — after tea we walked to our [bower] we sit there and sung a song or two and danced a jig. The evening was very pleasant; we returned home and retired early, as it was twelve oclock last night when we went to bead — *going to the well this morning I fell down* and hurt myself very much.

September the 12
I was carding and spinning all morning by myself — and Eliza has had a large wash of two pare of stockings — in the afternoon

* To lie in the same bed with one's sweetheart without undressing, a courting custom associated with New England.

mama and the girls came up in the spinning room with me. Eliza and Charlotte sowd and mamma helped me spin — after our work was over we went to the barn and had a swing and a romp in the hay — mama was to go to town but the rain prevented her — there was to be sum fire works preformed to night but the rain I sepose will put a stoop to it.

September the 13
This morning was spent very buisy in the spinning room and part the afternoon — Eliza took a nap this afternoon — Papa has bin to town this afternoon and Aunt sent for Eliza to come home — I went as far as Nanshill with hir — we meat Frederick and I bid hir good by and walkd home — Papa brote me a note from Harriet she is well — she sent me the musln I sent for — Eliza and me has bin rompin to day in the spinning room. We found time for that all tho we were very buisy — I shall feel quite lonsum know she is gon — but I live in hopes.

September the 14
This morning I was buisy washing — in the afternoon Mr Beamish came up and brout his hors — he spent this afternoon mending his gun and making me wate on him with the tuils — poor Pheby has meat with a sad miss fortun, a crow has taking a way one of her chikins and it was one of her favourits — Mr Beamish rode after it with his gun but cold not git it — the weather has bin disagreeable all day.

September the 15
In the morning I was making butter, and ironing and spinning — this afternoon I have bin sowing; I have bin making a spencer* for my frock — this evening I wrote a note to Harriet and one to Maria — nothing of any conciquence has happend to day and I do not feel very well and shall retire early — the weather has bin the same as usal disagreable and weat I am afraid much of our hay will spoil.

* A short jacket.

September the 16
It is Saturday to day and as usial cleaning house — after that was over I went to spinning and spun a large ball — Papa has bin to town to day; he brought me a note from Harriet, she promises to come over to morrow if fine — I took a run before night and got a few blackberrys. I got my feet very weat for it has raind every day this week — Mr Farquarson came here this evening; he did not stop long. Papa went with him to Mr Allens. I have bin sitting by the kitchin fire, knitting this evening; I am preparring for winter — for he approches very fast, wich prospict then how hopeless — we find the fire side the only cheerful compannion, when keen blows the north blast and heavy drives the snow.

September the 17
I spent my morning in reading — for it was so disagreable. I did not expect my friend — after dinner I made cake — a bout fore oclock Mr Beamish came up — I was quite surprised when I heard him below, I was sitting up stares reading not expecting to see anyone; he has not gon home this evening and takes my bead to night — I shall be preforced to seek a lodge ment else ware — Mr Wilom Allen came in a little while this afternoon for the news paper — I believe all the fates are against my friends comming over for this is the second Sundy appointed.

September the 18
I have spent the most of my day in spinning — Papa, Mama and Pheby went to Mrs Sturts this afternoon: Papa has jes returned with out mamma and Pheby; it rained so hard tha cold not com home — and I shall have to sleep without my bead fellow to night — Mr Beamish left here very early this morning befor I was up. Know dought he arrivd time a nuf for brakefast — this afternoon I went to the orchard and got sum Currents and took a walk and got sum blackberrys before the rain cum on.

September the 19
This has bin a nother spinning day with me — mamma and Pheby cum home this morning. Tha got very weat — I have jest wrote a note to Harriet — it has bin a very disagreeable day —

and I have bin up in my spinning room all day by my self — my spirits do not feel good for writing to night and as there is nothing nue I must wate till to morrow.

September the 20
I have bin spinning again all day. I expect I shall grow like a weed in the shade for I go no farther than my dairy and from there to my spinning room — Papa has bin to town to day he broute me a note from Harriet and a box of wafers — I am sorry to here that Mrs Beamish and Miss Beamish are not very well — Charlotte has gone to drink tea with Sarahann Allen, and papa has gone to Mr Allens this evening, I have bin sitting by the fire knitting — it is a fine evening and I sincerely hope it will be fine to morrow.

September 21
To day I have bin very busy, I have bin washing all the morning, Betsy and Maryann went to town this morning; tha did not git home till late this evening — all the afternoon I have bin making hay, and so has mamma — George came home with the girls, and returned home again.

September the 22
I had a tedious time making butter this morning, the weather is so cold — after dinner mamma and me walked to Dartmouth; mamma went to town to spend a day or two — in the evening Papa came down on horse back, and I rode home behind him; it was late when we arrived — I cald at Mr Colemans to see Mrs Macy her daughter was not home.

September the 23
I have not dun much to day except house work: papa has bin in town to day; mama has not cum home, the weather is so unpleasant, the house feels quite lost without hir — Pheby and me have bin sitting a lone this sum time for the girls are all in bead and Papa has bin in the palor reading.

September the 24
Sunday morning, first went to my dairy and did my ushal work,

secondly prepared dinner, thirdly sewd a little, forthly dressed myself, fifthly saw companny. Mr Beamish came up and dind with us, Papa went to town and took Gorgenia; after dinner George Coleman came up, Mr Allen came over a little while, Mr Beamish and me took a little walk to our little bower — George and Charlotte milked the cows for old Skinner went of and left us — it was late when Papa got home, and the two gentlemen have taking posesion of my room to night.

September the 25
The most of this morning was taking up with house work, and since I have bin spinning — I wrote a note this evening to my friend and sent it by the milk boy — Mr Beamish and George left here very early this morning, before we were up — nothing worthy of notice has happened to day; we git on as well as can be expectid without mama — Mrs Brinly has gon to town to spend sum time with Miss Mansfield, my candle is most out and I must give up writing for to night.

September the 26
I have not dun much to day, spun a little in the morning, in the afternoon saw compenny — Miss Macy, Mary and Eliza came up, and Eliza Allen and Sally came over to tea — Mary and me went and picked sum blackberrys while the other girls got read-ishes — I think Miss Macy a nice little girl — James cum up for them, and tha have jest gon — tha will have a dark walk — we have had a very fine day.

September the 27
I have bin spinning a little to day, mamma cum hom to day and Gorgina and Ann Coleman came up with hir. She has bin two days in Dartmouth; yesterday she drank tea at Mrs Albows — it has bin very cold to day and we have bin all seated round the fire like a winters night.

September the 28
I have bin very buisy washing to day; we had a large wash and not finnish till afternoon — Papa was in town this morning, he brought me a note from Harriet — Miss Beamish has bin very

sick but is gitting better — Mama has gone to Mrs Allens to tea
— papa has jest gon over — I hear Mr Osterman was marid last
night to Miss Eetter. I do not know how true the report is — it
has bin a fine day but very cold, I hear the children making a
famus noise below. I must go see what is the matter.

September the 29
This morning I was very buisy churning and making butter —
and the remainder of the day I spent in the spinning room —
Pheby went down with Ann this afternoon, I do not know what
I shall do with out hir for a bead fellow — I have jes wrote a note
to Harriet to send by in the morning — it has bin a very fine day
and Papa has bin improving it gitting in grain - there is nothing
nue at Colin Grove to day.

September the 30
To day I have bin busy with our ushal saterdays work — house
work — Mrs Thomson and Mrs Allen took tea here this evening
— Papa has bin in town twice to day — he broght me a note
from Harriet, I expect hir over to morrow if fine — it has bin a
beautiful fine day and very warm, the ladys have jest gon,
Charlotte is over to Mr Allens. She is going to stay all night.

October the 1
Sunday morning the girls came up and dined with us Harriet
and Maria, Mr Beamish and Salter; we spent our day sowing
and walking, I went home with the girls, we had a very disagreable time over; the boat was crowded with blacks, and the winds
blew very hard. When we arrived we found Mr and Mrs Osburn
— Mrs Beamish gave us a dish of hot coffe which was very acceptable after our long walk; we retired early — Mondy mornin
— we spent the most of our day walking — Tuesday we went
out to Shefrows to tea — Wensdy came home. Harriet and Mr B
— came with me; Harriet and my self have bin out with Thomas
gunning — we have bin sitting by the kitchen fire all the evening — Harriet is now sitting by me while I write — I feel my
eys drawing to gether, and I think it is time to retire so adiue to
writing.

October the 5
We spent the morning in running a bout picking blacberrys —
and after dinner Harriet Betsy Charlotte and my self walked to
Dartmouth to tea at Aunts — we took a walk up the roade a little
way before tea — the two boys came home with us in the evening: Charlotte has stade all night — we all feel fatiuged after
our walk and shall retire early.

October the 6
This morning I was very busy in my dairy, churning and making
butter; Harriet was helpping me churn; the remainder of the day
we sit up stares reading and knitting, Patience and Perseverance
is the tital of the book we are perusing. I think it a very good
thing, the weather has bin rather dul to day which prevented us
from taking a walk, have left them all seated round the table at
ther dometic imployments, sum sowing and others knitting,
and Pappa at the head reading — I must hurry to return to my
work or I shall be indisgrace — all's well!

October the 7
This morning has bin spent very busy cleaning house — in the
afternoon Betsy Harriet and myself walked up to Mr Prescotts
to tea; we spent a very pleasant afternoon; in the evening Papa
came up for us on horse back — Harriet rode home behind him,
Charlotte Patty Betsy and Liady came part the way home with
us escortd by there brother Johnthin.

October the 8
Sunday as soon as we dun brakefast Harriet and me walked out
to old Collys to git a horse to make up a riding party to go to
Mrs Stuarts at Cole harbour — but we soon returned disa-
pointed in our expectations of riding singel hors, we sit down
and read a little and then dresd our selves — Mr Beamish came
up and dind with us — after dinner we got the shoes and went
to Cole harbour. Harriet and Betsy roade, and Mr Beamish and
me walked; the lady of the manshin was from home, but we
stoped to tea with the gentlemen; we returned home early as the
evening was disagreable, Mr Beamish has not gon home to
night.

October the 9
This morning Harriet and me has spent in the spinning room; she read to me while I prepared for cold winters want — in the afternoon Harriet, Charlotte and me went to Mrs Farqurasons to tea, C came home last night — we had a very disagreable walk home — the night was dark and very foggy — Mr A F came home with us, I am afraid he git a compleat soking, for it has cum on to rain very hard — we have had potatoes and milk for our supper and shall retire early compleatly tired with our jaunt.

October the 10
I have spent nearly all my day in spinning and my book was all my compannion to day — this morning Harriet went home and Betsy went with hir to spend a few days — Uncle Brown cald here this afternoon but did not stop long — mama is not well this evening, she did not take tea with us — I feel quite lonly know Harriet is gon, I shall retire early to night as I do not feel well.

October the 11
I have spent my day nearly all in my spinning room with a boock; mama came to see me and told me I had better go and see Mrs Allen which I did — after tea Sally and me took a run over to Mrs Poots's, she was a little alarmmed when comming down stares to find us sitting in her room — when I rived home I found a note from Harriet by which I learn Mr B has gon to the fare in Winsor* — it is now quite late and I must prepare for bead with the sincer prayer for my distant Friend.

October the 12
I have bin very busy nearly all day washing till my fingers are all sore; this afternoon I read a little, and wrote a note to Harriet and sent by the milk boy — they have finished mowing the meadow to day; it has blown a gail all day and it seems to continue this evening — I have just left mama and Papa sitting reading, one the nuse paper and the other a novil; when mothers lead the way it is know wonder if daughters gos a stray.

---

*   A reference to Nova Scotia's oldest agricultural fair, held at Windsor.

EPILOGUE: LOUISA COLLINS

Nineteen year old Louisa Collins married her beau, thirty-five year old Thomas Ott Beamish on 21 September 1816. They had twelve children, the first born in June 1817 and the last in September 1844. Thomas was a butcher, clerk of the market and landholder in the city of Halifax. As a member of the city's respected middle class, it is unlikely that Louisa dressed in homespun or worked in the hay fields as she did in her youth. However, there is some evidence to suggest that the Beamishes experienced a number of financial difficulties which probably meant that Louisa was forced to draw upon some of the skills that she had acquired as a farm girl.

By the time Thomas died in 1860, the Beamishes were living on Dresden Row in Spring Gardens. Long before that time, on a Sunday in 1827, Colin Grove burned to the ground, while Louisa's parents and younger sisters were in church.

Louisa died in April 1869, nine years after the death of her husband.

MEMOIR

OF

MRS. ELIZA ANN CHIPMAN,

WIFE OF

THE REV. WILLIAM CHIPMAN,

OF PLEASANT VALLEY,

CORNWALLIS.

~~~~~~~~~~

Sold by John Chase, Wolfville—price 3s.

Frontispiece of Eliza Ann Chipman diary as published by her husband in 1885.

ELIZA ANN CHIPMAN
1807-1853

Eliza Ann Chipman was born in the Annapolis Valley on 3 July 1807. The Chipmans were New England Planters who had moved from Connecticut to Cornwallis Township soon after the expulsion of the Acadians from the region. Eliza began her diary when she was sixteen years old at the suggestion of Baptist minister Edward Manning.* A year later she joined the Baptist Church, an event which marked a significant turning point in her life. In 1827, before she had reached her twentieth birthday, she married another minister, her cousin William Chipman, whose wife had recently died leaving eight motherless children. Eliza herself bore twelve children. Despite her many family obligations, which were, no doubt, carefully scrutinized by the community, Eliza was also called upon to play a more official public role. As her diary indicates, Eliza led prayer meetings, taught Sunday School and played hostess to the many visitors who came to the parsonage. She was an important role model for young women in Pleasant Valley (now Berwick) where her husband was pastor. In the 1850s two young women from Pleasant Valley made the long journey to Mount Holyoke Seminary in South Hadley, Massachusetts, to study under Mary Lyon. One of these women, Alice Shaw, returned to Nova Scotia to establish her own female seminary and she eventually married Eliza's son, Alfred.**

Eliza Chipman's journal does not make easy reading. The rhetorical outbursts and stock phrases common to spiritual di-

---

* Edward Manning also kept a diary as did many devout Baptists of the period. See Edward Manning Diary, 1809-1846, Baptist Collection, Acadia Archives, Vaughan Memorial Library, Acadia University.

** James Doyle Davidson, *Alice of Grand Pré* (Wolfville, 1981).

aries of the period seem oddly juxtaposed with the events of Eliza's busy and often dramatic domestic scene. Nevertheless, there is a sense of psychological exploration in this narrative that is not found in any of the other diaries written by our gentlewomen. The evangelical pattern of doubt and despair, conversion and backsliding, served as a framework within which all events in Eliza's life were interpreted. Her emotional and imaginative life, indeed, her own female consciousness, was so completely dominated by the demanding conventions of 'born again' evangelicalism that she responded to earthly concerns such as courtship and marriage in ways considered unconventional even by many of her contemporaries.

As an adolescent Eliza was already imbued with a predestinarian world-view that divided society into the "chosen" who belonged to God and the "lost" souls doomed to eternal damnation. Preoccupied by the psychological tensions created by this duality, she relinquished the temptations of this world for a "sound conversion." Public, full immersion baptism and reception into the Baptist Church was a major rite of passage to adulthood in her Annapolis Valley community where nearly half of the population were Baptists. Yet, church membership did not save Eliza from a morbid preoccupation with fear, doubt, self-hatred and denial. On the contrary, it encouraged an even more rigorous self-examination. Her mental state is encapsulated in one sentence: "It is the fear of sinning that makes me afraid to live." In more metaphorical language she inquires: "has …. the sow that was washed and returned to her wallowing in the mire, returned again to the beggarly elements of this insidious world?" We are not more than 100 kilometers and ten years removed from Louisa Collins whose response to the world seems to have been determined as much by popular novels as by religious prescription. But Eliza offers a whole new discourse, peculiar to those raised on the Bible, Baptist doctrine and Watt's hymns.

To some degree marriage and motherhood tempered Eliza's obsessive spirituality. Although she continued to interpret events within a religious framework, she also foreshadowed the activities of the 'new woman' in her role as Sunday school teacher and prayer meeting leader. The alliance of women and the clergy in both resisting and shaping the values of the new industrial order in the United States has been documented by Ann Douglas.* From her diary, Eliza appears to have been a reluctant reformer but her religious conviction and position as a minister's wife made it difficult for her to use her domestic responsibilities — which were real enough — as an excuse to avoid her new 'calling.' A disciplining faith, curiously gender blind in its rigid prescriptions, encouraged Eliza to liberate herself from certain restraining aspects of women's role in nineteenth century Nova Scotia. She perceived herself not only as a wife and mother, but as a spiritual being whose worldly concerns infringed upon her personal development.

The modern reader cannot help but wonder what a woman of Eliza's determination and sensibility would have done with her life in another place and time. Domestic duties and a fatalistic approach to reproduction made it impossible for Eliza even to imagine other possibilities for herself. Nevertheless, she perhaps sensed that her 'otherworldliness' was a source of temporal as well as spiritual strength for women. Historian Nancy Cott has argued that the very act of recording their religious meditations was testimony for women like Eliza of their literacy and rising self-consciousness.** Eliza's decision shortly before her death to reveal her secret diary suggests that she had indeed developed a sense of self that transcended — or as Eliza might see it, extended — the spiritual concerns expressed in her writings.

Only a few excerpts from Eliza's diary which she kept from 1823 until a few days before her death in October 1853 are reproduced here.***

*   Ann Douglas, *The Feminization of American Culture* (New York, 1980).
**   Nancy Cott, *The Bonds of Womanhood* (New Haven, 1977), p. 141.
*** For a detailed discussion of Eliza Chipman and her times see, James Doyle Davidson, *Eliza of Pleasant Valley* (Wolfville, 1983). An annotated edition of Eliza Chipman's diary is presently being prepared for the Baptist Heritage in Canada series by Allen and Caroline Robertson.

ELIZA ANN CHIPMAN DIARY
1823-1837*

July 20, 1823
This little book was made yesterday, for the purpose of penning down a few of the exercises of my mind. But filled as I am with a sense of my own weakness and insufficiency, I rejoice that the Lord is able to bless the weakest means for the good of his chosen. Oh! I do feel assured that I am one of his chosen. If I am, why am I thus? why this dull and lifeless frame? I cannot relinquish the idea that the God of all grace and mercy called me by his mighty power and by his outstretched arm to attend to the things which belong to my eternal peace. O yes, he has called loud to me by taking my dear brother from me by death. Two years ago last May it sounded in my ears, "Be ye also ready, for in such an hour as ye think not the Son of man cometh." About six weeks before his death the Lord was pleased to afflict me with a slight sickness, at which time I was led to read the word of God more frequently than before, and never could think of lying down to rest without begging of God to have mercy upon me, and to shew me in a real sense the vanity of this transient world ....

July 27
Another week has rolled its round. I have let it pass imperceptibly away without ever dropping a word in this little book; but my thoughts have been often with it, and I have thought what material use will it be to me to pen down here some of the incidents that may occur during the short course of my life. Will it be to my own satisfaction and comfort, much more to the real satisfaction of those whose hands these lines may fall into? — But I have often heard my dear Minister, (Mr. Manning,) speak of the comfort persons might enjoy if they would pen down the first exercises of their minds, and how they then felt the strivings of the Holy Spirit; they might look back with joy thereon ....

---

* Published as *The Memoir of Mrs Eliza Chipman, Wife of the Rev. William Chipman of Pleasant Valley, Cornwallis* (Halifax, 1855).

Having taken a slight cold in my head it appears now to be resting upon my lungs, a hacking cough succeeds occasionally, which flatters me with the idea that time is short. I almost look forward with joy to the hour that shall free me from this body of sin and death. Willingly would I take a final farewell of my nearest and dearest relatives, and resign all earthly objects to awake with Jesus, and be forever with him ....

September 3

Three days ago my beloved Cousin arrived at our mansion, in a very debilitated state; but O what was my great surprise in seeing her so thoughtless and unconcerned about her future destiny, and so much allured with the fantastic visions of this nether world! Divine Redeemer, change the tenor of her thoughts, and let her realize that, although young, yet she must see; and O fit and prepare her for her great and last change, which will surely come.

January 30, 1824

My pen has long lain inactive, which at times has caused me many heart-rending feelings; to be so immersed with the concerns of life is a great hindrance to private enjoyments; but this is not all my excuse, because when a person's mind is rightly exercised, every thing will bow in subjection to the important concerns of their souls. Well, I must call in question what I have been about for these four months as well as all my life through. I would however observe, that in the omission of writing so long a time, I feel safe in saying that, during that time, I passed through what is generally termed a sound conversion. Such was the distress of my mind, that I knew not what to write clearly, and I feared at the same time that my convictions never had been such as they should be preceding conversion; and in addition to this I felt a heavy load of God's wrath hanging over my head, knowing that I was justly doomed to everlasting punishment. But I will say to the praise and glory of Jehovah's name, my greatest extremity was the time of God's opportunity. He brought my feet up out of the horrible pit, and miry clay, and set them upon the rock of ages; he put a new song into my mouth, even praise to our God. Though I cannot ascertain the identical moment in which the Lord passed by, and said unto me, "live," yet I can say, that whereas I was once blind now I see. Happy seasons were enjoyed by me; I would pray for the evidence of divine grace, while Satan would tempt me by telling me I was in possession of none. I am led however to inquire have I found that sweet confidence in my God which I had anticipated? has Christ become the ultimate end of all my wishes? the sow that was washed and returned to her wallowing in the mire, returned again to the beggarly elements of this insidious world? God forbid that I should ever be left to my own fleshly lusts!.

May 13
What a solemn transaction has taken place since I last wrote! I have entered into covenant with God's people, have cast my lot in with them, the excellent ones of the earth, and have been received into the bosom of the Baptist Church. What unmerited favours am I privileged with!...

January 5, 1825
With grateful acknowledgements, I trust, have I welcomed the commencement of another year. Great transactions have transpired during the last year that is forever gone; many delightful events connected with my own best interests, and I hope for the glory of God have taken place ....

July 3
Sabbath morning. Have this day entered upon my eighteenth year; but how stands my mind affected towards the lovely Jesus? Have I pressed on by the direction of the Holy Spirit to further degrees of grace since my last birth day? ...

March 1 [1826]
I have been enabled to arise from the bed of slumber at an early hour. I feel that I have too long indulged in that known sin. I want to deny self and all ungodliness, and I think I have experienced some good effects which proceed from it in two particulars, — in being (at intervals) abstemious in my food and (which I have reason to add, was only at intervals) in leaving the bed of sloth. Oh how little do I and many of my dear fellow

travellers to the celestial world know of the happy consequences of being conformed to the cross of Christ! ...

July 30

Sabbath evening. Have this day been prevented going to the house of God, by the too tender care (I think) which my parents have of my health. I however enjoyed, I trust, the privilege of retirement, and was led to reflect much on a speedy preparation for health, from a dream which I had last night. I dreamed of being at a meeting where there was a vast concourse of people; it appeared a very solemn time, as there had been many deaths around. One of God's Ministers came to me, namely, Mr. Harding, and said, "such a day thou must die." Not feeling much alarmed, on account of not hearing the sound distinctly, I yet felt curious to know when. After a few moments I thought I asked Mr. Harding how long it would be before the summons would be sent to call me hence? He answered "in three or nine days," this filled me with a sensation not to be described. I thought every one who saw me was gazing at me with astonishment, wondering why I was not more alarmed. I awoke, and it seemed to have a great impression upon my mind; how it is, the Lord only knows ....

March 31 [1827]

How shall I record the events of the past evenings, which are so important and weighty a nature! Oh that the God of heaven would direct me. I am now called upon to decide my situation for life, if it is the will of him who cannot err, and who is too good to be unkind. How much hesitancy do I feel on the account, if it should not be for the glory of God. Many things combined make me to shrink and almost recoil at the thought. The person paying his addresses is a widower and father of eight children, some older than myself, and one of them, especially, very much opposed. He is a beloved member of Christ and his Church, which is one particular inducement, as I always was opposed to believers and unbelievers being united. He is situated only half a mile from my father's mansion; every religious privilege granted unto me as at home (though I shall feel vastly different, having the charge of a large family). I was ever averse to leaving Cornwallis unless God in a very special manner called me. I have often thought (when reflecting upon heathen lands) that my nearest and dearest relatives would be no more than a thread to me, if God would only qualify and call me to go and tell the good news of a Saviour. What is opening for me in my own land heaven only knows. O guide me by thy counsel, dearest Parent, and afterwards receive me to glory.

April 12

Solemn and important have been the transactions of this evening. I have now, amidst opposition and conflict, given my hand to my nearest earthly friend. I trust it has been in the fear of Almighty God; and in the whole affair the glory of God and the good of a fellow creature have been the governing motives. Oh how arduous is the undertaking! May God sanctify me throughout, soul and body, and qualify for me to serve him acceptably.

May 24

The solemn day has arrived for my union with one of the household of faith and of the same name with myself; and in all probability the sun will never set again upon me (or at least for a time) in a single life. Oh how weighty and important does the subject appear! I hope I am not deceived, when I say, I feel that I am in the presence of Almighty God, and can make a free surrender of soul and body, all into his blessed hands, to lead, to guide, and to defend me through this thorny maze. Enable me, righteous Parent, to watch therefore (that I may not be overcome with the cares of this life and so that day come upon me unawares) and pray always, that I may be counted worthy to escape all these things that shall come to pass, and stand before the Son of Man. Solemn is a view of the transaction (my case being extraordinary, how can I ever perform the part of a mother to these orphan children on account of my youth and inexperience? But I can only say, if God has called me thereto, he is able to qualify me for the task; here I find safe trusting); but when I realize that heaven and earth are called to witness my engagements to an earthly friend, and that God and his holy angels are viewing me with minute inspection, I indeed feel weighty impressions. Oh that I may ever hold my precious Jesus up to view by my life and conversation, and be a fountain of praise to my covenant-keeping God. Lord, I implore thy grace to help me in this time of need, for soon must I go to engage in the important undertaking. Oh that the fear of God may be before my eyes.

June 28
Have been preserved through dangers seen and unseen while journeying to Chester to attend an Association,* and am with my companion, through the kindness of our dear Redeemer, safely returned ....

July 19
Am still the spared monument of God's saving mercy; have been quite indisposed the day past, but did not feel to murmur, or complain, knowing that God is my refuge and a never failing prop. The words of the poet are very sweet to me this morning:

> Amazing grace, how sweet the sound
> That saved a wretch like me;
> I once was lost, but now am found,
> Was blind, but now I see.

Twenty years of my life are gone, never to be recalled; and what have I done for God? Nothing, nothing. I am on a journey towards my eternal home; how it becomes me, to study, to honor and glorify my king and captain. How much I need journey bread! Lord, impart it to me, for there is enough in thine house and to spare.

January 27 [1828]
Lord's day. This is in some measure a quiet day after a week of confusion, arising from an election within two miles of our house, and my father-in-law being one of the representatives. Alas, how much wickedness has been manifested — enough to sink a world! Oh, if all were as anxious to make their calling and

* The Nova Scotia Baptist Association was an annual meeting of representatives from the Regular Baptist churches which practised adult baptism and close communion.

election sure as many have been in these political affairs, how much more safe would their standing be! ...

February 17
Sabbath day. Here I am, confined to the house (owing to peculiar circumstances) and suffering some privations, but they are small compared to what many have to endure. We have family worship statedly, bibles and good books to peruse, and the same God here as in the sanctuary; the most that is wanting is a thankful heart for the comforts and mercies, spiritual and temporal, I am favored with beyond many others. My companion always gives me an account of the meetings, so that I know almost as much as if I were present ....

March 7
A slight indisposition deters me from attending to the numerous avocations of life that devolve upon me, which leaves me more than usual time for serious reflection; but alas, if the spirit of God is not granted to quicken and enliven my mind, no outward means are sufficient of themselves. But ought I not to bless God for the smallest intimation of his loving kindness towards me? .... I feel to rejoice in the prosperity of Zion, which is about, we hope and trust, to lift up its head again in the eastern part of our Township. A number have been brought to profess faith in Christ; we hope it is saving faith in every one, but we rejoice with trembling, knowing that it is an easier matter to put on the livery of Christ than to wear it ....

April 27
Almost two months have elapsed since I have been able to notice my exercises; but O what thankfulness and praise is due to my covenant-keeping God and compassionate Redeemer for the displays of his unmerited mercy in my late confinement! I am now the mother of a living child, and am raised to a measure of health after a number of repeated indispositions; but the Lord has been kind, he has not suffered me to fall prey to disease and death; my obligations are greater than ever to live a holy and spotless life (but this is what I have never done, and doubt much whether I shall ever be able to; surely I cannot, only in the

strength of the Lord God of Hosts). I feel the weight of an immortal soul committed to my charge. God grant me wisdom and grace to conduct myself aright with it, and before it, for thou has given us a blessed promise that "wisdom and knowledge shall be the stability of our times, and strength of salvation." Oh if my son is only one of the heaven-born race, all my toil and care will be nothing, and I trust it will be unceasing for his spiritual interest. I already feel him to be a strong cord to bind me to earth, but long to feel, that he is only a lent favor, and to hold him and every other earthly enjoyment at loose ends. I have in my affliction to lament that I enjoyed so little of the manifested presence of Jesus; but I have also cause to bless God, that he has given me to feel quiet and submissive under it, though very crossing to my wishes.

July 27

This is a happy day (in some measure) to my immortal soul, having sat with great delight under the preached word by a Minister of the Gospel, Missionary from England (Mr. Tinson) to the Island of Jamaica, who has come hither by the good Providence of God for the purpose of improving his health; he appears to be a man of extensive information, good abilities and education, connected with ardent piety, as we must undoubtedly believe; what could have induced him to make such sacrifices as to leave his native land and many comforts for the thatched cottage in the burning Indies, but love to God and poor perishing sinners?

March 8 [1829]

Sabbath evening. The events of the present time are so important, in regard to my companion, myself, and others, that I cannot omit mentioning some of them; but (as a wise author says) "how can I sufficiently adore the patience of my Lord, my gracious husbandman who still bears with me, the weakest of all his branches? He has not cut me off yet, but still dresses to bring forth more fruit, though like a degenerate plant, I have yielded little else but wild grapes. Why, then, shouldest thou grumble, O my heart, at the application of his pruning knife? it is really for thy good. He is angry only with the degenerate, unfruitful branches; the more these are purged, the more fruit thou shalt bring forth." This I can say has been my case all through my life long, but particularly since I united with the church of the living God; and I view it more sensibly at this present time, having yesterday received a dismission from the First Baptist Church in Cornwallis, in order to be received into the Second Baptist Church in this place,* over which my partner in life is soon to be ordained (two ordinations have recently taken place with members of this Church; what hath God wrought?) Lord who is sufficient for these things? I trust I in some measure feel my weakness to perform the duties of Minister's wife, and also my responsibility to God, how I conduct myself; but oh my heart is very bad, a fountain of iniquity lies within, which has for a time back led me to hew out broken cisterns that can hold no water. I have experienced a long night of darkness. May the Lord sanctify it and all my trials. We have in expectation soon to remove from our present habitation to one more retired, twelve miles distant from this, where the little Church is principally situated, that if the Lord will we shall dwell among (at least for a time): we trust it is thy doing, for if thou build not the house, in vain do they labor that build it; it surely has been a subject of much prayer and deliberation (but alas, too little by me). How shall we go in and out before this people? Lord, counsel and direct us ....

March 30
I am now comfortably situate in my new habitation, and want much to be thankful for the mercies I enjoy; but alas, my mind is so secularized with worldly things, that I do not realize the importance of my situation as much as I ought. O for a right discovery of it that I may seek only for that happiness that flows from the right hand of God. O may the Lord of heaven dwell in me and I in him! Then I shall be richly supplied with every needed good. A new house is erected for the worship of God, near our dwelling; the sight of it from the window often creates in my breast a sensation not to be expressed. I hope I shall never get into such a state of mind that the house will not look pleasant.

* William Chipman had been appointed pastor of the Baptist Church in Pleasant Valley, later renamed Berwick, Kings County.

May 9 [1830]
How can I sufficiently admire and adore that hand that has upheld me and brought me through another sense of affliction (to enjoy almost my wanted health), while mercies are mingled with it? I am now the mother of a fine daughter. My obligations and responsibilities to God are increased. O why am I such a dull scholar in the School of Christ? ... Dear Jesus, take me out of this lethargic state ....

December 26
Sabbath day. I have just returned from visiting the grave of my first-born child, who three weeks ago to-day was in the enjoyment of good health (excepting a cold), and a week after he was removed from time to a vast eternity, aged two years and nine months. Five days before his death he was severely scalded (by sitting down into a kettle that had about two quarts of boiling water). Although he had two severe fits caused by the worm fever setting in, and was extremely ill, yet some symptoms appeared favorable, and we were too much encouraged until the day before he breathed his last, when the mortification took place which ended his mortal career. God has seen fit in his wisdom to hand me the cup of affliction to drink of, in common with the rest of his intellectual creatures, and although I have found it, and do still find it hard to be reconciled to this my lot, yet I know my dear Redeemer has chastened me for my profit, for he scourgeth every son whom he receiveth, and hath in faithfulness afflicted me ....

April 26 [1831]
A severe trial is presented to my view, and some others, to engage in the important duty of uniting to commence a female prayer meeting. I hope it is duty when I say so; I know I do not feel as I ought to about it; but the fear of the rod being laid upon me makes me desire to engage in it cheerfully, if it is for the honor of God. I want to see the path plain ....

August 7
Sabbath day. As no meeting is continuous to us to-day, I spend the day as much in reading as my eyes will allow me; but it

seems very strange to me that the precious word of God does not interest me more, and the blessed duty of prayer; but not strange, either, can it be, when I look at my wretched strayings and wanderings from God by sin ....

July 3 [1832]

This is the twenty-fifth anniversary of my life, and how little (if anything) I have done in the service of my Lord and Master! Nearly twelve years since I have seen an end of all perfection here below, and yet what poor progress have I made in my journey heavenward ....

February 15, 1833

Many, very many have been the changes of kind Providence towards me since I last wrote. The God of heaven has laid me upon a bed of sickness and raised me up again and committed to my charge a lovely babe (another daughter.) O how repeated are the obligations I am under to love and serve my blessed Redeemer, with all my *heart, soul, mind and strength*! but, alas, alas, instead of living more devoted to God, I feel myself to be getting farther and farther from Him who is the chief object of worship. Would to God I could be more disentangled from earthly objects, that is, my mind less diverted with them, so that I might use them and not abuse them. O Jesus, suffer me not to cast off fear and restrain prayer.

August 18

Five Sabbaths have elapsed since I heard the sound of the Gospel. My blessed Redeemer has seen fit to lay his hand of affliction upon one of my tender offspring and caused her to be entirely helpless, although much better on many accounts this fortnight past (her complaint the St. Vitus's Dance), yet the cause is not removed. How it will terminate is known only to Him who "rides upon the stormy sky, and manages the seas" ....

May 6 [1834]

The thing which I greatly feared has come upon me. My dear little Mary Eliza is no more: her immortal spirit took its flight (we hope to a mansion prepared for her) this morning, aged four years and nearly a month. Although this is what I have long looked for, and have tried to hold her as a lent favor, yet the bitterness of parting is great, with one so dear; nature cries, forbear, "but faith disclaims the hasty plaint impatient nature spoke, and said the will of the Lord be done." I hope I feel to acquiesce therein, knowing that her judge will do her no injustice. But now I want the supporting grace of God, that will enable me to feel that it is a stroke of mercy instead of wrath; such I found the death of my dear Leander. O what wise purposes there are in the designs of Jehovah! Make me, dearest Saviour, to seek for comfort and happiness only in thee, who art the restorer of the breach.

July 11
Have had a weeping time this morning in reflecting upon the subject of death, many of Watt's hymns upon the same appeared very comforting. I began to feel the strength of nature dissolving between me and my dear little Mary, although I have felt, I trust, to resign over into the hands of him who lent her to me for a short time ....

January 20 [1837]
...A Sabbath School has for some length of time much occupied my mind. I have hitherto felt that I had so many other duties to perform (too many of them temporal), that I could not attend to it, but I disposed now to try to surmount those difficulties (hoping the Lord will provide a way for me, if my motives are pure), and to cast in my mite in such a laudable undertaking; but when I look at my want of proper qualifications I am ready to shrink from the important work of instructing little immortals in the things pertaining to godliness ....

January 22
.... An inmate of our family was buried in baptism to-day, — a young woman that has had hope in God for three years or more, but for want of strong faith and decision for God, has conformed to the world (as she expresses herself) in a manner unbecoming the Christian character. May her future life truly evince her sorrow for the past, and her zeal to glorify God henceforward; may

her influence be of a most salutary kind wherever she goes. As she has friends and connections at a distance of a worldly character, may she not shun the cross, when meeting them. Here again I ought to be a nursing mother, particularly when I reflect that my influence is to be felt upon future generations in a religious and moral point of view. O Saviour, grant me strength equal to my day.

EPILOGUE: ELIZA ANNE CHIPMAN

Eliza Chipman died on 6 October 1853 at the age of 46. According to her husband who later published her diary:

> Three days before her death Mrs. Chipman informed her husband that he would find in a small trunk a sketch of her life and experience, in the form of a Journal. She hoped the perusal of it would be profitable to him. She added, that she did not wish it to be committed to the flames, for she had enjoyed much comfort in reading christian Diaries, and therefore, if there could be a selection of gleanings from her own, which might be useful to others, she was willing that her friends and the public should have the benefit. She was not conscious of pride in writing it, but rather of a desire that God's goodness might be acknowledged.

MARGARET DICKIE MICHENER
1827-1908

Margaret Dickie was born 4 July 1827 in Hantsport. Her father was a farmer and a shoemaker who not only taught his daughter how to bind shoes but also saw to it that she received a basic education. Like the Chipmans, the Dickies were of Planter stock and the Baptist faith, which probably accounts for their interest in 'schooling.' There is no record of where Margaret received her education but it was perhaps in one of the local 'dame schools,' that flourished in Nova Scotia in the early nineteenth century. The rich intellectual life described in this diary indicates that Hantsport was not a rural backwater. Visiting lecturers and access to books and newspapers from all over the English-speaking world kept the Dickies *au courant* with the most recent intellectual trends. The range of Margaret's interests, which included geography as well as the new psychological theory of phrenology, is impressive.

Like many Nova Scotians in the age of sail, Margaret Dickie's life was touched both directly and indirectly by the sea. During the period covered by this portion of her diary, Hantsport, located at the mouth of the Avon River, was emerging as a major shipbuilding centre and home for a fleet of sailing ships engaged in the world-wide carrying trade. Margaret often refers to the building, launching, departure and arrival of Hansport vessels, these seafaring activities counterpointing the routines of her own daily life. She herself never went to sea.*

* Hattie Chittick, *Hantsport on Avon* (Hantsport, 1968); Charles Armour and Thomas Lackey, *Sailing Ships of the Maritimes* (Toronto, 1975), p. 147.

From Margaret's diary it is possible to see how the absence of men for long periods from the community had an impact on the roles women played and the way they related to each other. Women often single-handedly cared for families, operated retail shops, taught school, performed civic duties and developed networks of female friends who helped in times of crisis. As Margaret testifies, Hantsport had its share of tragedies, many of which related to marine disasters. Given this cruel reality of seaport life, it is not surprising to find women urging their men to leave the sea for less dangerous occupations. Ironically, it was the decision to move to the American mid-west to take up farming that put a tragic end to Margaret's dreams of land-based domesticity.

Margaret Dickie apparently kept a journal for much of her adult life. Unfortunately for the modern reader, she learned various types of shorthand which made her diaries difficult, and sometimes impossible, to read. Thus only her early diaries (1847-48; 1849-53) and a transcription of an 1867-69 diary which chronicles a brief sojourn in the United States have survived. The following excerpts are drawn from her 1849-53 diary which the twenty-two year old Margaret began keeping four months after her marriage to mariner Simeon Michener. As well as the drama of her story, it is fascinating to note the richly textured fabric of family and community life described in the diary. Margaret's childhood home was within walking distance of the house she shared with Simeon, a frame cottage which was part of a clutch of Michener houses built near the centre of the village. Relatives belonging to the hopelessly inter-related Dickie-Michener-Davidson clan lived nearby. While Simeon was at sea, Margaret continued teaching day school and Sunday school, kept house for her sea-bound sister and hosted visits from relatives and friends. In her spare time she recorded daily events in her diary, a chronicle so immediate that even today we can share her love-hate relationship with the sea, the triumphs and tragedies which so dramatically punctuated her life.*

---

* We wish to express our gratitude to Allen Robertson whose genealogical skills and vast knowledge of Hantsport enabled us to better understand the context of one of our favourite chroniclers.

MARGARET DICKIE MICHENER DIARY
1850-1851 *

Jan. 2nd 1850

This has been a cold blustery day. I had prayer in my school this morning for the first time. I feel I need the help of God to do my duty to those around me and I wish to teach my scholars right. I lost my wedding ring since last night. I did not miss it until this forenoon. I prized it for the sake of the times and am very sorry to loose it. I have some fears at time that he may never return. I hope all is well with him.

13th

… As I was sitting here writing this morning Chipman David-son came in and told me the "Ready Rhino" had come and that he had seen Simeon and talked with him. A few minutes later and Nancy and I would have gone to meeting. She went but I was pleased to stop at home; it was not long before he came. How very thankful I am that he has been spared to return safely. Very soon John came in; he had gone to meeting but hearing of Simeon's arrival he came back. Then Maria and her father came; James Holmes and many others have called. John Michener stayed to dinner, then he, Simeon and James Holmes went to the shore. Ellen Dickie, Ann and brother John then came.

14th

I need not complain for want of company now, for since Simeon came home I have had plenty. Yesterday afternoon the house was filled, coming and going constantly.

23rd

We attended prayer meeting — had a good meeting. William Irish spoke well. The children seemed pleased and kept him busy.

---

*   Margaret Dickie Michener McCulloch's diaries and comments on her life appear serialized in the *Wolfville Acadian,* 23 December 1923 to 29 November 1929.

28th
We spent the evening at Father's in the company of Joe and Olivia, Hibbart and Mary. The tongues kept pretty busy, particularly about the rates, which are very unequal. The rate gatherer has been along. Mother has the greatest set of sons-in-law to make speeches and comparisons of any I know of. They are a jovial lot.

Feb. 16th
…I have been studying Navigation this week whenever I could get any spare time.

March 8th
This evening we have been studying Geography and talking over the news of the day. The boys and Ann with us.

21st
Yesterday was just like a Spring day, the children seemed to enjoy it greatly. Friday afternoon a company of sons of Temperance cadets from Windsor came down and formed a society of Cadets here. They marched down through the village with their regalia on and banners flying. Silas Hibbert was frightened when he saw them and ran home and told his mother there was war. I suppose he thought they were soldiers.

April 13th
I am so busy most of the time I neglect to keep my journal, though I might find much to write. Simeon went to Cheverie on Monday and came back this evening; it has been a lonesome week without him. I wish he might obtain work on shore so he could always be at home. I like my occupation quite well. Sometimes when I talk to my scholars they pay great attention and make free to ask questions. They appear to know what is right, and willing to do the right, but forget sometimes. Every day some little differences come up between them, but they are soon all friends again.

19th
My brothers and Ann came down last evening to study as usual.

Our attention is turned to Wisconsin and Michigan where Simeon, Capt. Curry and some others talk of emigrating to as it is good farming country. We women will be glad to have our husbands give up the seafaring life; we are willing to go — brothers, sisters and all, but what the outcome will be I know not ....

23rd
The "Hantsport" came on the beach from Halifax Monday, and yesterday morning John Michener came in and took breakfast with us; he has been busy today calling on the neighbours and giving them some oranges. We have a supply and they are delicious.

25th
We visited Abigail last evening. This afternoon Simeon told us he was to leave tomorrow. I was quite surprised that he is to go so soon, so I sent for my brother and Ann to come down ....

28th
Well, I am now alone as Simeon has gone away. I had no school yesterday as we were busy getting ready for his departure for Michigan, or some place that way. We arose early yesterday morning and took a walk; I suppose it will be our last one for some time. I was busy all the morning and got an early dinner; Capt. Curry and Simeon were running back and forth. After dinner Capt. Curry came in and asked me to take a walk with them to the shore. Maria would go if I would. So I got ready and we went. I suppose some thought if they were in our place they would not have gone, but they wished us to and we wished to see them as long as we could. They were taking some things to the vessel; we sat down on the bank watching them. John sung out to us — he being up in the "Hantsport" rigging. Mr. J. Frost came along and sat with us a long time, talking about the States and the people there; but the time soon came when we must be parted. They bade us Adieu with many good wishes to both parties, hoping to meet again ere many months shall pass. They stood waving their hats as we watched them sail away. We stopped at Olivia's and she came home with me, so I had my at-

tention engaged. Joe came up in the evening and then they all went home. Maria came over and we talked on the departed ones with many hopes and fears. We slept soundly, but I was dreaming all night about vessels. When I arose this morning I took a walk down the new road to the shore and back on the old one before breakfast. Sister Ann was here when I returned. I am glad Maria is so near by as we can be together often. I have been reading in Mason's Self Knowledge; it is a nice book and teaches one many things it is well to know.

May 1st

Mother was here to see me today and visited Mary also. It seems she and father are very much stirred up over our plans for going to the States. They do not like the idea at all and are feeling badly.

5th

I arose this morning with the sun and took a walk down to the shore. The scene is lovely. It was high tide. Six vessels are on the beach. The air was so clear I could hear someone singing over in Newport.* How calm and peaceful is a pleasant Sabbath morning ....

7th

My scholars number 32 now. I find it a trial sometimes to be patient, they are so noisy. I am kept busy. I would like to know where Simeon is. I hope he may make the journey in safety. I received my "American Messenger"** yesterday; there is some very nice reading in them.

25th

This day I have had rest from my usual task. I succeeded this week in moving my school into the big room. I have been down to Olivia's several times. She has been very sick. Ann is staying

---

* Newport is a village across the Avon River from Hantsport.
** The *American Messenger* was a Baptist-sponsored newspaper published in the United States and widely read by Nova Scotia Baptists. Their own paper, the *Christian Messenger*, often carried items from its American counterpart.

with her. The "Wanderer" sailed today for Fredericksburg. The weather is very pleasant. I would like to see Simeon very much.

June 1st

The month has come in cold and rainy. I went up to Father's after school last night, and called into Charlotte Barber's and Sarah Whitman's on my way. I found the men busy with the farm work and Mother was spinning. I went upstairs and heard rain on the roof; it reminded me of bygone days, and many pleasing recollections were presented to mind as I looked around. After the men came in Robert read aloud about the trial of Dr. Webster.* I arose early this morning and returned home. I read some in Comb's Constitution of Man, and find it a very good book. Jane Fielding is here and will stop the night with me. It is five weeks today since Capt. Curry and Simeon went away. I suppose they are in Michigan now.

6th

The "Orbit" came in from Halifax last night and brought some supplies to Mrs. Dorman for her store. There is great rejoicing among the old ladies as they all have been out of tea. I lent all I had as I do not drink it.

12th

John came down last night and went over to the Post Office. When he returned he had letters for father, Maria and me. Simeon wrote that they were fresh water sailors going to Ohio. They had a great time going from Albany to Buffalo in a canal boat. Simeon slept on the table and the cabin was crowded. They are going to cruise around for awhile before going to Michigan. They will write again soon. Maria and I had a great laugh at their description of their voyage ....

21st

Friday morning. I had looked forward all week to Thursday, hoping it would be a fine day so we might attend the exercises at the College.** I arose early and went up home. We started a

* Daniel Webster (1782-1852) was an American statesman and orator.
** A reference to Acadia College located in the nearby town of Wolfville.

little before seven o'clock — John, Robert, Ann and I. Robert called at Mr. Elder's for them. They soon came along .... in another carriage .... we went in to the College where people were gathering. We stood a while gazing at the beautiful scenery around and then went in and found the room all decorated with festoons and garlands of flowers, vines of evergreens and wreathes. There were many ministers there, among the number we saw Rev's Rand, Dickie and Burpee. Mr. Rand is the missionary among the Micmac Indians; R. B. Dickie is a relation, and one of our favourite ministers and Mr. Burpee is our foreign missionary just returned from India. The program began with singing followed by prayer by our Venerable Father Harding.

Mr. Henry Johnston delivered his essay on the Ice World .... Mr. Thomas Crawley received the B. A. degree and then spoke on the tendencies of the age to brotherhood, showing how society was advancing, new discoveries being made — the inventions, all calculated to bring the people of the world closer together. Mr. David Freeman spoke on Instinct, Reason and Faith, showing how we all are fitted to our station; the animals having instinct to guide them, and we, being so much above them have reason, reflection and faith united with reason, productive of happiness. The exercises were varied by singing, the last piece being the national anthem .... It was nearly six o'clock before we started for home.

July 3rd
... After school yesterday I took a walk across the fields back of the meeting house and beyond; the scene from the hill is delightful, looking down upon our pretty village to the adjacent river, with a glimpse of woods and houses in the distance. I was thinking of the last time I was there — about a year ago with Simeon .... I came to father's and stopped all night, and would like to have spent the day also, but had to return to my school. Shortly after my return Mary came in, wishing me to write a note for her to mother to come down. I went over [to Mary's] at noon and found mother, Mrs. Holmes and Mrs. Davidson there. After school was out I went over and saw my new niece that has come to stay. I was much pleased to find Mary had a girl and could hardly believe them, the five preceding ones being boys. There

have been a great many calling to congratulate her. I must go over there to stay all night.

July 12th
I went over to Mrs. G. Davidson's last evening to a sing; quite a company were there and I enjoyed myself well. I had a delightful ramble tonight, looking out a spot to have a picnic with my scholars.

17th
Last night I went up home to a sing. This morning early I took a ride with the boys and Ann up to the mill to get our wool. We took a walk around the mill, went in bathing and then took a row in the gundalow on the mill pond. Got back to father's at 7 o'clock. Ate breakfast, then came down to school and found some of the scholars waiting for admission.

18th
We arose early this morning hoping it would be a fine day for our picnic, so we were all much pleased to see such a beautiful morning. The scholars assembled as usual, except they had on their Sunday dress. We went through with the morning lessons. Marianne Davidson and Ann came down and I set them to making wreaths of flowers. Susannah Davidson was chosen as the prettiest girl and we decorated her to represent "Flora." Between eleven and twelve o'clock we started to march down near the shore. We marched by couples, "Flora" and I leading the way. We soon arrived at the spot I had chosen under some trees in Mr. Davidson's pasture. We took our dinner seated on the ground after which the children played around for awhile, then recited some hymns they had learned. They sang some pieces beautifully, then Ann played some for them on the accordion. We also gave each of them a present with which they seemed much pleased. We took a walk along the beach and up to the top of the bank, where we sat for a while to rest. Louise joined us there and then we marched back home quite well pleased with the day's enjoyment, and they asked when we could have another picnic.

Aug. 6th

I started last night after school to collect money for the Union Missionary Society.* I met with some repulses and some successes. I stopped in at Father's, then went out in the field and raked hay awhile. Hibbert came home last night. Mrs. Bezanson had a daughter today.

20th

...I met Mr. Harris as I was coming home and he said there was a letter for me. I found it was one from Simeon, written long ago from Cork, and there was some money enclosed. I wonder where it has been all this time.

25th

I had company yesterday afternoon; Ann Eliza West, Mary and Ann were here. We had a very pleasant time talking over days that are past and gone. Ann Eliza likes to talk on phrenology and physiology, and we agree there. They are good subjects for conversation. She stopped all night and we did not go to sleep till after midnight. This morning after breakfast Ann Eliza and her son returned to her father's and I went to S. School as usual.

Sept. 9th

It rained and blew hard all night. After supper I went over to Maria's. I read a while in the "Life of John Bunyan," then sat and thought on by-gone days. Every scene with which Simeon was associated came to my mind. I could not refrain from tears thinking "What if I never should see him again." At last such a desolate feeling came over me, I had to start for home in the rain. Maria came with me.

10th

Maria went to Capt. Holmes yesterday afternoon, and after

---

*   The Union Missionary Society, formally the Associated Society of Baptists, had been established by the Baptist Church in Nova Scotia in 1842 as a means of "rationalizing" the donations for various church activities, encompassing three educational institutions (including Horton Academy and Acadia College in nearby Wolfville), Sunday Schools, Temperance Societies, a denominational newspaper, a fund for infirm ministers, and both foreign and home missions.

school I went too. She, Elmira and I took a walk down to the brook. We had to make a bridge to cross over as the rains have raised the water quite high. We went over to a beautiful grove, the same place Rebecca Elder, Elmira and I sat and sang three years ago. There is a lovely view from there and we saw Capt. Toye's brig come sailing up. We looked forward to the evening hoping to get letters from our loved ones. I went to Maria's and watched, as the bridge by Bishop's is up, and the coach came this way and left the mail at Harris's. We went over, but there were no letters for us. We felt sad and fear they are sick. We think maybe they are coming home, or perhaps their letters have gone astray. Time will tell and we must wait patiently.

18th
Such lovely weather we are having now. The boys and Ann came in last night, after spending the evening at Mary's. Maria and I went with them as far as Marcia's. We then returned to Mary's to spend the night. The bed cord broke and let us down on the floor. We thought if we turned our heads to the foot we could sleep that way, but we kept sinking down till we could scarcely get up. At last we made our bed on the floor but could not sleep for some time for laughing ….

24th
I have been shopping over at Aunt Sally's. She sells a great deal; there is someone in there the most of the time. Grandfather got in last night. I have just received my share of plums, a peck or more. After school I went down to Olivia's. Maria went in the afternoon …. The boys came in and said there was a letter in the office for Olivia. Oh, how we wished there were some for us. We soon heard that Joe was in New York and was coming to Halifax. He said that on Sunday the 25th, Chipman fell from the top sail yard to the sea. It was a dark and stormy night but he was rescued. It made us tremble when we heard of it, and very thankful to know he was saved.

27th
Maria came in this evening and we have been taking turns reading aloud from a book called "The Young Emigrant"; it is about

two families who move to Ohio. It shows how many difficulties the first settlers have to encounter in a new country.

Oct. 2nd

How changed are all my prospects. What shall I write? I know not what to say or think. My beloved Simeon is no more! Can it be possible I will not see him again, or hear his sweet voice? I went to Mary's last night to wait till the mail would come in. Ezra went over and returned with three letters. I got a light and saw that two letters were for Maria. It was with fear and trembling I read my letter from Simeon; he was in quite good spirits when he wrote but not too well. I found Curry had received Maria's letter but Simeon did not get mine. I read my letter to Mary and Ann, and then in haste went up to Marcia's where Maria was. The road never seemed so long before; I could not go fast enough. At last I gave her the letters, wishing yet dreading to know the contents. I told her to read the latest one first. I arose ready to start at the news she looked; I saw her drop the letter and I went into the bedroom as I wished to hear no more. I knew Simeon was dead yet dared not ask.

Oct. 3rd

Simeon wrote to me on Sept. 10th and died on the 13th at 5 o'clock in the morning. Capt. Curry attended him until his last moments; he died easily as if going to sleep. If only I could have been with him it would have been a mournful pleasure. I walked the floor nearly all night. I cannot realize he is gone never to return. This forenoon I felt as if I wished to see my parents and glad I was to see my father coming in. Emily Ann and Mrs. James were in a while this morning and mother came in this afternoon. I am glad to have their sympathy. Aunt Sally came to see me. She well knows the bitterness of loosing a friend in a foreign port, but all the sympathy in the world cannot heal the wound. How many pleasant scenes I have to look back upon. How kind and good Simeon was! I was unworthy of such a good and loving companion. Oh, could I but see him once more, but the cruel grave has torn him from me. How can I bear it!

4th

I went up home with mother Wednesday evening; how lonely all things seemed, as all things remind me of the happy hours spent here with Simeon. I walked about from room to room and cannot put my mind on anything …. Oh, how rebellious my heart; how keen the smart when I see my sisters enjoying the society of their husbands. I feel I cannot submit to loose mine. Ann came down with me tonight. She will stay at Olivia's a while, when she and Joe go to Halifax. How keen was our grief upon entering my lonely home. Capts. Michael and Hibbart have been in. They seem to feel deeply the loss we have sustained. Maria is here to stop with me. May God help us to seek thee.

5th

This has been a lovely day as far as the weather is concerned. My friends came in to see me; little Simeon came over this afternoon. I could not help weeping over him when I thought of the one he was named for. The little fellow went to sleep in my arms. I find a consolation in prayer. I cannot say I feel resigned, but I pray God may sanctify his affliction to the good of each, and enable us to say "Thy will be done."

7th

I have come tonight to my lonely habitation. It is not the same as it has been all summer, for hope has departed. I was looking forward to winter when Simeon would be home. I took a walk down to Halfway River bridge and sat on the fence by the marsh to watch the flowing tide. I sat there till it came all around me as the tides are high — and ebbed again. I read while there Pope's "Messiah," which Simeon had learned and wrote it off for me before we were married. It sounds so like him, I almost think I hear him repeat it. I seem to envy Maria the hope she has of Curry coming home, but why should I? Let me give up, and wish others all good success. Maria is here now; my friends are all very kind. I wrote to Rebecca Elder today. I feel some consolation in scribbling. I pray God may direct me.

9th

... I was looking over Simeon's letters this forenoon; it seemed my heart would burst. I had to leave off and could not get my mind settled for a long time. I try to pray but I fear I am too much attached to the creature rather than the Creator ....

13th

... I feel comforted whilst reading the many promises in scripture. I trust in the promises and hope although this affliction is for the present grievous it will work for my good. I feel to cling more closely to him who has promised to be the widow's God ....

21st

Monday evening finds me alone at my table scribbling. Yesterday was a drizzly day and a melancholy one. Rev. Vaughan preached a funeral sermon from the text, "Be ye also ready, etc." It seemed as if it was a call to all of us. I felt as though I wished to have the body before me while the services were being held but alas! that was denied .... Oh, I felt if I could only see his body there to be interred, it would be some consolation, but perhaps I would feel no better ....

22nd

Fine, clear weather. Elmira came and stayed all night with me. She is truly a good sincere girl. I love to have her pray with me. We arose early and had breakfast, but no sign of daylight yet, it was just moonlight. I am going up home today to stay awhile.

28th

Monday morning. Well, my house looks as lonesome as ever when I enter it. I came home early this morning after having been away nearly a week .... While at father's I took a walk daily down the glen below the house and to the bridge to gaze at the flowing waters. It reminds me of the stream of time thinking our lives are going as fast. Saturday afternoon I had a great ramble around the most rugged and steep bank I could find, and up to the spot where Simeon and I sat so happily a little over a year ago. The melancholy winds and wild rambles suit my spirit better than anything I find ....

As I was going to Hibbart's this forenoon he said, "There has more trouble come to our family." I asked, "What?" He said, "James Holmes has been brought home dead," I felt my grief afresh then, as I though of poor dear Abigail. I came home and then Hibbart came for me to go to tell Abigail; he said he could not do it. She had gone to Ann Barker's with her boys to spend the day. I went over, but could not go in the room where she was. "Oh," I thought, "if she only knew it, I could see her." After awhile I went in and talked of what had happened, saying we knew not who would be affected next; then I spoke of James and said Hibbart had heard from him, and I went out of the room. Abigail followed me and demanded to know what I meant. I told her to be prepared for the worst. She began to scream. "You tell me he is dead," and she shook me. After she knew, we thought she would loose her mind. Emily Ann came in and we talked to her about her children and tried to calm her. Capt. Michener and Mrs. Kendal came in and after awhile she prepared to go home; her father, Mrs. Kendal and I went with her, Emily Ann and some others following after. A short time afterward the body was brought home .... There he was in his sailor clothes looking so natural. I feel great sympathy for Abigail. She has her three little boys to be with her in her widowhood; they look like their father, only gone a week last Saturday from his home, and now returned a corpse ....

Dec. 4th

Here I am at my lonely dwelling for a few minutes writing. Father and I went to Windsor Tuesday afternoon. I called at Dr. Harding's to pass an examination to get a license for teaching school. Mr. Murdock gave me the license. In the evening we attended a lecture at the Temperance Hall. We stopped at Mr. McHeffey's all night, then, after doing some shopping we returned home ....

13th

Ann went down to Mrs. E. Holmes to watch, as her child is very ill.

14th

Saturday night I went to stay the night [at Mrs. Holmes']; about half past eleven the child died in my arms. It was the first time I had ever seen one die; it sank away so gently I hardly knew it was gone. I thought how sweet to die and be at rest from the tumult of this world. Dear little babe, it looked more beautiful in death than when living, for it was a great sufferer. Mrs. Hicks and Jane Lynch sat with me. Mrs. Hicks is a widow for three years. She has six children. I feel a nearness to widows.

Jan. 4th 1851

Two years ago tonight, I sat as a bride beside my husband. I knew not then what time we would spend together, but now I know, for it has fled. Dear Simeon, how happy we were .... I have taught school for a week now and like it.

EPILOGUE: MARGARET DICKIE MICHENER

Margaret Dickie Michener continued to grieve for her dead husband comforted by the concern and company of relatives and friends. During the winter of 1852 she attended Miss Kidson's academy in Horton to further her education. New faces and academic challenges seem to have lightened the burden of widowhood considerably. She returned to her various duties in Hantsport and, in 1856, married Robert McCulloch (1817-1901), who was drawn to Hantsport by opportunities in the shipyards. The McCullochs had two daughters, Nettie (b. 1860) and May (b. 1865). Robert worked as a ship's caulker while Margaret taught school and served as the town's telegraph operator. In 1867 the family moved to Delaware to join Margaret's brother Robert Dickie in a fruit farming venture. Carpetbagging did not have much appeal for the McCullochs who returned to Hantsport the following year. Meanwhile, Robert Dickie moved to

Bay City, Michigan. In 1880 Nettie and her father visited the Michigan relatives. Robert McCulloch had no difficulty finding work in the Great Lake shipyards and in September 1881 Margaret and May joined the other half of the family in Michigan.

The McCullochs bought a farm near Tuscola and Margaret began to sink roots into new soil. She became a school inspector and joined the local Baptist church. As in Hantsport, she was active in missionary and Sunday school work. When Robert McCulloch's health began to fail, Margaret resigned from her various public duties, and Nettie and her husband, James McKay, moved to the farm. Nettie reported that:

> Mother then had more time for visiting and work of other kinds: she used to knit double mittens for the woolen factory, as did many of the other women, and thus added quite a sum to their income. She used to read and knit. One picture I have of her in my mind is seeing her churn with the old-fashioned dasher, having a paper pinned to the wall and reading as the work went on: the paper was generally "The Christian Messenger" or "The Presbyterian Witness" which was father's paper.

Robert McCulloch died in 1901 and May, who followed her mother in the teaching profession, died in 1903. Meanwhile, brother Robert returned from California where he had been living since 1893 and Nettie's father-in-law, Alexander McKay from Glengarry, Ontario, spent his last three years of life in the McCulloch-McKay household. Margaret died in 1908, just a few weeks prior to her 81st birthday.

There is a wonderful irony in Margaret's life story. The values relating to religion, education, domesticity, material well-being, gender roles — and diary writing — brought to Nova Scotia by New England immigrants were replanted in the North American west by women from the Atlantic seaboard. A wonderfully mobile people, Nova Scotian women were full participants in this cultural imperialism which would soon spread beyond the shores of North America.

COMERS AND GOERS

MATHILDA FAULKNER CHURCHILL 1840-1925

Born in 1840 in Colchester County, Mathilda Faulkner attended the Normal School in Truro and spent more than a decade as a teacher in her native province. In her spare time she served as a volunteer missionary among the black population of Truro. Mathilda longed to serve as an overseas missionary but single women were discouraged from such endeavours. When she was 31, she married George Churchill, a Baptist minister bound for the foreign mission fields. They were among the first group of seven missionaries to be sent out by the newly established Independent Maritime Baptist Foreign Mission Board in 1873.*

Mathilda was not the first Nova Scotia woman to take up a missionary career. Richard Burpee, the first missionary from British North America, was accompanied by his wife, Laleah Johnston Burpee (related by marriage to our earlier diarist Rebecca Byles Almon). They and subsequent missionaries sponsored by Maritime Baptists travelled to Burma under the auspices of the American Baptist Mission Board until Maritime

---

* For a discussion of the role of Maritime women in the missionary movement, see E. C. Merrick, *Those Impossible Women — 100 Years — The Story of the United Baptist Women's Missionary Union of the Maritime Provinces* (Fredericton, 1970); Denise Mary Hansen, "'Sisters Unite': The Maritime Baptist Women's Missionary Movement, 1867-1914," BA Honours Thesis: Acadia University, 1979; Wendy Mitchinson, "Canadian Women and Church Missionary Societies in the Nineteenth Century: A Step Toward Independence," *Altantis*, Vol. 2, No. 2 (Spring 1977), pp. 57-75. A more general treatment is provided by R. Pierce Beaver, *American Protestant Women in World Missions* (Grand Rapids, 1980); Patricia R. Hill, *The World Their Household: The American Woman's Foreign Mission Movement and Cultural Transformation, 1870-1920* (Ann Arbor, 1985).

Baptists felt strong enough to mount their own organization. Much of the impetus for the creation of an independent Maritime Board in 1873 came from two single women missionaries, Minnie Bishop DeWolfe and Hannah Maria Norris. DeWolfe initially went to Burma with the American Baptist Mission Board in 1867, while Norris founded the Maritime Baptist Women's Missionary Aid Society in 1870 to sponsor her missionary activities when she was told that regular funds were being reserved for a man. Despite the obvious preference for male missionaries, women consistently outnumbered men on the mission fields throughout the history of Maritime Baptist missionary activity.

In 1873 the Baptist Foreign Mission Board of Ontario and Quebec joined forces with the Maritime Board. Two years later, Cocanada, India, was chosen as the location of a united Canadian missionary effort. As Mathilda Churchill hints in her letters, this decision disappointed many Maritime missionaries who had spent years learning Karen and Siamese only to be forced to learn yet another language in order to communicate with new Indian charges. There was also resentment over the allocation of funds. Such difficulties prompted Maria Norris Armstrong and her husband to sever their connections with the Maritime Board in 1881 and return to the American field in Burma.

While only a handful of Maritime women went overseas as missionaries, a much larger number belonged to the Women's Missionary Aid Societies that sponsored the careers of women missionaries. The following excerpts from Mathilda's diaries and letters were published by author Grace McLeod Rogers to encourage the activities of those who laboured on the 'home front.' Even making allowances for the drama that she might wish to convey to the women of the missionary societies, Mathilda's story gives readers a rare insight into the world-view which made her stick to her convictions at great personal sacrifice and against all reasonable odds. Her words convey the strong sense of purpose that she brought to her chosen career, the special relationship that she developed with the women among whom she worked, and the determination with which she carried on despite tragedy, heartbreak and, finally, the infirmities of old age. Although Mathilda's smug sense of superiority may seem misplaced, her pragmatic approach to missionary work yielded success in her own terms and enabled her to love her adopted India as much as her native Nova Scotia.

MATHILDA FAULKNER CHURCHILL
LETTERS 1871-1879*

Retreat Cottage, Truro, Nova Scotia, December, 1871.
... I must tell you of the great and abounding joy that has come
to me this day. Mr. Churchill, who is under appointment to go
to the foreign field, has written and asked me to accompany him
as his companion and colabourer. At last I am to be a missionary! For many longing years my heart has yearned to go to the
heathens to tell them of the wonders of God's love and grace. I
think that the impulse first was born at the time of my conversion, a little girl of fourteen. How well I remember that happy
time. Our home was then in Stewiacke, and through the consecrated zeal of a Mr. Banks and his wife, newcomers to the community, a series of wonderful meetings was carried on, many
being converted, seven of us cousins among the number. We
cousins were all baptised on the one occasion, and ever since
then I have wished to be a missionary. Reading the wonderful
story of Dr. Judson's life** and labours raised the fire in my heart
to glowing heat — a burning desire that naught else I could render would quench, a motive power in all other aspirations and
undertakings.

When we moved here to Truro and I was thus enabled to attend the fine Model and Normal Schools, I prosecuted my studies for the different ranks, always with this aim in view, to fit
myself for proper service. But there seemed no open door to my
great Desire. We had no independent Mission Board, and few
were the women who from this land had pointed their footsteps
to the foreign field. When possible opportunity offered, my
parents kindly but firmly opposed it, not willing that I should
venture alone to such strange and distant climes. Wise and
loving guides they have been to me in all else, and I was not led

---

*   Mrs George Churchill, *Letters From My Home in India* (New York, 1916).
** Adoniram Judson (1788-1850) was a missionary who served under the
     American Baptist Mission Board in Burma. His experiences and those
     of his three successive wives who accompanied him to the mission
     fields made compelling reading for the faithful in North America. As a
     result of Judson's career the concept of a resident missionary family
     with wife and husband working in partnership became the North
     American missionary ideal for over half a century.

to override their decision in this. At such times I would say to myself — Is it the Lord calling me, or only a wish for something new and unusual — am I fitted or worthy to carry on His great work abroad — should I not instead be throwing my full strength into activities at home? Then I would teach my Model School with redoubled zeal, confronting myself with that wonderful scripture that Christ who gave unto some to be "Apostles" and "Preachers," gave also to some to be "Teachers." But though somewhat encouraged by this, yet always the other claim stayed in my soul. Next the thought came to me that perhaps by giving a portion of my substance to support a native preacher, I could be doing my "portion," and gladly did I yield a full third of my salary toward it, eagerly receiving tidings from time to time of the labours and successes of my "substitute." But why try to buy with money what I should render in flesh and spirit, and I was not "satisfied." Then one day, while especially troubled over it all, a new field of labour came straight to my hands. Sitting in the church choir, one Sunday, I saw two coloured men come up into the gallery, and something seemed to say to me almost as distinctly as if I heard a voice — "Who cares for their souls? You are longing to go to the heathen but why not try to save and teach these people?"

"I will care for them, Lord Jesus," I answered; and straightway that week I secured consent from the trustees to have the church open on Sunday afternoons, also visiting the "Island" where the coloured folks live, from house to house inviting them to come to a service on the following Sunday.

Large numbers attended, and the Mission became well established, many students from the Normal School assisting, and some members of the Church also giving us great aid. On week evenings I have had a night-school for any of them who wish to be taught reading, writing and arithmetic; gathering in our home kitchen at first, and as they increased in numbers overflowing into the big dining-room. It is a glorious work and I love it — something really definitely mine to do. Yet my heart has not been at rest, the old fire still burns for foreign service. So when the letter came to-day telling me of Mr. Churchill's decision and asking me to share his life and labour, I felt that at last the way was opened up. And I took the letter to my family, leaving them to read it together, confidently believing that if it was God's will that I work for Him on heathen soil, He would so rule their minds to give me consent; that if He needed me there, He could raise up someone here, to care for the loved and loving sister whose long illness had hitherto made me appear necessary in the Home. It seemed to me, I must have the long vexed question settled, and if ever I prayed about it, I prayed then, that God would make me willing to be used as He saw best to further his kingdom — here in Truro, or in far Burma. When I came down for my answer, they gave their consent, not gladly perhaps, but willingly, and devotedly. I feel that theirs is the greater sacrifice, for I go to my long Desire, and my happy heart is full of joy — God's work and earth's love included, how rich has been His blessing! ...

Philadelphia, November, 1872.

... You will want to hear how I am getting on in Philadelphia. It seems wonderful that Miss Eaton and I could get here at study so soon after our momentous decision. Miss Eaton is to be one of the outgoing missionaries. She is a great worker, and grand comrade. As our Board earnestly recommended that the missionaries equip themselves with the best culture possible, general and theological, Florrie and I determined we should be no whit behind our men in this preparation. Both Miss Norris who is already in the field, and Miss DeWolfe who has returned on furlough, impressed upon us the great value of medical knowledge, as an aid in reaching the heathen women in their homes, so we felt we must come here to Philadelphia, in attendance upon the Women's Medical College.* It was hard to leave the home nest. A tinge of the long parting so soon awaiting us all, coloured our leavetaking at this time. My beloved sister from whom I have not been separated since the beginning of her illness, seven years ago, was loath at first to let me come, but yielded with patient and beautiful grace when fully under-

---

*   Because most medical schools in North America were still closed to women, the Women's Medical College in Philadelphia was an important institution for women who wanted to take medical training either for domestic or overseas purposes.

standing my great need of the equipment. It was sad, too, giving up my school — all those young, eager lives committed for a time to my hands to teach and fit for their place in life. Sometimes when the pang of parting was sharpest the Tempter would tell me that this work I loved so well was labour enough, and that I did not need to go hence to "desolate places." But only momentary would be the temptation, for great as is my interest in my school, this work for my blessed Saviour in heathen lands is filling my very being with sacred joy that I am accounted worthy to undertake it.

We rented a room in a small house across the street from the college, and here we study, cook, eat, and sleep, finding little time for recreation, much as we could see for both profit and pleasure, in this beautiful city, had we opportunity. Three evenings a week we spend in the Dissecting Room where we often remain till near midnight before our findings are accomplished for next day's recitation. You remember my nervousness, so you will not laugh when I tell you how Florrie is to me, going into the rooms ahead always, and lighting the lamp, and allowing me to pass out first again while she remains to extinguish the lights. But I will overcome my shrinking in time, and though we neither of us greatly love this portion of our work, we are here for knowledge, and will neglect no part of the course.

Last evening we attended a large missionary meeting. Prof. _____, who has from our arrival been much interested in us, because students for mission work, took us up to the front after the service, and introduced us to the speakers — Mrs. Carpenter and Mrs. Hovey, sisters — one of them a missionary from Burma. We had a very pleasant profitable talk together, upon nursing, medical knowledge, and many other phases of service most valuable as aids in the work. Before parting, they seemed to feel it necessary to inform us, most earnestly and gravely, that there were no matrimonial opportunities on the foreign field, except with a widower whose helpmate had gone on before to the Better Land. As we had deemed ourselves such staid and assured "single" women, taking our work so seriously, we were rather surprised at their counsel, but accepted it in a kindly spirit, and I did not think it incumbent upon myself to announce to strangers that my own future in that direction was quite assured.

There will be a series of missionary gatherings here next week, some of which we plan to attend. The instruction and information given by the different speakers will be of great value. I hope to be able to remain throughout the entire college year, but we have not very long purses, and money fairly melts away even with most careful expenditure.

To supplement our funds we have each taken a hand at canvassing for a book, and when we can find a few spare hours we go to get subscriptions ....

Bangkok, March, 1874.
... Thanks be unto our Heavenly Father we are now in Siam, after a series of short water trips from Tavoy, occupying about twenty days in all. When I first set foot on Burman soil I felt to say, "My God, I thank Thee for allowing this great and precious privilege to be mine;" and each day since then I have echoed those words.

Miss Norris and Mr. Armstrong were married in Rangoon, on Saturday evening January 31st, and on the following week we all started for Tavoy, they leaving the steamer after entering the river, and going on ahead, that they might be in the Mission House at Tavoy to welcome us when we arrived. There we all tarried together for a month, studying the Karen language, and getting accustomed to Eastern sights and sounds. The first hymn I tried to learn in the new tongue was, "How can I Sink with Such a Prop." It was sung at a little Karen prayer meeting on the Mission House verandah, and never will I forget the emotions that swept me as I tried to join my faltering voice in the strange speech of these people with whom I am to labour — my privileges, my responsibilities, rolled upon me, almost overwhelming — and with all my heart I prayed to be fully, wholly consecrated to the work.

But pleasant though our life was at the compound in Burma, we did not feel content to be merely supernumeries, and after much careful deliberation, it was decided that Miss Eaton and ourselves should remove here to Bangkok, Siam, where we hope there will be opportunity for mission work as well as study ....

We are providentially provided with a dwelling place, a vacant house belonging to the American Baptist Union, placed at our disposal by Dr. Dean. Mrs. Dean sent her servants to assist us in unpacking, and we have commenced housekeeping. In addition to our studies Miss Eaton and I have decided to get some pupils, as a start in our mission work. We hear that a number of Chinese and Siamese boys, anxious to study English, will pay for instruction. Their payment will cancel any necessary output, and if we can be teaching them to read and speak English, also teach them of one true God, we meanwhile getting some knowledge of Siamese in return, we shall feel that our labours are not in vain.

In the heart of the city is a neat little chapel built by the American Baptist Union, in which the Christian Chinese worship is held. We often go there with Dr. and Mrs. Dean who conduct the services. There are also services at the English church every Sabbath, the missionaries taking part in turn, and we have a union prayer meeting every Wednesday afternoon. Last Sunday we attended our first sacrament since arriving here. There were present at the table of our Lord, Siamese, Chinamen, Karens, Englishmen, Portuguese and Danes — so will it be in Heaven when we sit before the Throne.

Bangkok, September, 1874
... We have been teaching our little school since June. For a week only one pupil attended, but we did not despair, for he was a precious soul, and God could direct our efforts toward leading him to the light. At the end of the week another arrived, and about a month later seven more enrolled. One has to be patient in this land, and learn to wait, for nobody hurries, and our western energy and fervour are constantly getting a check. We meet the listlessness and procrastination in all ranks, and are told that the climate itself, its languor and its burning heat, is largely contributive to this characteristic ....

Bangkok, April, 1875.

... Many things have transpired since I last wrote you. During my husband's absence on tour my twin babies were born — a boy and a girl — but only the boy lived — the little daughter never opening her eyes on earth, not breathing the air. If it had been God's will to leave her with me how I would have loved to train them together, watching their separate development. But He cannot be unkind, and I must feel it is best. Since the very moment my boy was born, I have tried to consecrate him to the Lord's service, and over and above all else I wish, do I desire that from his youth up, he will be truly God's child.

Not until baby was ten weeks old did my husband return from the tour, and glad and thankful I was to have him at home again.

Cocanada, India, August, 1875.

... On May 28th we received our "mandate," in the form of a cablegram from our Foreign Mission Board, instructing us all to proceed to Cocanada, Central India, where our Independent Mission is to be carried on among the Telugus. The message took only six hours from St. John to Singapore, Mr. and Mrs. Boggs who were visiting there making all haste to bring it to us at Bangkok. We were somewhat surprised at the decision, and perhaps at first a bit disappointed, but all else was soon lost in satisfaction that the question was settled, and the waiting time at end ....

And here we are at Cocanada, safely brought across the waters to our "desired haven." Mr. McLauren* met us at the boat, extending a most cordial welcome and bringing us all to this home for a few days till we could get established in our own quarters .... We call our new abode the "Nova Scotia Barracks." We have not yet decided upon the best division of our forces, nor the final establishment of the respective fields to be occupied. But we women feel that while we are acquiring the language we ought also to be carrying on schools for children, and the matter is resting heavily upon our hearts, because to do this

---

*   John McLauren was appointed by the Foreign Mission Society of the Baptists of Ontario and Quebec to establish a mission at Cocanada in 1873.

we must have funds to pay the salaries of native teachers, without whose help we could not successfully undertake the work. The building operations for our several missions will, we know, be a heavy drain upon our Board, without extra grants for school purposes, and we are hoping that the sisters of the Aid Societies will decide to assume all expense of school equipment. Though education should not have first place in mission work, it should play a very prominent part, both in the foundation and throughout the whole structure. The older people have within them, from their youth up, the knarls and kinks of heathenism, even though converted now, but the young of the land, trained in schools, are our hope. If we can gather some of the little girls around us for a few years, early in life, they will present a very different type of womanhood. And we do so yearn over those children, to be able to have a place and means to call them together a while each day, away from the surroundings of their heathen homes, that we may exercise a fitting influence over their habits, as well as instructing them in their studies.

I had a talk with my teacher one day lately about the women of this country. He belongs to the Rajah (King) caste, and he told me that the girls of his caste were never allowed to go outside their homes after they were six or seven years of age, and that education for them was prohibited, "for they were wiser than the men anyway, and if instructed would be too wise, and the men could not manage them!"

But the "morning light" is breaking over such benighted views as this, and just as our girls at home, to-day, are thronging college halls and reaching out for higher learning that fifty years ago no women even there could obtain, so here in this heathen land the women shall not remain in darkness, and I believe I will live to see all over India colleges established for education of their girls. Do not forget to pray for this. Earnest believing prayer will do much to bring it to pass.

Bimlipatam, August, 1877.
… We had an eventful and exciting day in our quiet life when the box arrived from the dear homeland. I was teaching my little

school on the verandah when the bandy drove up, but it was very near closing time so I dismissed the pupils, and as soon as Mr. and Mrs. Sanford joined us the parcels were taken out and opened. Everything came in perfect state, hams, apples and all. We could not wait long for a taste of beans and apples, but had some cooked that very day for dinner, and I can assure you they were delicious, the home savour making them doubly good ....

I teach a little school on our verandah. The attendance waxes and wanes, but on the whole is very good indeed. They are getting quite a start now in reading and sewing, and in memorizing portions of scripture. I like to see their sparkling black eyes uplifted so eagerly to mine when I am giving the Bible lesson, and how I wish the words would come faster to my lips, for until a missionary can feel and think in the language of the people he will be anything but satisfied with his efforts. Besides the school, I am trying to do some work outside. There are many small villages within a radius of half a mile, and when the sun is low enough not to threaten sunstroke, I visit among them, taking with me Miss De Prazer, a young woman from my Bible class, to be mouthpiece in explaining the meaning of the precious words I can read to the women and children who flock around us.

This young girl has been converted, and baptised, and her Christian course thus far has been most consistent and beautiful.

The villages are made up of ten, thirty, or perhaps fifty mud huts, all huddled together, without any order, without streets, and only room left to walk around each hut. We are never asked to go into a house, and indeed do not greatly desire it unless we are needed within. The roofs come down so low, you must stoop to enter, or to look in, and the interior is usually very filthy, for these are mainly Pariah settlements, the lowest class of natives about here. We walk around among the huts, talking to such women as are outside, tell them our errand, and ask them to follow us to where we can get an open space. There we sit down on a cot they will usually bring out for us, and the people squat around on the ground. We seldom have fewer than twenty and sometimes nearly fifty before we are through. They are often quarrelling among themselves, seeming not to listen, once in a while asking foolish questions to try to trouble us, and even scoffing, and our hearts are very sore and sad for them. When we tell of the love of God they will say "Yes, He loves *you* and gives you everything you want, but He does not love us or He would not let us starve as we often do. We keep crying 'Davoor-doo,' but he does not give us rice, and we have to work so hard we have no time to worship as you do, we are so ignorant we cannot understand Him."

Once in a while we meet with encouragement, and hope the good word has fallen into good ground. One day a very aged man joined the group, listening most attentively to all we had to say, and just before we left came to us, asking us to tell him all over again the way to believe in our Jesus. Another time, we found a fine looking old lady who treated us so well and answered our questions so intelligently that we hoped she was not far from the kingdom; she was very earnest. But they are so deeply, darkly ignorant of everything spiritual. What shall we eat and how to keep from breaking caste, seem to occupy all the thoughts they have. Some of the villages are caste, but very low caste, yet when we ask the parents to send their children to our school, they refuse indignantly, giving as reason that we have not a caste servant on the place and that children might drink water a Pariah had brought, and thus break caste. A "Pariah," we feel like exclaiming, who can be lower than you are yourselves, for all the little ones are naked and filthy alike, and to distinguish between them by appearance or conduct would be an impossibility. But such is their slavish prejudice to this terrible system.

A number of these Pariah women consented to come to us on Wednesday afternoons, and we teach them on the verandah. You might be disgusted to look upon them. They are filthy and ragged, their hair matted, and so forlorn and despairing looking; not pleasant to labour with, nor are their children, but I think of the people of the streets who thronged and pressed about our Lord Jesus Christ, and He "suffered them ...."

Bobbili, August, 1879.

... Here we are at last, in our home in India! And happy I am, and thankful, every hour of the day, that after all the weary years of waiting, wandering, and anxiety, we are in God's good providence now settled in our especial field of labour....

...Next to Truro, Bobbili is now the dearest place on earth to me — it is Home, in India, and home wherever it may be is a loved spot to a woman. If you could see our tiny shack here you would note a great contrast between it and my old Truro abode, but we might have a very much worse place, and are thankful indeed for even this shelter, small and rude thought it may be. My only complaint is because we are cramped for room to carry on our work. Last Sabbath we were overrun. I had invited Mr. Churchill's day school class to come to learn to sing on week evenings, and they begged to come Sunday afternoon as well, so last Sunday I had more boys on the verandah than I could manage, while the dining room where the children's cots have also to be kept, was filled to overflowing with young men listening to Mr. Churchill's instructions. To refuse any of them admission might be to lose the chance of reaching them altogether.

... I long so to reach the women of this land. Some of their lives are very hard and bitter. Especially is this the case with widows, who are the drudges of the household, never allowed to marry again even if widowed at the early age of seven or eight. The Zenana work is most interesting ....

...The Zenana is the room in the house in which the women are secluded. They are never permitted to walk abroad through streets and fields as we are but must stay in the one bare room, which rarely contains more furnishing than a mat, a box or two, a cot, and a few brass utensils for cooking. In many instances this apartment is very dark, so that entering it from bright sunshine without, you can scarcely distinguish different persons or objects. Here the mother and daughters spend their days and their nights, never leaving except to go to the little cookhouse in the high walled backyard where they prepare the food for their husbands and brothers — waiting upon them, and receiving for their own portions only what remains from the men's serving. The rooms which the men use are always much larger, brighter and lighter. Women of the lower castes, and the Pariah class, do not live in these Zenanas, they go out freely as we do, but most of the higher caste are thus secluded, as it is considered more respectable. Very few of them can read or write or sew, their time being spent in idle gossip, telling stories of their gods, adorning themselves in their jewelry, quarrelling and sleeping. How can we ever expect to enlighten this dark land until we better the condition of these poor prisoned sisters of ours, making possible for them light and joy in life, and hope beyond the grave. For even here among these heathen women, it is the mothers who may and must play the most important part in national character building. Give us right-minded, highsouled women, and we will have righteous noble men and children, a truth which should be recognized everywhere, both here and in the home land.

EPILOGUE: MATHILDA FAULKNER CHURCHILL

For almost fifty years, Mathilda served in India which became her true "home." She had four children, three of whom died in India.* The remaining daughter, Bessie, was sent back to Nova Scotia to receive her education but later returned to India to help her parents in their work. When George Churchill died in 1908, friends expected Mathilda to return to Canada. She, however, had no intention of leaving the schools and mission they had worked so hard, physically and spiritually, to build. Despite old age and ill health she carried on until 1921 when she finally came back to Canada on her last furlough. Acadia University awarded her an honorary degree in 1923. She died the next year at the age of 84 and was buried in Mount Pleasant Cemetery in Toronto, not far from the grave of another pioneering missionary, Hannah Maria Norris Armstrong, founder of the Maritime Baptist Women's Missionary Aid Society.

---

* Mathilda Churchill's tribute to her son William was published after his death as *Reminiscences of Willie Chandler Churchill by his Mother* (St. John, 1882).

ANNIE ROGERS BUTLER
1841-1906

Lucy Anne Harrington Rogers Butler was one of twelve children (ten of whom survived to adulthood) born to Benjamin and Elsie Rogers in Yarmouth, Nova Scotia. Although we know that the Rogers raised their offspring in the strict discipline of the Wesleyan Methodist tradition, there is little information about Annie's childhood and early adult life. We do know that her father was a ship builder and that at least one brother, the William mentioned in her diary, was a sailor. It therefore comes as no surprise that on 9 June 1870, at the age of 29, Annie married a sea captain, John Kendrick Butler. One month later they set sail for South America in the brigantine *Daisy*.*

Despite popular superstition that women on board ship brought bad luck, it was not uncommon for a wife, and even children, to accompany a skipper to sea on the various established trade routes. Without his family to keep him company, a captain's life aboard ship could be a lonely and isolated one. All decisions regarding the handling of the ship were his, and he assumed full responsibility for any disciplinary action. Protocol required that he not fraternize with the crew, and he was unlikely to socialize a great deal with the mates unless they were related to him by blood or marriage ties. To choose a life at sea often meant being away from home and loved ones for very long periods at a time. Small wonder, then, that many captains brought their wives and children along for companionship.**

From Annie's diary it is clear that she was well educated and

---

* The *Daisy*, 337 tons, was built in Yarmouth in 1863 by George and S.M. Ryerson.
** Stanley T. Spicer, *Masters of Sail* (Toronto, 1968), pp. 161-172; Judith Fingard, *Jack in Port: Sailortown in Eastern Canada* (Toronto, 1982).

held strong religious convictions. Sunday church services, prayer meetings, and the opportunity for "a good sing " were among her great pleasures, as was socializing with other women. She was particularly close to her sister Maria (Rie), who was two years younger than Annie and was raising her own family back in Yarmouth. The extent to which 'home,' both in the physical and spiritual sense, dominated Annie's thoughts is evident throughout her journal. We are always aware that this was not just a honeymoon voyage but her first extended trip away from home. While Annie was often able to amuse herself with the simple pleasures of reading and needlework, she nonetheless had to contend with uncomfortable conditions, hard work, monotony, sickness, and danger which the long, slow sea voyage entailed. She often suffered from headaches, depression and anxiety, symptoms of the homesickness which frequently overwhelmed her.

Annie's diary provides a vivid picture of life on board a small vessel. It also reveals how a captain's wife established her own domestic enclave in an all male context. Undaunted by her surroundings, Annie pursued a remarkable number of domestic tasks: sewing, knitting, housecleaning, washing, ironing, cooking, baking and preserving, nursing the sick and comforting the sorrowful. Letter writing and reading also helped to pass the time. Annie's reading materials included conventional nineteenth century popular literature and religious tracts. Such classics as Thackeray's *The Virginians* and the ubiquitous *May Queen*, a popular early poem by Tennyson, were standard fare for English-speaking people all over the world.

Despite her success in establishing a familiar domestic routine, Annie remained hopelessly homesick. The coarse language of the crew, their failure to observe the sabbath and their reliance on alcohol to relieve tensions made Annie feel uncomfortable. Different cultures based on class and gender also existed on land but differences became more obvious within the confines of a sailing ship. Troubling dreams, fits of crying and constant thoughts of folks back home testify to her unhappiness. Annie's grief over parting with her sister Rie is particularly heartfelt.

Annie's diary calls attention to the close relationships that women shared in their productive and reproductive lives. Even the language in which she expressed female interaction differs considerably from the way women discuss each other today. Visiting on board another ship on 3 April, 1871, Annie writes: "One night the gents did not come from the shore, and Mrs. Wade made her bed on the sofa so we would all be together. I slept with Mrs. Fulton. I loved her dearly. The night was very boisterous. " Carroll Smith-Rosenberg has argued that in the nineteenth century female world of love and ritual a different kind of emotional landscape encouraged a loving and trusting relationship among women.* Annie would probably be shocked to think of how her words would be interpreted by twentieth century readers who separate loving relationships into mutually exclusive political categories described as 'heterosexual' and 'homosexual' and who describe love primarily in sexual terms.

Confined to a sailing ship, Annie and John were forced to rely on each other for companionship and comfort. In the following passages from her diary we share Annie's frustrations with the "old tub" of a vessel, cramped surroundings and the absence of family and friends. We also sense the warm relationship shared by this newly married couple sailing down to Buenos Aires in the early months of 1871.

---

* "The Female World of Love and Ritual," *Signs*, Vol. 1, No. 1(Autumn 1975), pp. 1-29.

ANNIE ROGERS BUTLER DIARY
1871*

1871, January 3rd Tuesday afternoon

Well we are fairly launched upon another year, and I trust we may profit by our short-comings in the past and strive by God's help to do better in the future. 98 days out today and have not yet weathered Cape St. Augustine but I am thankful that kind Providence has brought us thus far. John thought he would have to go to the North again but I guess that danger is over now. I spent a very happy New Year much pleasanter than I antici-pated. The weather is beautiful and we have some glorious sun-sets; how often I wish for some of the dear ones from home to enjoy the beauties of sea life. We have been in around the coast for 3 or 4 days. It looks so good to see the land once more even tho tis far off. It is quite pretty in some places, along the shore is white sand. I fancy it is hot enough too when the sun shines. There are a great many trees also to be seen but none of a very tall growth. This morning we were just opposite a small town called Natal. I have a piece of pink coral that came up on the lead when they took soundings. There was a Steamer went into Natal this noon. I hope we shall soon make some port and get something fresh to eat in the shape of vegetables, it is a long time since we tasted any. I often wish for a piece of Mama's bread and butter. We have been eating bread made up with washing soda for we used our saleratus** up long ago and I wanted a piece of her plum pudding too; but alas no plum pudding for this child Christmas or New Years but we had a cock for New Years that a Capt's wife sent me from the schooner we spoke.

January 5th Thursday morning 9 o'clock

I have just been bathing my husband's head with some bay water, he has had to be up so much at night for the past week and spying with the glasses it has made him feel rather badly in

---

*   We are indebted to Mr. Raymond Simpson, Annie's grandson, for his invaluable assistance and support in preparing Annie's diary for publication. Mr. Simpson has recently completed a manuscript entitled *If We Are Spared To Each Other: Love and Faith Against the Sea*, containing Annie Butler's diaries and John Butler's accounts of his voyages.

**   Sodium bicarbonate or baking soda.

this region. Just think we have been at sea one hundred days. All hands begin to feel quite blue. The mate said, this morning at table, he began to feel so badly at night when out pacing the deck all alone and plenty of time to think. I expect the poor man wants to get home to see his wife. Her health is not very good and of course it makes him anxious. I went on deck this morning before breakfast to have a look at the coast. There are a great many of those stunted trees and a number of little huts in among them. One of those Cattamarans came up close along side and I had good look at them. John asked what they called the land ahead, but we could not make out what they said. One of the sailors said they said half a league. I suppose they thot we wished to know how far we were from shore. We made a good bit yesterday; I hope we may be as favored today. It is slow getting along and it worries John very much, but we are very thankful for even this help; it would have been so unfortunate if we had had to put back. I got thinking of home and dear Rie last evening and had a good little cry to myself. John did not know I was crying and asked me to sing a little for him. It struck me so ridiculous that I got laughing and crying at a great rate. I have not had many hysteric fits since I left home but once in a while I get taken but it is no wonder I am nervous for I guess John is himself. Mr. Mac says he was never out so long but once before and *my boy* was never out so long. With this brig we cannot expect anything better. We did think however we would be on our way back by this time instead of not having reached our destination — but we have been so blessed with health that we must not murmur but trust for a quick despatch when we do arrive.

January 7th Saturday afternoon, 4 o'clock
Yesterday my head ached so badly I could not write and it don't feel very well today. I have been very fortunate in regard to my head since we left St. Mary's. We are still beating along and I hope we shall soon reach a place called Pernambuco where John intends to call and get some provision and get some of the barnacles scraped from the vessel.

The mate went out where he could get a good look at her bottom when she came out of the water and he says it is fearful to look at. There have been several ships in sight today in the same plight we are but everything beats us. It is rather trying but we will have to keep cool.

Yesterday after dinner I felt very blue. I got all worked up and had a good cry. I felt as though I should never see my home again, but I know God is good and will take care and bless me if I put my whole trust in Him. I thought of the little band who met for the first Friday in the New Year and was with them in spirit; I trust God willing I may be with them in person before many months have elapsed. The weather is charming, beautiful sunshine all day and lovely moonshine all night. We saw the eclipse the other night.

It is a good thing that I had so many articles to work with or I should have been very lonely. I have made a pillow and sheet sham for our bed and John thinks they are very *becoming*. I do myself. Our men have been making hats of the Palmeto.* I guess they have all got one ....

January 9th Monday afternoon
I have been sitting on deck for a while sewing. Making a frill for an apron; I got tired of it and thought I would like a talk with my journal. When I got in our room, I found my darling napping. He awoke as I entered and informed me the sun was very bright. I immediately took the hint, returned to the deck and closed the lattice. I humor him just a little at present as he has to be up on deck so much at night these coasting times. I'm sorry to say we did not make much headway the last twenty-four hours, but the wind has brezzed up now and I guess we will do something this time. This morning I arose at five and went on deck to see the southern cross. It is four stars which appear all at one time and form a cross.

It was a lovely morning, the sun was just beginning to throw his cheering smiles upon the earth and sea. I stayed upon deck until the horizon was all aglow with his roseate hue. I think I shall try it again sometime as I got treated so well. The mate seemed very glad to have my company. The steward got my chair out and brought me some coffee. The men are all very respectful and polite to me. I wish they were all serving God as they ought to be doing; some of them seem to be rather seriously

*   Small palm trees with fan shaped leaves.

inclined and say they think christians are the happiest people, but think the forecastle a very hard place in which to do right. I told them they will not have to fight the battle alone and they believe all that I say is true. I gave them a Bible from the cabin and Tom told me today that they all read it but he did not think it did them much good. I do pray most earnestly that God would send His Holy Spirit into their hearts and convince them of their sins.

I wish I had the gift to talk to them better but I can never find words to express myself when I do say anything I feel that I am so unworthy myself that I am not fit to teach others. I hope God will give me more love in my heart for those who know him not. I do want to be a blessing to those around me

I often think of all our loved ones at home and in the social gatherings and long to be among them but when I think how lonely my dear John would be then, I'm glad I'm here. I do trust we shall yet spend many happy winter evenings at home, sweet home ....

'Tis [seven] months since we were married.

Tuesday afternoon January 10 five o'clock
We have been doing a little better today than yesterday, but it is trying to see everything sail us out of sight. John spoke [to] a St. John Capt. bound for New York. He had been to Montevideo. Had 72 days from Montreal. He had his wife with him. They had a nice looking vessel. Were loaded with hides. I wish we were bound for the same place. Maybe we shall get a freight as good if we get safe out. John is reading me a book called A Year in Spain written by a young American. It is very interesting indeed. The mate lent it to us.

I have just been ironing a linen coat for my husband to go ashore in. I hope he may soon get a chance to wear it. The weather has been pretty warm today, 86 in the shade. John has made me a foot stool, painted it green with a five pointed star in white on the top of it. Mr. Mac and I have had quite an amusing time for a few moments watching the ants at work, they have a road from the pantry around to the aft part of the boat and they carry their burdens to and fro. This afternoon they had a dead cockroach and fun to watch how they persevered and carried him along and such little creatures as they are, they did not give him up until they reached their nest and such a time as they had to get him in, however they mastered it. They certainly teach us lessons of perseverance.

My darling has just come down and says come Annie to tea dear and off he goes and seats himself at table so Annie dear must run too.

January 11 Wednesday afternoon four o'clock
We had a good brezze last night after ten and got along famously. Did the best work since we have been beating. We do feel so thankful to the giver of all good for we prayed that he would send a good wind, and he answered us. John is in hopes that by tomorrow night we shall have reached Pernambuco. I do hope we may for we are sadly in want of some vegetables and fresh food, although we are not suffering as yet. We have one barrel of flour left. The land along the coast today looks very pretty. I feel as though I would like to be among the beautiful trees, but I've no doubt I should soon wish myself on the water again. It is very hot here and it must be scorching there. We had it calm nearly for a while after dinner but it has breezed again now. After dinner I read the May Queen for my husband's bene-fit. He admired it very much; then we went on deck. I took my crochet-work. I am finishing Aunt Chloe's toilette set and John read from the History of Spain awhile and then came below for a nap. I let him sleep for an hour, then called him. He came up looking as though he had had a good drink of whiskey to him-self and acted so too; he got a blanket and wrapped himself in it and then came and rolled it around me ....

Friday morning January 13 nine o'clock
Last night we arrived at Pernambuco and this morning we went into the harbour. It looks very pretty all along the coast and tis quite a stirring city. There are a great many ships lying and steamers too. My gentleman has gone ashore and I am left here to look out for myself. It is getting very warm now. This morn-ing before the sun got high it was nice and cool. It is considered a healthy place and I should think it would be for they have a nice seabrezze all the time. I am expecting some fruit when my

boy gets back. There are a great many strange things to be seen and heard. The bells have been ringing nearly the whole morning, they sound very cheering to ears that have heard only the music of the wild waves for [a] hundred and seven days ....

January 28 Saturday
We are fairly out at sea again after spending ten days at Pernambuco. We have three men and a mate down with a touch of yellow fever but they are doing nicely now. The mate was delirious for a little while. I hope they will continue to do well for it is rather hard for my husband and he needs rest so much as present. He had so much running around to do in P. in the hot sun. It was fearfully hot there at noon time.

One night the wind was off land and it was suffocating. I woke in the night and I could scarcely breathe. We opened the window but the air was hot. We left the Rosses there waiting for the mail boat. I trust they will soon get off for it is becoming very sickly there. I was very sick the first Sunday I was there but our kind Heavenly Father granted me my health again. I do not know how to be grateful enough for it. I earnestly hope he will still be gracious to us and keep us all in health and guide us in safety to our Port. My dear John does not feel well tonight. He has had to much work to do lately. He has only one man in his watch. Old Frank said to me the other day, I guess you will have to come in our watch. I do hope the sick ones will be enabled to get around next week.

I have been thinking of the dear ones at home and wondering what they are all at. I long for the time to arrive if God spares my life when I shall be in dear old Yarmouth again. There's no spot on earth so dear to me.

Last Sabbath I was very homesick. I went up to our room in the Hotel and was looking at my Album and the tears would flow in spite of all that I could do. I had to walk back to Mrs. Rosses room and when she told me of her trials I thought I had not any. However it is but natural that I should get a little down and long for home at times. But tonight I am happy that I feel in my heart that Jesus helps me to trust in him and keeps my mind in peace and quietness. I feel my faith growing stronger and my hopes brighter. Oh I do trust in God with my whole heart, and

I know that all things shall work together for our good ....

February 14 Tuesday afternoon
Yesterday was my boy's birthday. He is thirty four now and I shall soon be thirty. It don't seem possible that I can be so old but oh it is *true, my youth is fading.* We have had very light winds for the last twenty four hours so we shall not make headway but I hope the wind will brezze up tonight. We have got company along. The Daisy has really got up to a vessel. John compared Long. this noon.

February 15 Wednesday afternoon
Dear sister Rie's birthday. How I would like to be near her. I wonder what she is doing. Frying doughnuts maybe. Wouldn't I like to have one or two or a dozen to eat.

It is a beautiful afternoon. The sunshine is cheering and beside we have a fair wind which I hope we may keep until we get into port. I have had pretty good spirits since we came out but today I had a downfall of them. Once in a while I get so very nervous but I try to keep my feelings down all I can. Now and again they will give way. I hope the time will not be very long e'er we shall be sailing off with a fair wind for home but I must have patience for that time to come. If we are spared it will be a good time of the year to get back. O I do long to be in dear old Yarmouth once more. I trust I shall get faces to look at when we get in. John just says this wind would take us right fair up the river. I do hope we shall be favoured with it, he says too we may arrive on Sunday. I have been thinking perhaps Annie Lewis is spending the afternoon up to Ries. Dear Annie I dreamed of her last night. I so often see them all in dreamland. God in tender mercy grant that in a few months I may be with them once again. Darling coz Liz, how often I think of her and long to be in Hebron* having a good sing with Han and herself. I hope I may yet have that pleasure and my John too; *he can sing grand.*

March 9th Thursday afternoon
Sometime has elapsed since I last wrote in my journal. We have been in Montevideo and spent a few days very pleasantly with

* A village near the town of Yarmouth, Nova Scotia.

some of John's former acquaintances.

I was very sorry that we could not unload there but John got orders after lying a week to proceed to Buenos Ayres. A great many tried to persuade me to remain in M__ while John came up here on account of yellow fever; but I could not see that it would be wise to do so. I would have worried all the time for fear John would get sick. We have concluded to live aboard ship and I do expect to see the city only in the distance. We are 6 miles from the shore. Everybody that has been on board says the sickness is not so bad. One thing we do know that the hand which had kept us from disease so far is still as powerful as ever. In God is our Trust. It is nine months this evening since I was married and oh how rapidly the time has flown; how many new acquaintances I have made and how many different scenes I have witnessed since that eventful eve.

This morning the barque Prowess passed close to us on her way out to Antwerp. Capt Hibbert Master and right before my eyes was dear old Lou. I did feel so disappointed that we could not have been here together. They had been here three months. What fine times we might have had if we could have only got here sooner but I must not repine. Dear little Frankie stood on the top of the house waving his kerchief as he saw his mother doing. Lou called out: "Ain't this too bad Annie. " I said, "Yes, I'm cross, " I meant at this poke of a vessel. We could put up with ill-winds but she don't go any when there is a good one. Everyone gets sick of her. Our Pilot from M__ said he would not sail her if she was given to him; and the pilot here got out of all sort of patience right away. He said he did not know where my husband got his from. He thought he should jump overboard if he had to be long in her. Well poor John has been pretty well tried to, I can assure you, and borne it as well as anyone else would I know. I do hope we may be spared to sail in a good ship sometime that will not cause him such annoyance. I think I would enjoy going to sea then ....

March 10 Friday afternoon
John got back about seven last night and I was very glad to see him; but tonight alas he cannot come for it is dark and dreary and raining very very hard; thundering and lightning too.

This morning we had a slight Pampero.* I thought it bad enough, it grew very dark and the wind blew fearfully. I do wish we could go in nearer. It is five or six miles to shore. I am so glad Capt Young stayed with us today. I won't be so lonely as long as there is a Capt aboard.

John saw Amiel Crawley yesterday and several Capt's of his acquaintance. From one of them he learned that two months ago dear brother William was here, and I think ten years have passed since last we met. O I do so wish we could have been here at that time but I know God moves in a mysterious way his wonders to perform. He may have kept from us and that would have made me feel worse to know he was here and not want to see me; our steps are all wisely ordered. 'Tis one consolation to know he is still alive. O I do pray most earnestly that God would work upon his heart and reclaim him from his evil ways and guide him into Virtue's path from which he has so widely strayed ....

1871 March 16 Thursday evening
I feel very lonely tonight. John went off this morning at six and Capt. Young went too and now the day has passed and gone, nearly eight o'clock and my husband not back yet and what is worse I don't expect he will come tonight. I don't like this sort of thing at all. I cannot bear to be left here all alone at night, but life is such. The mate and steward have just seated themselves for a game of chequers in the forward Cabin. I want to hear from home so much. I did hope John would get off tonight and bring some letters. I have been ironing the clothes and cutting out work today, and tomorrow if I live I must get up early and go to washing. We do not dare send the things ashore. The news today was the fever was over. I trust it is for then I shall not be left all alone sad and lonely among a set of roughs. Oh I do not like it. If they would not get angry and swear at each other it

---

* A strong cold wind that blows from the Andes across the South American pampas.

would not seem so bad. One of the men had a fit this noon, and one is sick with a cold. I sent him some sage to steep and drink. [I] hope he will get better soon.
My head aches and I think I'll retire.

March 20 Monday Afternoon
Sat John (when he came from shore) brought Capt. Wade and his lady to tea; they spent the evening as we had a nice moon. I have made a promise to visit her soon. Sunday they came alongside for us to go aboard the Ella, Capt. Fulton's brig. John had told Mrs. Fulton the day before that we would come. I did not feel just right about going and after we got there we found his men at work stowing cargo. I did not enjoy myself as I would have done had it been a week day for we could not have the quiet I like on Sunday. I will never leave the ship again on a Sunday. I have promised to go there on Tuesday next but I do not know I shall get there for our boat leaks so I am afraid of her ....

April 3 Monday Morning
I have been so busy lately that I have neglected my journal. Since I last wrote I have been away on a visit to Mrs. Fulton. The following Wednesday after the Sunday I was there John took me down just before tea. It had been blowing Pamperos all the first of the week and as it calmed down some we thought we would take a sail. It was pretty rough but I did not get frightened until we got alongside the vessel. They were so long throwing the rope and Jack was unable to fasten ours quickly. The boat kept going up and down and striking against the Ella's side that I was very much alarmed. Mrs. F__ said I was white as a ghost. I could not get over it for a long time. John went back after tea and I remained until Saturday eve, then John came for me to go home. I had a very pleasant time indeed. Mrs. Wade was there too. Her husband and Capt Fulton were great friends and always went ashore together. Capt. Wade's cargo smelt so badly while they were taking it in that Mrs. Wade did not leave Mrs. F__ until they were ready for sea. One night the gents did not come from the shore, and Mrs. Wade made her bed on the sofa so we would all be together. I slept with Mrs. Fulton. I loved her dearly. The night was very boisterous ... John started in our boat only one

man with him and got lost among the shipping; he could not find the Daisy and then tried to find the Ella but could not and had to put back to the shore again. I would have been worried enough if I had thought he was out that night.

Since I got back I have been washing, ironing and mending nearly every day. I've been very tired some nights after my day's work but rest was the sweeter for it. I find that the work agrees with me. Last Sunday week we had a fearful thunder storm. The sky was one continual blaze of light for some time. I never heard such pelting rain or saw such vivid lightning. It was very bad for the sickness. It was called Black Monday. The next day there were so many deaths 600 and some say nine, the fever is still raging and a few cases of cholera have been known. I do trust God will soon in infinite love stay the hand of disease. It must be heartrending for those who are losing their loved ones. I wrote to Papa and Sarah Ben last Sunday. I do hope the time will soon come when I shall greet them all again. John is heart sick about the voyage; he knows he will sink so much money but we must try and be patient and look to God to help us through, and bear with our difficulties. There are a great many vessels lying here and it is slow getting along with business at present.

April 5 Wednesday Afternoon
Dear me how the days, weeks and months fly off. We have been up here ever since the 6th of March and it is hard to tell how much longer we shall be here. John has gone ashore today to see what can be done to hurry matters. I have been making a rag mat. It is so cold now that the bare floor is rather cool to step on at night. It is quite a fine looking affair. I dreamed of home dear home last night. Oh I do long to be there once more. God grant that we may be taken there in safety. The fever was not any better the last day John went off. For the last few times he has found some one with whom he has had conversation or dealings with the time before dead and buried on his return. The weather is growing cooler all the time. I do hope it will stop the progress of the fever. I have been thinking of M.M. Hilton and wondering what has made her treat me so. I did count so much on her letters knowing her to be such a good correspondent. I do feel really hurt when I think about it. I'm very sure I should not have

treated her in like manner. I suppose they are beginning to think about housecleaning at home. Well they will be all through by the time we get back if we live. I have been reading the Virginians and I think I will go have a read now for a while.

The cargo is nearly out and the carpenters have nearly got the rudder fixed, and if we could only get ballast we would soon be off.

April 8 Saturday Afternoon
It is a lovely afternoon; clear and cold. Just cool enough to be pleasant. I suppose we shall soon be in hot weather again if spared to resume our voyage. I have been making some gooseberry jam this morning. I have a little spirit lamp and I have made preserves two or three times with it, it is very handy. I have got my husbands and my own clean clothes all out for Sunday and have been patching up our old towels to save our good ones. I would like to get some curiosities from here but everything is so very expensive and I cannot go ashore to look up anything. John does not have time for anything but his business. My eyes are very sore and have been for a week. I don't know what is the matter with them. John has been reading to me since dinner. I shall be glad when I can read with some pleasure and less pain. Lying here so long in the fresh water I have got the rheumatism.

I dreamed of Nellie last night helping her put her house to rights ....

April 12 Wednesday Afternoon
John has gone ashore today. He did not get off yesterday and we did some washing, he put the clothes out for me and he did some of the washing too as I had a good many pieces. After he left this morning I went at some wollen shirts of his that needed washing badly. I knew he would not let me do them if he was here; however I got through grande. 1 got Billy to get my tub down and the steward brought me water and then he hung the shirts up for me. The worst part was emptying my tub; it is so heavy, but I managed. I have washed up our cabin floor and got my bed made and all fixed up and it is not quite 11 so I think I'm pretty smart. John went aboard a German vessel yesterday and there heard the Custom House is to be closed for a month after

yesterday. I hope we shall get off before that time but is no use to worry about it. I must try and keep my courage up. Last evening I felt pretty blue when I thot how matters were and John seemed so bothered. I hope things will turn out all well in the end. John knows he will be found fault with but I wish his owners had to worry through matters as he does every day. He has hard work to keep from being out of sorts all the time.

April 18 Tuesday Morning
John has gone ashore and I am into housecleaning strong. I have got one of the men helping me. We have got everything cleared out of our room and I have got Tom white washing and got things so he can go right ahead with cleaning so all I shall do now is look on and see he does it well. John was sick nearly half the night. I was sorry he had to go off today. He should have kept quiet and he went before I knew it and has forgotten his overcoat. I'm afraid he will get cold, the air is very keen after the sun goes down; he ought to have thought of it himself but he may get back early so I won't fret. It is a lovely morning and I am so glad as we can have all the windows open housecleaning, how I do long to be at home once more. I do hope we shall have a quick passage if we are spared to get from here and I hope that will be very soon. Well I must not take any more time to write but go do some work. I have got to fix up my woollen stockings. It is to cold to wear cotton.

April 22 Saturday Afternoon
I have been very busy starching and ironing this morning, and I have some more to do this afternoon. I had to leave of[f] for the steward to lay the table for dinner. Just after we were through our dinner the boat arrived and of course I thot John had come but only the men came with a letter for me saying he would be off in a whale boat tonight. Last night I was dreary enough. I don't know when I have felt so homesick before. I had a real good cry to myself after tea, then I felt better. Every woman knows the blessedness of tears. After that I killed three mammoth roaches; and settled down to my work. How I did wish for someone to speak too but no there I sat sad and alone on the River Plate.

EPILOGUE: ANNIE ROGERS BUTLER

The *Daisy* finally set sail from Buenos Aires on 11 May. After calls at Barbados, Saint Thomas and Puerto Rico, John and Annie arrived in New York on 16 August 1871. It was not until 2 March that Annie was back in Yarmouth and settled in her "own parlour. " She never again went to sea with her husband. In April 1872, a son, Frank, was born, and three years later in October 1875, she gave birth to a daughter, Elsie. In 1876 John was made master of the brigantine *Clarence* (145.58 tons), built by Annie's father and named for her brother. The *Clarence* embarked on its maiden voyage in December bound for Martinique with a cargo of lumber and fish. It never returned. John was lost at sea at the age of thirty-nine, leaving Annie a widow with two small children.

For a brief time, Annie ran a nursery school, mostly for children of the Rogers-Butler clan. In 1891 she accepted the position of Matron at the Halifax Protestant Orphans' Home. Elsie lived with her mother at the orphanage while Frank boarded with several families in Halifax. In 1900, when the children were old enough to support themselves — Elsie taught elementary school and Frank trained as a mechanic — Annie retired from her post. The three shared a house in Halifax until Annie died in 1906. It was not until after her death that her children married, and that Frank, like his father before him, went to sea.

Yarmouth Harbour (circa late 1800s)

HANNAH RICHARDSON
1844-1880

While a few dedicated women like Mathilda Churchill were carving out careers in foreign mission fields in the late nineteenth century, many more were drawn to job opportunities in industrial centres. As the 1889 Royal Commission investigating labour conditions in Canada documents, some women found jobs in Nova Scotia factories, manufacturing such commodities as textiles, biscuits and candies.* Many more went to the nearby United States to find work. Very few of the single female migrants left accounts of their experiences and their letters written home seem to have been all too often destroyed in one of the periodic housecleanings mentioned by many of our diarists. One exception to this generalization is the diary of Hannah Richardson of Carleton, Yarmouth County.

Located on the southwestern tip of Nova Scotia, Yarmouth County is just a short boat ride away from Boston. Many young people in the region took advantage of the regular steamship service to seek their fortunes in the 'Boston States.' Hannah Richardson, the eldest in a family of seven children, was 27 years old when she left Yarmouth in 1871 to work in the P. P. Sherry shoe factory in Lynn, Massachusetts. Her brother Nathaniel, the "Than" of the diary, was already located in Lynn as were many other 'provincial' sojourners. From her meticulously kept accounts, we learn that in the year 1872 Hannah earned over $500.00 and on occasion made as much as $3.40 a day. As a 'lady stitcher' acquainted with the subtleties of the new "Singer"

---

* Gregory Kealey, ed., *Canada Investigating Industrialism* (Toronto, 1973); see also Susan Mann Trofimenkoff, "One Hundred and Two Muffled Voices: Canada's Industrial Women in the 1880s," *Atlantis*, Vol. 3, No. 1 (Autumn, 1977), pp. 66-82.

sewing machines, Hannah was among the elite of factory workers. Her income was high even relative to that of many men in
this period. The prospects of making so much money would be
a strong inducement for a single woman to become a 'working
girl,' at least for a few years before marriage. Hannah sent
money to her father and lent money to Than who was setting
up his own household in Lynn in 1872 but most of her income
was spent on the purchase of consumer goods which were faithfully listed in her 42 cent diary.

The move to Lynn seems not to have been a difficult one for
Hannah, in part because her brother and several Yarmouth
County friends were already located there. When not at work,
Hannah's social life revolved around family and friends, church
and community, much as it would back home. She had a network of female friends, including her sometime room-mate
Abby Moody from Rumford, Maine, with whom she shared the
contents of her diary. She also spent a considerable portion of
her spare time sewing for the men in her life, a traditional occupation for women and one particularly well-suited to a lady
stitcher, with access to a sewing machine.

Hannah's diary is curiously silent about conditions on the
shop floor. We sense that her job was less noteworthy and perhaps no more demanding than work on the farm where she had
grown up. Although she occasionally admits to being tired,
most of the time she had the energy in the evenings to go 'calling,' attend church functions and participate in the busy social
life of urban lodging houses. Only the mention of weight loss in
a later section of the diary not published here and her several
moves to new lodgings suggest that boarding house fare might
not always be adequate for a working girl. Hannah easily solved
this problem when she returned from her summer vacation in
Yarmouth by taking her board with Than and his new wife. This
solution, significantly, soon netted her a gain of 10 pounds. In
short, kinship and community ties served and survived the migration experience remarkably well and, as Hannah's diary
suggests, Nova Scotia women in the 'Boston States,' were never
far from home.

Hannah's daily diary entries are sparsely written and some-what repetitious. Only an edited version of 6 months' activities, noted faithfully every day, is published here.*

* Hannah Richardson's individual experiences nicely confirm general conclusions reached by Alan Dawley in *Class and Community: The Industrial Revolution in Lynn* (Cambridge, 1976). The background to women's role in the shoe manufacturing process is described in Mary H. Blewett, "The Sexual Division of Labor and the Artisan Tradition in Early Industrial Capitalism: The Case of New England Shoemaking, 1780-1860," in *To Toil the Livelong Day: America's Women at Work, 1780-1980* (Ithaca, 1987), p. 35-46 and in her forthcoming book, *Men, Women, and Work: Class, gender and protest in the New England Shoe Industry, 1780-1910* published by the University of Illinois Press. We wish to express our thanks to Mary H. Blewett for making excerpts from this book available to us and for her assistance in interpreting the context of Hannah's life in Lynn.

HANNAH RICHARDSON DIARY
1872*

Monday, January 1, 1872.
Mild and warm, but cloudy all day. Went out in the morning
with Abby Moody, we each bought a Diary gave [for] 42 cents.
In the evening Jenny & Susy Smith and I went and spent the evening with Than. Joe** gone to drawing school. He got home just
before we left and came home with us.

Tuesday 2
Clear and cold. Went to the shop in the morning, did not have
any work till most noon. When I went home to dinner stopped
on my way, bought me a hat gave 50 cents. Went to the shop
after dinner and had work till night. Went to singing school in
the evening with Than and Joe.

Wednesday 3
Cloudy and cold. To the shop at work all day. May left the shop
to night. Home in the evening sewing, fixed the neck of Joe's
shirt and sewed a little on Than's. Retired at ten.

Thursday 4
Wet and rainy all day. To the shop hard at work. May went in
Miss Patch's shop. Home in the Evening. Sewing on Thans shirt.
Retired at half past ten.

Friday 5
Cloudy all day. To the shop all day. Got a letter from Sam at
night. In the evening Than and Joe came in. Than & I went to
Mrs. Williams to see the Smith girls. We went home. I retired at
ten.

---

*   Hannah Richardson's diary is in the possession of Mrs. Wyndham
       Morton, Framingham, Massachusetts. We wish to thank Mrs. Morton
       for permission to publish excerpts from the diary and also Gwen Trask,
       who located the diary and helped us to interpret it.
**   Joe Bain is the brother of Sam Bain, Hannah's Nova Scotia beau,
       mentioned below.

Thursday 11
Fine in the morning, clouded up just before night. To the shop all day. One caller Jenny S. In the evening Joe and I went down to Nehemiah McCormack,* found his wife very sick. She wanted us to sing, we did. Wrote part of a letter to Sam after I got home.

Sunday 14
Cold, windy and cloudy in the morning but cleared off in the afternoon and a little warmer, went to meeting both parts of the day, took dinner and tea with Jenny & Susy S. In the evening Jenny & Susy & Susan Chisholm went to the boys room, had a nice sing and went home.

Wednesday 17
Cold and snowy. To the shop. May in a while in the morning, Jennie Smith in the afternoon. I ran over to the boys room a while after tea, came back and went to work on Thans shirt. Nehemiah McCs wife died this morning 9 o'clock.

Thursday 18
Fine but cold. To the shop. Jennie Smith brought me a letter, it was from home. In the first of the evening Joe, Than and I went to N. McCormack. He started for home at half past eight to take his wife. I went to the room with Joe. Than went to division.**

Friday 19
Fine in the morning but cloudy before night. To the shop all day. In the evening I went and spend the evening with Joe, spent a very pleasant evening. I sewed part of the evening, we sat and told stories the rest. Than gone to Boston.

Tuesday 23
Fine. To the shop. Went to the young ladies reading room to get

* Nehemiah McCormack and his wife Sarah were also natives of Yarmouth County.
** Temperance Division.

a boarding place.* Got the ladies name went after tea to see her, think I shall go there. Went to church and singing school in the evening ....

Friday 26
Fine. To the shop all day. In the evening May & I, Miss Hilton and Wilson, Mr. Hamilton and Charley Potter went in to Mrs Davis' where Than and Joe board. Spent a very pleasant evening, had a nice sing.

Saturday 27
Fine. To the shop all day. Went out in the evening, Joe with me. Bought me a waterproof cape and a pair of kid gloves. Went to the room with Joe, stopped a while and came home. Than went to Boston.

Sunday 28
Snowy in the morning but cleared off at noon fine. Went to the meeting morning, afternoon & evening. Susy & Gusty Walsh, May and I went to the boys room after dinner and sang till meeting time. Went to the young mens meeting and to Mr. Lions to prayer meeting.

Tuesday 30
Fine, snow on the ground. To the shop in the forenoon. No person working in the afternoon because Mr. Sherry's baby died. I washed a little after dinner, dressed and went and called on Susy & Gusty Walsh, Susy, Jennie Smith. Went to singing school in the evening.

Wednesday 31
Fine. Not to work in the shop. Home in the forenoon, ironed a little in the afternoon. Jenny & Susy Smith and I went and had some pictures taken together. I took tea with them and went to prayer meeting in the evening.

---

*   Hannah seemed to find her boarding house less than satisfactory. See entry for March 23rd. The young ladies' reading room also served as a clearing house for boarders.

Wednesday, February 7
Fine. Spent my 28th birthday in P.P. Sherry's Shoe Shop. Had a birthday gift, a silver thimble. Susie and Gustie Walsh gave it to me. Went to meeting in the evening with Than, to Mr. Turnbulls. Got a letter from Sam.

Saturday 10
Not very fine. To the shop. In the evening Joe, Than and I went and spent the evening with Susie & Jennie. Jennie cut my wrapper. I bought a valentine to send Joe & Sam. Abby Moody bought one for her mother.

Wednesday 21
Fine. To the shop all day. In the evening I went to the Grand Army Fair. One of the girls in the shop gave me a ticket for two nights. Joe with me. Susie & Augustie were with us.

Monday 26
Fine but cold. To the shop, moved in our new shaking room. In the evening Abby Moody, Susie Walsh, May and I called on the boys & had a laugh. Went to the next woman's, stopping at Majors room on our way back & played on the organ.

Monday, March 4, 1872
Cloudy, To the shop, Home in the evening, sewed a little. Susie Walsh stitched my morning dress on the machine while I played for her on the flutina.

Sunday 10
A rainy day. Home all day and evening. Wrote letters to sisters Susie and Tabbie & Sam B. Played on the flutina a little, read a little and retired at eight. Lonesome.

Monday 11
A fine warm day. To the shop one caller, Jennie Smith. In the evening Than & I went out to Mrs. Pattersons.* Had a splendid time. Miss P played on the piano. Emma Wright gave me her picture.

---

*   Mrs. Patterson was also from Yarmouth County and a future in-law of Than who married Hattie Patterson.

Tuesday 12
A cold blustering snow storm. To the shop. In the evening May
& I went and spent the evening with Than and Joe. Came home
and retired at ten. No letters yet.

Monday 18
Fine. To the shop all day. Steam came on this morning but we
did not work by it. Home in the evening, finished my wrapper.
No letters yet.

Tuesday 19
Fine. To the shop. Worked by steam, it seems good to have steam
again I tell you. Got a letter from Sam and one from Emma
Thomas. Home in the evening sewing, retired at ten.

Wednesday 20
Fine but very windy. I to the shop but had no work in the fore-
noon. Mr. Sherry fixing the shafting. Work in the afternoon.
Home in the evening, washed a little, sewed a little.

Thursday 21
Fine, but windy. Worked in the forenoon. In the afternoon Susie,
Gustie, May & I went and got some pictures taken. Than & I
went down to Mrs. Elwells, and spent the evening.

Saturday 23
Not very fine quite a snow storm in the afternoon. May & I left
Mrs. Pearls and came to Miss Patch's to board. Seems like going
from a prison to a Palace.

Sunday 24
A splendid day, but snow on the ground. Did not go to meeting
in the forenoon. Wrote letters to Sam and sister Tid, & Mother.
Like my new boarding place, nice so far, had roast turkey for
supper tonight. Went to meeting afternoon & evening.

Monday 25
A lovely day, snow melted very fast. To the shop, one caller
Jennie Smith. Susie & Augustia Walsh & Abby Moody moved

from Mrs. Pearls down here next house to us. May and I went to see them tonight. They happy as can be. Two letters from Sam to day.

Friday 29
Fine. To the shop all day but sick enough to be home and abed. Home in the evening sick. Than came in and spent the evening.

Saturday 30
Fine, better and to the shop. Had a letter from Sam. In the evening Than, Joe, Ned Clements & I went out to Mrs. Pattersons and spent the evening. Had a nice time. Tonight I put $25 in the bank.

Thursday, April 4 Fast day
A splendid day. Joe, Than, Susie & Augustia Walsh, Abbie Moody, Hattie Patterson and I went to Boston. Started at eight o'clock in the morning. Went on the boat & had a nice time going and while we were there got some pictures taken all together. Went to a saloon and had dinner first then went and got the pictures then we all went in to the Boston Museum. It was very nice. Then we took the half past five train and came home, all but Than & Hattie.

Tuesday 9
Wet & rainy all day. I to the shop. Home in the evening sewing. May went back to Mr. Sherry's shop to work to day.

Friday 19
Fine. To the shop. Went to meeting in the evening. A year ago tonight I was to Mrs. Bains sitting on the lounge beside Sam. I did not feel very well in my mind.

Saturday 20
Fine. To the shop. Went down to Mrs. Williams in the evening to get my bask and over shirt. Joe called there to come home with me. It was very pleasant and we took quite a walk before we got home. Had quite a chat about Bill & Mary. A year ago to night I left Yarmouth for Lynn.

Sunday 21
A lovely day, warm as summer. To meeting all day & evening. Went down to Mrs. Elwells a little while between meetings. In the evenings Joe, Susie Walsh and I went to a lecture in the Methodist Church. It was very good. He was very much against the Catholicks.

Saturday 27
Fine. To the shop. Susie called at five o'clock and went to the bank with me. I deposited 10 dollars. In the evening Joe called and he & I went in to see the girls a while.

Sunday 28
Fine but windy. To meeting all day and evening. Went to the Methodist in the evening with Joe heard a nice lecture on the evils of intemperance. Wrote to Sam, Father & Tid between meetings.

Saturday, May 4
Raining all day. To the shop. Katie Carroll died this morning. One of my shop mates. Down to Mrs. Williams in the evening. Slept with Susie & Jennie Smith. I left Miss Patch to night.

Monday 6
Fine. To the shop. Went to the depot at half past eight A.M. to see Susie & Gustie off. May and I came in to room with Abby Moody to night.

Tuesday 7
Fine and very warm. To the shop. Had a letter from Mother. In the evening Than, Hattie, Kiss Patterson and I went down to Mrs. Hamiltons. When I got home found May gone. She went to room with Katie Edwards.

Saturday 11
Fine till most night then came in foggy, a little cooler. In the evening Abby & I went shopping, Joe with us. We bought new hats & bows alike. I gave myself a new shawl. Had a letter from Sam. John Patten brought it for he came to day.

Tuesday 14
Fine. To the shop. One caller, Sis Hamilton. In the evening went to the ministers to a sociable. Presented him with a silver service.

Friday 17
Fine. Did not feel very well in mind. Got a letter from Sam. Went to prayer meeting in the evening. Abby & Joe went for a walk.

Saturday 18
Fine and cool. Hard at work all day. Kiss Patterson and I went down to Mrs. Crowells in the evening to see Joe. Had a nice time eating oranges and mending Joes pants and coat. Also a pleasant walk home.

Friday 24
A lovely day after the rain. Too pretty to work in the shop. I went to prayer meeting in the evening.

Tuesday 28
Showery thunder storm at night. I did some stitching on Mrs Mitchel's machine.

Thursday 30
Decoration day.* Fine the forenoon but rained most night. In the forenoon I went to the saloon with Frank Sawyer and had some pictures taken. Abby worked. In the afternoon Abby and I went out a while, did not stop long for it rained. Willy Preble came home with us and stopped till tea time.

Friday 31
Rainy. Mr. Mitchel moved from Lloyd to Johnson street. Abby & I with them. We went out in the evening for a walk. Will Preble met us on the street and came home with us.

Saturday, June 1
Fine and warm. I went to Boston in the afternoon. Hattie & Kiss Patterson went with me. We had a nice time but we got awful

* Memorial Day, held in honour of those who died in American wars.

tired. I got myself a set of hair curl a set of jewelry and a sun-shade. Will Preble and Abby met me at the depot. I saw Jim Miller & Lyman Kelly in Boston.

Wednesday 12
Fine in the morning and very warm, but clouded up most night and rained thundered & lightened very heavy. I had my feet doctored by a negro.

Monday, 17
Fine. Home in the forenoon sewing. After dinner Abby & I laid down and had a nap then got up, dressed and went to the beech. After tea Will Preble & Abby, Sawyer & I went out, saw the tight rope performance, then went to the beech for a walk. We left Abby and Will at the hotel sitting on a seat. We walked around on the walk to an ice cream saloon, went in and had an ice cream and came home.

Saturday 22
Fine & warm. To work all day. Sawyer came in the shop to see me. Stopped till I got ready to come home. In the evening Than, Joe, Hattie P., Abby and I went to West Lynn to Abbys uncle's Mr. Elliott's. Spent a very pleasant evening. Came home in the horse cars.

Tuesday 25
Not very fine, a little rain. To the shop but not doing much.* Came home at three o'clock and sewed on my dress. Abby & I took a walk in the evening.

Wednesday 26
Not very fine. Worked a little in the forenoon. To the shop but did not do any work on shoes in the afternoon. In the evening Abby and I took a walk. Went up to Mrs Pattersons but did not stop long. Came home and went to bed.

---

*   The slacking of work in the shop was typical of the summer season in the shoe industry.

Saturday 29
Fine and hot. Abby started for Rumford at eight o'clock. I went to the Depot with her. Then went to the shop with May and helped her finish her work. In the afternoon went to the shop for my pay and stayed with Miss O'conner all the afternoon. Up to Mrs. Pattersons in the evening. Joe & Than there.

Sunday 30
Fine but awful hot. Went to meeting in the forenoon. Stopped to Mrs Preble's the afternoon. After tea Sawyer & I went up on high rock to meeting. Wrote letters to Susie & Gussie Walsh. My last Sunday out on the hill in the afternoon back of Mrs Preble's, on Washington St. *first time there* in Lynn for a while I suspect.

Monday, July 1
Fine but very warm. I went to the bank in the forenoon and drew my money, went in Mr Mullens shop to see May a while. Came home and went down to Mrs Williams in the afternoon. Bid them goodby. Up to Mrs Pattersons in the evening. Than & Hattie Married.

Tuesday 2
Fine but very warm. Left Lynn at eight o'clock for Yarmouth. Came to Boston on the cars. Took the boat. Left Boston at half past ten. Fine on the water, one shower at three oclock. We all went to bed at four oclock. Very cold on the water.

Wednesday 3
Got up at half past nine. Went up on deck. Did not feel very well. Stayed on deck till we got in to the wharf. Went up to Sis Bain, got tea then went up to Mr Bains, stopped to Hebron corner and got Sam.

Thursday 4
Foggy most all day. Went down town in the morning, met Father in town, went to Anna Bains and got dinner then started for Carlton. Got home at six oclock. Having a great time in Boston to day I expect. Found the folks all well at home but Mother. Charl and Will Nie came out in the evening.

Friday 5
Rain in the morning, not very fine the rest of the day. Got our trunks home and I washed a few things. Went down to Mrs Kelleys in the afternoon. Home in the evening sewing. Got a letter from Abby Moody.

Saturday 6
Foggy in the morning cleared off fine the rest of the day. Home in the forenoon went out to the mill in the afternoon. Did a little work on Susan Durkee's machine. Came home before tea. After tea Hattie & I went down to the lake to bathe.

Sunday 7
Fine and warm. Went to meeting in the morning. Home afternoon and evening. Wrote letters to Abby Moody & May.

Monday 8
Fine & warm. Home all day. Washed in the forenoon, ironed a little and sewed a little in the afternoon. After tea Than, Hattie, Tid & I went up to Mrs Eldridge's a while.

Wednesday 10
Fine & warm. Festival day. Aunt May Crosby came up in the morning. Sam came at ten o'clock. Joe & Cad Trask, soon after. All to Fathers to dinner. We all went to festival in the afternoon. Had a nice time.

EPILOGUE: HANNA RICHARDSON

In 1873 an economic depression put an end to high wages in the shoe industry and left many factory operatives umemployed. We do not know if Hannah was a victim of these larger forces or if personal reasons influenced her to quit her job. In any event, she returned to Nova Scotia in 1873 where she married her beloved Sam on August 2nd of that year. They had one son, Eugene Frederick, born in October, 1874. Hannah died in 1880 at the age of 36. Eleven years later, Sam married Tabitha Richardson, Hannah's younger sister.*

---

*   Genealaogical Records, Yarmouth County Museum. Interview with Mr. and Mrs. James Nickerson, Carleton, 20 August 1982

MARY MACDOUGALL MACDONALD
1853-1940

Mary MacDougall was the sixth of twelve children born to Maria Sanford and William MacDougall in the West Gore area of Hants County. Like many of our diarists, Mary was an enthusiastic student. "O happy childhood, how I love to go to school," Mary proclaimed when she was sixteen. In June 1873, at the age of 19, she married her childhood sweetheart, Peter MacDonald. In July the newly-weds set out for California by rail through the United States. En route they stopped to visit Mary's sister Sarah, her husband Tom Loney and a host of other relatives and friends in Grass Valley, California. They then proceeded to Stockton where they worked on a farm owned by a Mr. Sloan with whom Peter had apparently been employed before returning to Nova Scotia to marry our diarist.

Mary and Peter's long journey to the land of "milk and honey" was repeated many times by Nova Scotians in this period. In an earlier dairy written in 1869, Mary noted that the "California fever" had become "very infectious" in her community. Although men were often the first to 'go West,' the absence of women on the frontier often spurred men to look for wives 'back home,' once they had decided to settle in distant lands. The journey by railroad across the continent was much easier for Mary than it was for women who, prior to the completion of the first transcontinental railroad in 1869, had made the trek by horse and wagon. Yet Mary's problems, including homesickness and an excessive dependence on her husband for companionship, were similar to those experienced by an earlier generation of pioneer women. They, like Mary, never quite forgot the kinship networks and community ties left behind.* For Mary and many women like her, a diary became a welcome outlet for feelings difficult to articulate or control.

Mary also has much in common with Annie Butler. As married women their extensive travels were dictated by the work and ambitions of their husbands. Both women became homesick, not just for their native province but for their kin and community networks which comprised the basis of their identity and power. We watch both women become desperately dependent upon their husbands and even enlist them into helping with the household chores. Because there were no female companions in whom to confide, their diaries are more forthcoming than the other chronicles in our collection. Mary resorted to poetry to express her fragmented feelings for her husband, her distant home and her distraught self. Her closing lines: "But chide me gently dearest one/ You know I'm but a child," is particularly revealing about the way Mary perceived her status within the marriage.

Like Annie Butler, Mary MacDougall found consolation in her religion. She belonged to the Church of Christ's Disciples, an evangelical sect which had a considerable following in her Hants County community of West Gore. When Mary discovered that strangers did not observe Sundays in the same way that she had been accustomed to, she gathered friends from home for a soul-sustaining hymn sing. "O, it reminds me so much of home when I hear our good old tunes sung again that we used to sing away in the dear old home with brothers and sisters," Mary observed on 7 September. The emergence of such institutions as churches, schools and voluntary organizations on the agrarian frontier of North America almost certainly owed as much to the urgent demands of the womenfolk as it did to the men who were preoccupied with 'getting ahead.'

---

*   On the experience of women on the overland trail see Lillian Schlissel, *Women's Diaries of the Westward Journey* (New York, 1982).

Mary's sharp eye captures much of the excitement of travelling across the North American continent in the early days of rail transportation. Her apparently callous reaction to the Indians they encountered en route was typical of white attitudes which helped to produce the desperate situation she described. Although native people were still able to win victories over white generals — as George Custer found to his regret at Little Bighorn River in 1876 — the western frontier of North America would be dominated by people like Peter and Mary MacDougall from West Gore, Nova Scotia.

MARY MACDOUGALL MACDONALD
DIARY 1873*

July 26th

Saturday the sun is shining brightly down upon the pretty little way side towns as we go whizzing by them. Change cars, Conductor says, so we pick up our baggage and off in a jiffy. It is just half past 8 and we are to wait here till eleven A.M. This is Albany. At eleven we took the Emigrant train and stopped at one, waited till two and took the Express. Landed again at Amsterdam where we are now. We have had a little walk around and are now sitting in the station room waiting for the train .... 6 O'clock and we are again on board an express. The car is very much crowded. The scenery along here is lovely; we are passing along a large river; the banks are covered with verdure and bushes the greenest of green. The broad river is rolling along so peaceful and grand and, O, how it reminds me of home, Dear home, now so far away in the distance. At about 9 we landed at a pretty little town, Herkimer. We went to a hotel and found the Land Lord so crusty that we were obliged to take our leave. Next door we found a more agreeable one and there took up our quarters for the night.

July 27th

It is Sunday. The day is pleasant, though very warm. We have had a splendid night's rest and feel quite refreshed. The streets are nicely shaded with trees. The gardens here look beautiful but, Hark, the church bell is tolling out its solemn to warn us that this is the Lord's day and we must spent it aright. We stepped into the first one we came to and found it to be a Methodist chapel. The Organ was pealing its grandest notes; it

* This diary is in the possession of Edith and Munro MacDougall of Dartmouth, Nova Scotia, and has been transcribed from the original by Austin MacDougall of Bedford, Nova Scotia, who kindly brought this diary to our attention. We also want to thank Peter MacDougall in Halifax who patiently answered all our questions concerning Mary's life and community.

was lovely and when the Choir united their voices the music was perfect. We walked home, had a drink of nice cool water, took a lunch and a nap and then had a walk away out of the town to the river. There is a nice large canal running alongside the river. There are a great number of boats. We climed up a steep bank to get some cherries. There we had a nice view of the village. Went back to the hotel, had a lunch and then went to Methodist meeting in the evening and retired for the night.

July 28th
Monday fine. We left Herkimer at ten, stoped at Rochester and changed cars and changed again at Detroit. We have lovely scenes along the road. We passed the falls at night.

July 29th
The day is fine. We left Detroit and came to Chicago in the evening. The place looks quite old and spoiled; I suppose because of the fire.* Changed cars for Burlington at 11 P.M. We passed lake Michigan before we came to Chicago. It is a very handsome lake. We are passing large meadows and prairies with flocks of horses and cattle roaming wild.

July 30th
It is a lovely day, as cool as need be. It is six o'clock; we have just got up for we made a bed on the seats and had a splendid sleep. We had crackers, ham and bread for lunch this morning. 8 A.M. we are passing large tracts of prairie land, nice fields of wheat oats and corn. Corn seems to be the chief product here; we just passed a large stone quarry and are now stoping at Sagetown station. O, here is the Mississippi and over on the other side is a pretty little town built on a hill. I don't know the name. What a noble river, wide and deep. The banks are lined with green brush and alders and what a large bridge, 9 piers, and all made of iron. Right across is Burlington, quite a large town. We kept on, are going at a great rate and still passing the great rolling prairies, dotted with pretty little country cottages, fields of wheat and corn, cattle and horses. We have to whistle them off the track sometimes. Ten o'clock; here we are at Council Bluffs.

*   A reference to the 'great' Chicago fire of 1871.

We intend to stop on this side of the river. Free bus to Bryant House. We steped into the bus and rode to the hotel where we found a nice room and bed and breakfast for 2.00 dollars. But we unfortunately met with a little mishap. Mc found that his pocket book was gone from his pocket with tickets and all. We did not know how to account for its disappearance and concluded that it must have been taken; Mc went back to search, hired a team, went to the station but it was not there. When he returned he found the Bus driver had found it in the Bus. I waited his return with many anxious thoughts; he came at last, was gone two hours. We were all right then.

July 31st

This is the last day of July; how the time is going. It is very cool and pleasant this morning. We rose at six, took breakfast 7 and left the hotel for the depot. A policeman with gray whiskers and a long cane came and packed us all into the Emigrant train. We took good care to secure two seats for ourselves. The train started at two P.M. and from that time till five we were shifted to and fro, back and forward a few inches at a time. 5 O'clock we were actually started in earnest … and did not see anything very remarkable. We were nicely fixed up for sleep that night when we were disturbed by a band of Indians in the shape of a lot of little barbarians, rushing into the car and shouting at the top of their voices: Coffee, hot Coffee, Eggs S.S. as soon as they got out again they set up a desperate war cry, used some filthy strong language and had a general fight. Some of the folks were very much amused.

August 1st

The day is fine, cool in the morning. We are still passing prairie land; the scenery along is very interesting. We can see the pretty hills in the distance away beyond the prairies on either side. Once in a while we see a large herd of cattle, a caravan crossing the plains, gentlemen on horseback. Indians with red shawls and bundles on their backs, squaws carrying the little things on their backs; they look so comical. Noon; it is very warm we are going on slowly but surely and will soon be to the North Platte river. We have not seen much but a big black wolf today and that turned out to be a dog. Towards night the sky began to grow dark and lowering. The big black clouds looked threatening and there was every appearance of a storm. Soon our attention was attracted to the western sky. It was beautifully lighted up by sheet lightning. It was very faint and distant at first but it gradually grew brighter and more brilliant until the whole heavens were, or seemed to be, one vast sheet of fire and flame with now and again a bright quick flash, almost dazzling, in its piercing brightness. It was brighter than day. We could see away to the river and hills in the distance. We could even see the cattle on the plains, so bright and constant was the lightning. Soon the thunder began to rumble and roar. The scene was perfect, nothing could exceed the splendour and magnificence of the scene. We gazed out upon the night with the deepest awe and admiration and our thoughts were irresistably drawn to him who spreads the heavens abroad, whose voice is heard in deep rolling thunder and his mighty power displayed in lightning's flash which mocks the gazer's eye, and contains such mighty power to destroy. Only think, one flash might strike us dead if our Father willed it. O, how much we need his tender care and how best, how comforting, the assurance that he will love us and care for us ever if we will humbly trust him. The storm continued a long time, and the rain was heavy; it came through the roof and nearly drowned us in the night; however, we managed to survive.

August 2nd
It is fine cool and pleasant this morning the thunder storm left the air pure and settled the dust nicely. The train stopped this morning at day break. We found out the cause: a bridge was washed away by the night's storm and we must stay here all day. This news was received with a good deal of murmuring at the delay. We took a walk out after breakfast and examined some deserted mud huts. They were comical constructions, you may believe. We have a lot of soldiers in an Express train ahead; they are disolute desperate looking characters. We took a walk away over the plains to some cliffs, and quite a view of the surrounding country, found some moss eggets, gathered some wild flowers, and sat down to rest on a great big boulder. We soon

got tired and steered for the train. The ground here is covered in some places with sunflowers and sagebrush. We took some dinner, and it being very warm and sultry, we went off by ourselves and had a nice long nap. We awoke not until four o'clock. The rest of the day we spent pleasantly in viewing the scenery. It was nice and cool in the evening. We went and found a room where we had it all to ourselves. Well, we were nicely esconsed in bed when we were suddenly aroused by a tremendous thump on the side of the car. They are going to run this car off so we must move into the other. Hurrah, here we go off again at last at ten P.M.

August 3rd
Sunday morning. The day is fine but how strange that this is Sunday morning when all is bustle and business and we travelling on in the train. How strange it seems to those who are accustomed to seeing Sunday strictly observed. Well, we are away out on the plains and are very much interested in the scenery. We pass some pretty little places; it looks so nice to see human dwellings away out on the plains so far from home. At noon we arrived at C[h]eyenne. It is quite a city to be in such a rude, desolate place. We have just passed the Summit house and this they say is the highest point of the mountains where the track runs. We are going at pretty good speed and are on the look out for some sights. O, look at the pretty little prairie dogs. They are such cunning looking little things. It is quite amusing to see them stand up and look at you. They live in villages. The next phenomena we witnessed was an antelope. They are the prettiest little things imaginable. They look just like Antelopes, are mostly red and a white patch on the back. We saw a good many flocks but did not have the pleasure of chasing the Antelope over the plain. Well, we rode on a long time with nothing to relieve the monotony of the barren plains but some herds of cattle drivers on horseback, a snow shed once in a while and any amount of snow fences with here and there a few little mud huts and parks, a solitary traveler or caravan crossing the plains. Well what next? Hurrah a wolf, a wolf! We looked and behold a large wolf was actually roaming over the plains quite near. A very

quiet evening. Sang some of our good old tunes and then retired for the night.

August 4th
When we awoke this morning we found the folks were afraid of freezing and had made up two great fires in the cars to the great danger of roasting me and mine. We threw up the windows and at last succeeded in getting cooled off. We had considerable fun over the affair. Well, by this time we arrived at a little mountain town where we got some coffee and made quite a comfortable meal. It is a very bleak looking place and the wind is blowing a hurricane almost. We can see the dustsand drifting like snow. We are coming along through the Rocky Mt Desert and will soon be where we can see something worth looking at.

2:00 P.M. we are now passing along between Oh such high rocks on either side. The scenery is most enchanting, it surpasses my wildest expectations. I did not imagine anything half so grand. Why we can scarcely see the tops of the cliffs; they rise almost perpendicular away above our heads and we can only look up in wonderment, awe and admiration. There are besides the huge mountain rocks some detached peeks, castle shape. They look like vast towers or chimneys built of stone. Oh, they are so magnificent, so sublime, I will never tire of gazing. There is a pretty little river running along between the cliffs. It looks so peaceful as it gently winds its way among the wild mountains. We are going along quite a wide little vale between the craigs. The scenery is so interesting that the time is passing very swiftly and pleasantly. It will soon be evening now, and we are approaching Ogden. Here we are between huge cliffs on either side and right to our left is a long perpendicular passage or Slide and is quite a curiosity ....

August 5th
The day is fine; it is Tuesday. We breakfasted on eggs, jelly bread and onions. We are getting along very slowly. The train stops several hours every five minues (comparatively speaking). We are passing through great sandy plains covered with sage brush. There are great high hills on either side. One comfort we enjoy

[is that] it is very cool and not dusty. The scenery here is not very sublime, you may believe, nothing to be seen [but] sour Alkilie sand and here and there a few squaws. It is almost night and we have not noticed any thing of importance as yet; we had a glimse of a Lake. We have been going down grade all day, passed some snowsheds. One of our lady passengers will leave at this station, Humboldt Wells. She is a Missourian and expects to meet her husband here. It is 9 O'clock; she is alone, so the conductor very kindly offered to pilot her to the Post Office ....

August 6th
It is bright and cool this morning. We are still passing through a desert sandy region. We stop at a good many stations. We came to Elko this morning and came through the Palisades about 9 O'clock. We were quite amused with some squaws with babies who came to the train to beg; they are poor miserable looking creatures and so comical. We had a walk out at Elko; nothing there; they gave us ice water this time Noon; we have seen nothing but sand all day and expect to see nothing till tomorrow. 3 P.M. we are stopping at a way station called Battle Mountain situated on the plains; it has been very hot today. And sometimes the dust comes in clouds into the car. At dusk we came to Humboldt Station. There is an ellegant manshion there for station and hotel. At ten we went to bed.

August 7th
We awoke quite early this morning. It is very cool and pleasant and the sun is shining brightly enough. We have had a nice night's sleep and are stopping in front of a nice large station house with shade trees and fountains in front. It was pleasant to see something green after so much sand and bare hills. We came to Browns about noon. It is very cool yet.

2 P.M. It is getting quite hot now. We are going to have a nap. We came to Wardsworth at about 5. It is quite a place; a large house is the chief ornament. We came to a pretty little river farm at a place called Clarke. There are some nice looking trees here. It is getting cool again. We are living in the blissful anticipation of getting to Colfax tomorrow morning and this we hope will

be our last night on the train for a time at least, for we are getting pretty well tired of seeing and traveling. I am beginning to get a little anxious to see California. That renowned land of gold that sunny "clime" that "flows with milk and honey," but we must have patience and wait. We came to Reno at dark. The moon was shining so brightly that the town looked lovely by its light. At ten we retired.

August 8th
It is a beautiful day. When we awoke at daylight we were passing through the snow sheds. When we get out we will see something a little different from what we have been seeing all along. We are in the State of California now and expect to arrive at Colfax at 9. We are having nice scenery now. The Nevada mountains are quite picturesque; stunted pine and spruce are the chief vegetable product. Here we at Colfax at 9 O'clock A.M. It looks to be rather an insignificant place, though I see there is considerable business carried on here. We went to a hotel to change our dusty clothes and were a little too long and so lost the stage. We then got our dinners and took an express waggon 5.00d[ollars] and started for Grass Valley where we arrived at about 4 P.M. Our friends Mr Peter and Lady left us and we proceeded at once to my *sister's*. We found the house, were dissapointed in the appearance but I thought I would just peep in the windows and see if there was anything there that I knew and the first thing I saw was Sarah's spool stand. Sarah came to the door. She seemed some surprised to see us; she is very thin; and the next thing we saw was a little Johnnie, the prettiest little fellow I ever saw and six weeks old. That evening we went over to *Aunt Katie's*. She reminds me of Aunt Rachel very much. She has quite a large house, very airy and cool. Mc and I stoped there that night.

August 9th
Saturday, fine day. We went back to Sarah's in a buggy and stayed all day. Mc went into town in the evening with *Loney*.

August 10th
Sunday very fine. We all went to meeting in the morning. Mc

and Loney walked and Sarah and I rode, we had a nice meeting and saw *Uncle Levi* and family. Stopped at Aunt Kate's to dinner, saw *Uncle Nathan* and went home in the evening.

August 11th
Monday I washed and helped Sarah cook and took care of Johnnie who was some sick. Mc looked around and helped me.

August 12th
Tuesday I ironed and mended our clothes, kept the baby good and chored around. Mc was cutting wood for Loney. I unpacked and took out my *sewing machine* and showed Sarah my goods. I sewed some. Mc was cutting wood part of the day.

[They spend two weeks visiting relatives in the area.]

August 26th
Monday fine. At 4 we rose and prepared for a start again. Miss Eva came to drive us out to Colfax as we were going to Stockton. We bade them good bye and drove away. The train left at ten and we found that we were just ten minutes too late so we waited there till 2 P.M. and took a passage on the Caboose to Rocklin where we stoped at a hotel until 4 in the morning.

August 27th
Tuesday. At 4 we started again and reached *Sacramento* at 6, too late for the Fruit Express. We waited until 2 P.M., had a walk round the city and visited the capitol. The view was very lovely. At 2 we took the Express for Stockton where we arrived at 4 P.M. The scenery was very nice. Mr. Sloan lives 3 miles out from the town so who should we meet but Mr. Sloan himself as soon as we got onto the platform with his Buggy. So I rode with him and Mc came along with the team. O what a cosy little place was my first impression of the grounds. The house I expected would be white, but is nice and large. I was very much pleased with the appearance of Mrs Sloan. She is very pleasant and friendly. Mr Sloan did not seem to want to make an acquaintance with me at first. I think I shall like him very well in time. Mc took me around the garden. He seems very pleased to get back to the old place.

I am glad that he is pleased and hope he will be contented. I mean to do all in my power to make him so.

August 28th
The day is fine. It is Wednesday and we intend to take the rest of the week to look about us. Mc has gone away somewhere with Mr Sloan and I am sitting all alone in my room. There is a nice outlook from my window. We can see broad wheat fields as far as the eye can reach, scattered all over with tall oaks. They look very beautiful. The garden is very shady and nice. The greatest ornament I see is the number of windmills. You will seem them flying in every direction. I don't think I shall be lonsum here at least I hope not but I cannot help thinking of home away so far in dear old Nova Scotia.

Farewell my childhood's home and friends
I bid you all adieu
Twas hard to leave My native land
But harder for to part with you.

This land seems very strange to me,
So different from my own
And I feel so like a stranger here
So faraway from home

Perhaps I'll see them once again
When years have rolled along
But O that hope's so very dim
I fear the day will never come.

But I must trust my father's God
And banish all my fears.
Tis useless now to waste my time
In vain regrets and tears.

I am not sorry that I came,
For him I'd go this world around
For husband is the dearest soul
That ere on earth was found.

The folks are very good and kind
And the sun is shining bright today
But O I feel so lonely now
Whenever he's away

It must be that I love him so
I feel so different then.

When he's away my sunshine's gone
Until he comes again.

O husband you will never know
How dear you are to me
For in your Mary's loving heart
Forever will your image be

And Dearest Peter listen now
My faults they are not few
But if you only will forgive
I try my best to do

You know I am a reckless one
So stuborn willed and wild
But chide me gently dearest one
You know I'm but a child

August 29

Thursday. Mc and I put up 11 cans of peaches, churned and all the rest. Mc stayed in the house and helped me part of the time. I had a busy day, was pretty tired but I intend to get used to it.

August 30

I washed today, finished at 11. After dinner was cleared away was so tired and sleepy and as my head ached Mc told me I might take a nap. I starched and ironed some before tea. We retired at eight.

August 31st

Sunday Mr. Sloan and Lady went to church and did not come home until 3 O'clock P.M. Mc and I kept house. Sandy Gordon* and a friend of his came to see us. They stayed until afternoon. We had a very pleasant day.

September 1st

Well I do believe this is my birthday and I am twenty today, growing old. I will soon begin to say when I was young. I am twenty today; can it be possible that I am out of my teens? Well

---

* Alexander Gordon was also from West Gore.

I suppose it is not much odds now as I am married and happy. I worked today.

September 7th
Sunday has come again, blessed day of rest. What would we do without Sunday? Mc and I went to Methodist meeting in the morning. Mr. Anthony spoke from the 3 chapter of Cor 11 vers. We came home and spent the afternoon very pleasantly and profitably. Sandy Gordon came in the evening and we had a sing. O, it reminds me so much of home when I hear our good old tunes sung again that we used to sing away in the dear old home with brothers and sisters. O, I would like to be at home tonight. It seemed very strange to me to look around upon the people in church and see none of the old familiar faces.

September 8th
I washed today. Mc helped me and I got along nicely, finished at 3 P.M. We then took a nap and just shelled out in time to do the chores.

September 9th
Ironed some in the forenoon. Mr & Mrs Sloan went to town today. Mc went to town and left me to keep house all alone. It was rather lonesome. Mc and I had a nap and then peared some peaches.

September 10th
I finished ironing in the forenoon. Mc went to town with a load of wheat, got back at dinnertime and brought a present for me. Mr & Mrs S were away, I was all alone. We peared some pears and apples to dry.

September 11th
I staid home all day and baked some cookies. Mc went to town in the forenoon and over to Colbyville in the afternoon with Mr Sloan. The day was warm but quite cool in the evening. I was very lonesome when My husband was away. They got back at 6 O'clock. I was skimming milk and Mc came down to get a — a walk.

September 12th
I made a pair of sheets in the morning and helped get dinner. Mc churned and dressed the butter for me. After dinner Mc went to town and I peared some pears to dry. Mc and Mr Sloan are still speculating. It has been cooler today than usual. I had a ride on horseback and think it quite a critical place to ride.

September 13th
Mr and Mrs Sloan went to town and Mc went with barley so I was left alone. I called on Mrs Boice and did my scrubbing in the morning. After dinner Mc and I canned some tomatoes. I made pies and cake and had a bath before retiring.

September 14th
Sunday has dawned again. We must stay at home all day. I would like to have gone to meeting but could not. Alex Gordon came in the afternoon and we had a sing. I heard some news from home. Mother married, and Mrs Grant is dead. Sunday always makes me think of home more than any other day. Sunday was always a pleasant day at home, how I would like to be there now.

September 15th
I washed this forenoon. Mc churned for me and dressed the butter like a dear good boy, and went to town in the afternoon. I had a nap, mended some clothes and cut out an apron. Mr Sloan had a headache in the evening.

September 16th
I did up the morning work and intended to go to ironing. Mc was to town and I had a fine chance but just as I got fairly begun Mr Wm Murdoch and his lady came to stop the day with us so work was put aside and we had a nice social time. They left at 5 O'clock. Dear Mc got a tooth filled.

September 17th
I finished my ironing and made some cookies, Gingersnaps and apple pies before dinner. Mc put up some grapes to day. Afternoon we peared some tomatoes and canned them. Mr Sloan

went to Willets. I had a hum drum up stairs to myself after Mc went out. I am just as lonesome as ever when my darling is away from me. I cannot tell what is the reason.

September 19th
Friday Mc stayed at home and helped me all day. We made some jelly, some pickles and canned some pears. We had a nice cosey time to ourselves. Mrs Boise came over to get some figs. Mr and Mrs Sloan went to town.

September 20th
This is Saturday so we will have an other busy day but Mc is going to help me and so I am all right when my pet is with me. We finished putting up fruit, baked some snaps and pies and prepared for Sunday. Mc was so kind as to wash the floor for puss, the darling, just like him. We were expecting some folks this evening.

September 21st
Sunday Mc and I went to the Christian church in the forenoon. I felt very much at home there with the brethern and sisters. The disciples always seem near to me where ever I see them. We came home to lunch and went to take a nap when we were disturbed by a great racket down stairs. Mr Sperry's folks were come and the little scamps of girls lugged my darling off to play with them and I had to stay by myself. I don't like them girls. Sandy Gordon came to tea.

September 22nd
Monday Mc went away to town and left me alone. Mr & Mrs Sloan were away too. I washed before dinner and Mc did not come until 3 O'clock. I was beginning to get uneasy he staid so long. My darling boy was very sick that evening.

September 23rd
Tuesday. We packed up today and Mc took a load of stuff over to our cabin fast by the wildwood among the oaks and coons. I ironed and prepared to leave. I left very lonely and unhappy all day, and I was so glad when Peter came back.

September 24th
Husband packed up the rest of our things and I got ready to go too. I rode with a lot of chickens in the express wagon. Our cottage is a perfect little palace about ten foot square and some of the boards are not rotten and there are nice large holes through the walls, so we can see in. I washed it out, and Mc went to haul a load of lumber. Mc went over to Charlie Sperry's in the afternoon and my tooth ached so badly that I was obliged to go and get it out. I rode with Mc on the wheels. I got two teeth pulled and Mr S took me home.

September 25th
Mc went to town. Sandy Gordon, Murdock and Lady called. I sewed some and found it very lonesome.

September 26th
We went to the fair; Charlie Sperry took us to town in his express. We saw some curious performances and slight of hand tricks in a tent, we took lunch at a hotel and then went to the pavilion. We examined the machinery and everything belowstairs first. The display upstairs I thought was very grand. There were among every variety of other things some very handsome engravings. One I thought perfection; it was a picture of a New England farmhouse and grounds just after a light skiff of snow had fallen.

September 27th
Saturday, Mc went away again and I stayed at home alone. He did not get back until 2 O'clock, and brought a load of things from Sloans. I felt quite pleased with the things. This has been a long, lovely day.

EPILOGUE: MARY MACDOUGALL MACDONALD

Mary and Peter had four children. When Peter died in 1879 Mary returned to West Gore to raise her children at 'home.' She later married Jacob Mason, a hard-rock miner, and had 7 more children. She is remembered as 'Aunt Mary Mason' in West Gore where she died in 1940.

Nova Scotia.—VIEW OF PICTOU, FROM MACKENZIE'S POINT.—From a sketch by W. O. C.

MARGARET POTTINGER CONNELL
1833-1899

In the 1870s, Margaret Connell moved from Pictou to Fall River, Massachusetts, with her husband Thomas and daughter Mabel. Although both Thomas and Mabel found work in the textile mills, their family income was barely sufficient for survival. Margaret's letters home to her sister, Jessie Pottinger, are a poignant reminder of the hardships experienced by many Maritimers who joined the exodus to factory towns in search of work.

An older sister, Mary, also lived in Fall River and the two women were very close. Mary's new baby, Willie, was probably named after their father, William Pottinger, who was a cooper in Pictou. The William of the letters is their younger brother, also a cooper, whose problem with alcohol was a cause for concern. William eventually "saw the light," gave up drinking, married and settled down in East Boston. Another brother, John Wallace Pottinger, was a sailor, and a third brother David, worked for the Intercolonial Railway and eventually became General Manager of the Canadian Government Railways. The aunts mentioned are their father's sisters, one of whom, Charlotte, married John Sparrow Thompson. Their son became Sir John Sparrow David Thompson, a premier of Nova Scotia and Prime Minister of Canada, 1892-94.

As these letters indicate, the new industrial order expanded opportunities for men. Meanwhile, women struggled to recreate their domestic realm in vastly transformed circumstances. Margaret's role as domestic manager stands out in bold relief as she goes about her household chores, nurtures her immediate family, and worries about the fate of her many relatives. Even the economic cycles had a clear meaning for Margaret who recognized that the 'bread winning' roles of her husband and daughter depended on the health of the capitalist system.

In industrial communities such as Fall River, women seem even more firmly bound to the household than they were in earlier times. "Mary and I have been indulging a hope that we could go to see you all this summer," she writes to her sister in Pictou. "I dont know how it will succeed, it will be harder for me to get away than her; I cant leave Mabel without some-one to keep house for them and that someone i dont know where to get." With her unmarried daughter working outside the home and her other female relatives scattered along the Atlantic seaboard, Margaret was virtually imprisoned in her domestic sphere. Middle class women, of course, could, and increasingly did, hire domestic servants to do household chores but for working class wives like Margaret Connell, the housework was literally "never done."*

---

*   Susan Strasser, *Never Done: A History of American Housework* (New York, 1982); Ruth Schwartz Cowan, *More Work For Mother* (New York, 1983).

MARGARET POTTINGER
CONNELL LETTERS
1876 - 1881*

18 September 1876
Dear Sister
I suppose you have been expecting to hear from us some time ago but we had a much longer passage than we expected we was 10 days from the time that we left Pictou until we anchored in Boston harbour. We anchored in Arichat and went on shore the Captain asked us to go to his house and we went and stayed all one night he has a very nice house and his wife was very kind to me. But she has very little *English* so on that account our conversation was rather limited but she managed to show her kindness in various ways. They have four children two boys and two girls the oldest girl is 15 and the youngest is twelve months. Two fine little boys one six and one four. It was very amusing to us to hear those two little fellows chatter away to each other in French. Well we anchored in Boston Bay tuesday the 13th and on thursday the 15th we arrived in Fall River. We had two pretty severe gales one on the 4th and one on the 11th and the day after we got to Boston it blew a perfect gale. O how thankful we all felt to think that we was not out on the ocean. We was both pretty sea sick. Mary was as bad and I dont know but worse than I was. She had one of them bad spells that she used to have before she went away. I gave her some mustard and water to drink and it made her vomit quite freely and she soon got better. The folks in Fall River thinks that she looks miserable. All our acquaintances were very glad to see us When Mrs Dunfee saw Mary she said O you dear creature you aint agoing out of this house again you must come back and live with me. So she is going to live with her again and I think she get along nicely.

Jane Hart is tickled to death because she came back. She will write to you herself and tell you all the particulars. I expect to go to work in my old place next week. All my friends were glad to see me back again and just as soon as they heard I had arrived

---

*   Margaret Connell's letters are housed in the Hector Centre Trust, Pictou, Nova Scotia.

they came to see me. The first two days after I got back they kept comming in all day, and they never thought of such a thing as me calling to see them first. Mary is going over to New Bedford next week to see her acquaintance there before she goes to work. Tell Mother that I found that pair of drawers that I had thought I had lost. I did not take them with me when I went home Mrs. Nicols found them on the cloths horse after I went away. She said that she knew that I had forgotten them so she put them away in her drawer. You dont know how glad she was to see me she is a good kind woman and she is a true Friend to me.

The weather is quite pleasant now but the summer here has been very cool. Mrs Blake seems to be quite smart since she got home. She was not much sea sick comming back.

Mr Johnson is in a great *panic* for his wife to come home. I am afraid he will have a *cat nip* fit if she does not come soon. You will please excuse this poor writing for my hand troubels dreadfully. I have not got quite over being so long on the water. I shall now have to bring this communication to a close for it is time that it was in the office.

Mary and I joyned in love to you all Aunt and David and give our love to Mrs Griffiths. We did not see Jessie Tollison in Boston. Let us know if you heard from William and let me know if Cousin James or any of them came down and if they sent a letter to me. Send it inside of yours. No more at present.

Write soon to your affectionate Sister

20 March 1877
Dear Sister
I received your welcome letter wensday the 14th and was very glad to hear from you and also to hear that you were all in good health. I was just thinking before it came that I should write to you again. We are all quite well and hope this will find you all the same. Thomases eye is about the same it is not any better. The bump gathers and then he takes a needel and opens it and lets the matter out it does not pain him much only by spells. And then once in a while he will have a regular abcess which is very painful but it is almost a year since he had one of them. Mrs Nichols youngest Daughter Eva, died of consumption yesterday

and is to be buried tomorrow there is only one left she is married and lives in New Bedford.

I think the winter here has been very much the same a .t has been with you the first was very severe then the month of Feb was just like spring but what we have had of March has been very cold and stormey. The 17 and 18 we had a regular snowstorm and very cold the seasons come and go and the years roll round and when we look back it seems but a little while since we was all children together and now we are growing old and are scattered over the world. I am glad you heard from John. Poor fellow I am so sorry for him what a hard life he must lead. And he might be so comfortabel and happy and make those around the same if [he] would only do *right*. The times here have not improved much yet altho every one thought that as soon as the Presedential question was setteld * business would brighten right up but there has not been much change yet. I was at Marys Friday afternoon I took your letter and she read it and was so pleased to hear from you as I was and indeed we both wished that you and Mother was there to have a cup of good tea with us. Many a time we wished that. She has not commenced her mat yet she has not got quite enough rags. William is with her yet he has been doeing better for a few weeks. He always pays her his board if he gets behind when he is drinking he always makes it up afterwards. I told him one time last fall when he was spending his money so foolish that it would be better for him to send Mother some of it and he promised me he would but I know he never did. I am going to have a talk with him again about it. But he does not like very well to be talked to or advised he knows he does not do right and he knows what right is. So he dont want to hear any thing about it. But Oh dear he would be so angry if he knew I told you a word about him I would not have him know for anything. I am sorry to hear of the death of Mr Bayne and also of Dr Johnson they will be very much missed

---

* In the presidential election of 1876, votes for the Republican, Rutherford B. Hayes, and the Democrat, Samuel J. Tilden, were so evenly divided that Congress created an Electoral Commission to decide the matter. On 2 March 1877, Rutherford B. Hayes was declared President.

your letter was very interesting to me. I like to hear about the peopel I used to know in the days of my youth.

I have been washing to day my hands are rather stiff and sore so I will have to stop pretty soon. I did not get my cloths dry however for the weather today has been very pecular cloudy until about half past ten then a smart shower of rain then sunshine for about one hour then high wind and more rain. Sunshine again until about 8 oclock then rain thunder and lightening about three flashes and two peals of thunder. Steady rain up to this minet or rather hour for it is just ten oclock. So I had to take them off the lines dripping wet and dump them into the tub and cover them with water to await fair weather so I will now bid you good night. Thomas is reading at the other side of the tabel he joins me in sending love to you all. Mabel has been in bed an hour and a half she goes to work in the morning at half past six so I make her go to bed early at night.

Please write soon while I remain your affectionate sister

1 July 1877
Dear Sister
I thought I would write you short letter telling you how we get along. I am sorry I waited so long but it is so hard to get started at writing. I suppose you are quite busy now and would like to hear from us all. We are all pretty well or about as well as usual, and get along about the same. Business seems to be a littel better than it was when I last wrote to you. Provisions are very dear meat and flour are up to the old *war prices** you know they have been shipping a great deal of those two articels to *Europe* and then they put up the prices here. We have had an abundant crop of strawberries here this year and I never knew them to be so cheap. You know they dont grow wild here they are all cultivated and are very large but not so sweet as your wild ones. Some of the cultivators went into the business so extensively this year that the markets was over stocked and they did not bring such a high price. Consequently they did not gain as much as

---

*   The boom that followed the close of the Civil War ended with the crash of 1873. This depression reached its lowest point in 1877 and was followed by a slow economic revival.

they expected. The market is full of everything you can think of. New potatoes, green peas, string beans, cabbage, beets, turnips most all kinds of vegetabels and fruit, but takes *money* to buy them. What a sad thing that fire in Saint Johns* is and still it would be worse if it was in the winter there will be time to get clothed and prepared for winter, altho it will be a long time before they will get over the loss.

How good the peopel of Boston are to them they are sending vessel and steamer loads of every thing needful to them. And all the other places are making up boxes of clothing and bedding for them besides money — there was a large box sent from Fall River last week and we are making up another as fast as possabel and see by the papers that Chicago & New York have sent money. I wonder if Mrs Agnes Stewart was burnt out. If she was I suppose she will go to Pictou. I was sorry I did not see Miss H — when she was in Providence. If I had knowen where Mrs Fowler lives and just when she was there I would have gone to see her for your sake but I thought it was useless to go on uncertainly. She need not be afraid of warm weather we have not had any to speak of yet, all june has been very cool with nice rains every thing looks green and beautiful. She must have enjoyd her visit Providence is a pretty city. William is still in FR he is not with Mary but has a good boarding place and is doeing pretty well. He bought a nice suit of cloths and looks real well. He boards with Mr Colemans wifes mother a very nice lady and she thinks a great deal of William and she will as long as he tries to do right — but with all his faults Mr Colman says he never had a man like him for honesty and excellent work he overlooks other things on that account. I am very sorry that he has grown so hard hearted toward home and Friends but we will hope for the best he may soften I would like to see you all and have a long talk. I have almost filled up this paper you must excuse all mistakes my hand is a littel shakey let me know if you have heard from John. Mary will soon write try and write as soon as you can.

---

* The Great Fire of 1877 destroyed over half of the city of Saint John, New Brunswick.

With love and good wishes to all I remain you affectionate Sister

11 November 1877
Dear Sister
I thought I would write and let you know that we are all well. Mary has a young son born the 7th of this month. She is doeing very well the baby seems healthy and likely to live. He is a bright little fellow and weighs about 8 pounds. William was to see them last night and seemd quite pleased with the baby. He is still here and I think will stay this winter he is doeing better for a few week past. We heard that John has got home. Has he got steadyd down any. I wish you would write soon and let us know how you get along and how you all are. Mary would have written to you but she not been well all summer. She has had them billious attacks very often and very severe. She thought if you and Mother knew how things was you would be worried all the time. I was worried enough about her all summer you know she is not very young and I was afraid it would go hard with her. So we ought to be thankful that she has got nicely over it and perhaps her health will be better now. Jane Murray has gone home to spend the winter among her Friends. She will call to see you when she goes to town. I sent a small parcel by her. You must not be offended it was hardly worth sending. But I can tell you I have not much about my hands. You know how it was that time we was home last. Well its about the same all through. Mabel has been working but the works has shut down and dont know when it will start up again, wages of all kind is very small but what she earns is quite a help she is a big girl now almost sixteen and it takes a good deal to keep her in cloths and shoes. I suppose you heard that Mrs Blakes youngest son was murdered out in California last June it was a tirrabel blow to his poor mother he was shot dead by a ruffian while trying to defend a friend of his own Jane M. will tell you the particulars. Mrs Blake has moved away from Fall River with her daughter Susan and her husband I suppose they will move back when Susans husband can get work here. Her daughter Margarets husband has built a house and they are quite comfortable. You remember Christyann Shaw her husband has built a very nice

house and they are near neighbours to Mary and she is a very kind one too but her health is very poor. We feel sorry for her she is a great sufferer she has not got any children — Mary lives all of a mile from where we live. I try to go to see her everyday now but by and by when the big snow drifts comes I cant go so often it is quite lonesome there in winter but beautiful in summer. I will have to stop writing now. Thomas Mabel and I are going up to see the baby this afternoon if it does not rain too hard …. I hope the dear little fellow will be spaired to us.
I remain your Affectionate sister

25 March 1878
Dear Sister
I suppose you are anxious to hear how we are getting along so without waiting for a reply to my last letter which I hope you received, I will write you another but I cant promise it will be a very long one; we are all quite well at present. Mary has got quite well again and the baby is growing finely as you will see by his picture. O how we all love the little fellow; you may think he looks *odd* in high neck and long sleevs, but that is the way they dress babies here now, and a good sensible way it is. His dress is made with a tucked yoke pointed in the front and back; in the front is a littel gold pin that I gave him for a Christmas present we tied a plaid sash around his waist to relieve the whiteness of his dress if you had seen him just before his picture was taken you would wonder how he could possably keep still long enough to have any kind of a one taken he was so delighted with seeing the horses and teams in the street passing to and frow. How I do wish you all could see the dear littel fellow Mary and me often wish you could, but the picture looks just like him. Mary is going to try to write to Aunts and send them one. William has gone to Boston to work, I dont know how long he will stay there I am sorry he has left Fall River. I am afraid he will not do so well there, but perhaps he will come back here again; Thomases eye is about the same as when I last wrote to you. Every kind business is very dull; wages has been reduced at a fearful rate; but rents and provisions are still high; we cant get butter fit to eat less than 30 to 35 cents pr pound and every thing else in proportion but we must not grumbel as long as we have

our health. I hope times will brighten up before long. I hope you will write soon and tell me what you think about the dear littel *face* and tell me how you all are; Mary sends her love to you all; from your affectionate sister

March 1879
Dear Sister
I have been expecting a letter from you for a long time. I have not heard a word from you since Kate Fraser was here last November. I hope you nor any of the rest are not sick. I thought I would not wait any longer but write to you and hope you will try to write as soon as you can. Well the winter has about passd away with all its joys and sorrows sickness and death it has been a very hard winter and a very unhealthy one. Fall River has had a fear full shakeing only think of it three of the leading men in *Prison* the last one sent there is Charles P. Stickerly once a member of Congress with an *Honorable* attached to his name we are all wondering who the next will be for every one thinks there is more yet but I hope not, I hope we have seen the worst of its for times have been dreadful hard this winter. Last fall I thought I would try and save a littel money and maybe make out to go to see you this summer but I could not do it. For we had all we could do to get along and not go in debt. Thomas had very littel work and Mabel very littel. But we had our health and could eat our hearty meals, for which we ought to be very thankful. I dont know what may turn up, but as far as I can see now I will have to give it up I wanted very much to go but it is so hard to get money. Marys husband had a letter from brother William about a month ago, he is still working in East Boston and has been doeing very well for sometime and said when the hurry was over he would come and see us I wish he would come, it was a year the 19th of this month since he went away from here. Mary and her family are well now but littel Willie E. has been very sick so sick that the Dr. had very littel hopes of him. In the first place he had seven fits the first four in succession out of one into another the next three, five hours between, the one before the last almost finished him we thought he never would come out of it. He could not have lived through another as hard as that but the last one was lighter; the dear littel fellow I shall never

forget how he looked. Well that was the beginning of his sickness then Dysentry and inflamation of the bowels set in, and the
Doctor came every day for three weeks and the first two he did
not have much hopes of him; but he got better and is nearly as
fat and strong as ever, it was about the first of January that he
was taken he has a running sore in his ear; it is some better now
the Dr gave something to syringe it out with and it has helped
him. Poor Mary had a hard time of it I helped her all I could but
I could not be with her all the time, and to take care of him was
all one could do what passd from him was blood and matter -
His sickness put him back in walking he does not quite go alone
yet and only has six teeth. I am afraid he will have a hard time
getting them in the summer. I am sending a littel peice of his hair
his littel duck tail I cut it off the other day when I was up there.
Mary sends her love to you all and hopes you will excuse her
for not writing as her will is good but she cant find time; I will
close now hopeing to hear from you soon let me know what you
are all doeing and how you got along this winter.
Your Affectionate Sister

December 1879
Dear Sister Jessie
I received your welcome letter yesterday and I thought I would
sit right down and answer it this afternoon hopeing you may
receive it about Christmas. I want you and Father and Mother
to have a good Christmas *Dinner*. tell Mother I had a letter from
Brother William on the 24th of November, he was well and
doeing well. He wrote me a very nice letter told me he was still
trying to walk in the *strait* and *narrow* way and daily looking to
his heavenly Father for strength for guidance said he had not
been in side of a place where *Liquor* is sold for over a year and
does not associate with those who drink, he told me not to be
anxious about him and I think he would wish you not to be also.
I think he will come to Fall River and spend Christmas with us,
I wrote to him to come, if he does we will all be together at 31
Annawan St. He got your letter he told me so at the time. He
said in his last letter to me that a Daughter of Joseph Davises call
to see him and he had a long talk about home. Littel Willie E is
quite well, is fat and *rosey* and full of fun and play as any littel

one can be. You say you fancy you can see him running around. I wish you could in reality many a time poor Mary wishes it too; O if they only could see him, she will say to me, how glad I would be. He said *Grandma*, meaning Mother for he knows nothing about his other one she is away *out west*, has been for over a year. Mary tells him about Mother and he will point to her picture and say Grandma, he talks very plain and understands every word we say, we are going to have littel presents for him at Christmas; Thomas is very fond of him and they have great fun when he is down here. He calls Thomas: *Antie Tom* instead of uncel Tom but he will soon learn to say *uncel*. Poor brother John. I am sorry that he is on the water this cold winter weather I often think of him, he has been away a long time, it is such a hard life to follow the sea. I am glad to hear that Aunts are so comfortable; I heard about them from Jane Murray; also about *David* I hope he may long enjoy his prosperity he earnd it honorably and is what the Americans call a *self made man*; he has workd faithfuly and steadly step by step without aid from any one except what he justly merited; Jane told me how nice you done her bonnet & how hard it is for you to get blocks, I thought it would be more convenient by this time; but if I knew of any possabel way to send you some I would gladly do it. Thomas had a letter from his brother James he wrote soon after leaveing the *hospital* he was hardly abel to write when he did; poor man he has had a terrabel affliction and feels dreadfuly about looseing his son. Thomas will write to him in a short time. It made me feel sad to hear of Mrs Browns death but I hope she has made a happy change; I am so glad that you went to see her. I have not seen any of her Friends for some time her father is quite old but was smart when I last saw him about a year and a half years ago he came to Fall River and took dinner with us and walkd all the way up to Marys to see her. I am quite sure he told me he was nearly 85 years then. Now dear sister I hope this will reach you safely it is not much I would gladly send you more if I could say nothing about it, I have not seen Mary since your letter came she was here the day before I got it. But I will give the boy all the kisses and them all the love when I do see them. Write me a few lines soon after receiving this so I will know you got it all

safe and with love to Father Mother and yourself
I remain yourAffectionate Sister

I came near forgetting to tell you about Ts eye, it is pretty well just now, but was very sore in the fall it gathered and broke twice but since then has been better; he had been on the salt water a good deal which is very bad for it, got cold and so bad to suffer the consequences.

23 May 1881
Dear Sister
I know you will think it very strange that I have neglected writing to you for so long, I have thought many times that I would write and then I would wait a while longer and so on until now I think it is nearly four months since I had a letter from you, but I must arouse myself and try to do better for the future. I hope you all are well as when you last wrote to me. We are all quite well and getting along in about the same old way. I have been and am still busy cleaning house and sewing I dont get ahead very fast, my eyes and head troubels me a good deal and I am very nervous. Sometimes I am about good for nothing. But I hope it will wear off after a while. I had a letter from William about a week ago he is still doeing well and is now foreman of the shop. His employers puts all confidence in him and would not like to part with him. I suppose he writes to you sometimes. He writes me such nice letters and always speaking of the change in his life and the one he owes it all to. Mary and I have been indulging a hope that we could go to see you all this summer. I dont know how it will succeed, it will be harder for me to get away than her; I cant leave Thomas and Mabel without some-one to keep house for them and that someone I dont know where to get. Mabel works in the mill, and even if she did not work she is not capabel of leaveing the care of the house to. I dont know how I can arrange things. O I wish I could go away and have no care on my mind, if I could have confidence in them I have to leave, all would be right but I have not, and feeling so I could not enjoy my self nor feel contented but I dont know how it will be yet I will try very hard to get away. It is about the same as it was last summer when I think things are going on all right and my mind is easy then it is that something will happen to

upset it all. It is a hard thing to loose confidence in a person. I think Mary will go anyway and of course take the Boy, as Brother William calls him. He grows very fast and talks very plain. Last Thursday night he staid and slept with Auntie and was a real good boy and his mother came and took him home Friday. If we do make out to come home we will go to see Aunts too it will seem very strange not to have their house to go to in Pictou, when you write let me know if John has got home from voyage to *Ireland* and how he gets along and let me know if you are taking straw work to do this summer. I hope the next time I write that I will feel more encouraged than I do now and can write a more cheerful letter.

So good night from yourAffectinate Sister M C

EPILOGUE: MARGARET POTTINGER CONNELL

These brief letters are the only record we have of Margaret's life. She died in Fall River in 1899.

NEW WOMEN

REBECCA CHASE KINSMAN ELLS
1856-1928

Rebecca Ells' diaries, written in lined scribblers, cover much of the period from 1901 to 1906. They provide a detailed account of one woman's daily routine on a commercial farm in the village of Port Williams in Kings County, Nova Scotia.* Although the men had taken over the orchard and garden to grow commercial crops, women still managed the egg and butter production. Rebecca's labour was an essential part of the farm economy and her work reflected the seasonal rhythms of rural life.

For all practical purposes, Rebecca was a 'single mother.' In 1899 her husband, Cyrus Ells — the "Cyde" of this diary — went to the Yukon in search of gold. He left behind his 43-year-old wife Rebecca and her 18-year-old son Manning to manage the farm. For cash income, Rebecca and Manning depended on crop sales, especially apples which, at this time, found a ready market in Britain.** They also benefited from the sale of Rebecca's butter, chickens and eggs. They could afford to hire a man to help Manning in the fields and, sometimes, a woman to help Rebecca in the house. Clarence, Lee, Perry and Roley, who are mentioned

---

* See Port Williams Women's Institute, *The Port Remembers: The History of Port Williams and its Century Homes* (Kentville, 1976) for a good introduction to Rebecca Ells's "Port."

** On the development of the British market for Annapolis Valley apples see Margaret Conrad, "Apple Blossom Time in the Annapolis Valley, 1880-1957," *Acadiensis*, Vol. 9, No. 2 (Spring 1980), pp. 12-39; for a useful discussion of farm women in the Canadian context see Marjorie Griffen Cohen, "The Decline of Women in Canadian Dairying," *Histoire Sociale/Social History*, Vol. 18, No. 34 (November 1984), pp. 307-40.

in the diaries, were hired to help Manning while Mrs. Inglis, Fannie, and Mrs. Steele, at various times, worked for Rebecca.

Close family ties are documented in the visits of Rebecca's father, the poignant memories of her dead mother and Rebecca's relationships with her three sisters, two of whom — Ann and Olive — were dead, though fondly remembered. Mary, her remaining sister, was married to Robert Rand, the "Rob" of the diaries. Lorne was their son. In the absence of her husband, the close network of family and friends sustained Rebecca through her difficulties and her triumphs.

Rebecca's first child, Willie, died as a result of a school yard accident. As with many of our diarists, a strong Baptist faith offered consolation: "I know he would have been a comfort to me had he been spared — but God knew best. I gave him to Him." Manning, the remaining child, was the apple of Rebecca's eye and proved to be a good farm manager. In this portion of the diary Manning is courting Minnie Messenger, who, once married, came to live in the Ells household.

Rebecca's headaches, rheumatism and bilious turns punctuated her accounts of energetic work. "Just hurried all morning," was a familiar refrain for the hard-working Rebecca. Hard manual labour, financial worries and anxiety about the animals and crops were a constant source of stress and sometime wore Rebecca down. "We churned 11 3/4 lbs butter — I do get tired working the butter sometimes," she remarks, "but it brings in quite a lot of money." Modern domestic appliances were still absent from Rebecca's household in 1901, but not for long. She purchased a sewing machine in 1902 and a washing machine in 1904 which offered her "a great saving in time and labour." A telephone, installed in 1904, was considered "a great invention" by Rebecca, who was now able to keep in closer touch with her kin and community.*

Only a selection of Rebecca's diary entries for the year 1901, offering a sense of the seasonal rhythms of a farm woman's life, is published here.

---

* Rebecca Ells Diary, 15 and 17 February 1902; 29 March, 25 May, 31 July 1904.

REBECCA CHASE KINSMAN ELLS DIARY
1901*

Tues. Jan 1st 1901
The first day most passed of the new Century. It was lovely and mild this afternoon with alternate sunshine and snow squalls — Cleared off cold this afternoon, and this Evg is a perfect moonlight night. Father came over in a sleigh to dinner, and Rob came up this afternoon and fixed the ceiling in my bedroom. It looks fine now. Manning has gone to Canard to Mrs. Waltons with the girl of his choice I expect. I hope he wont get more cold for he has been laid up for days with a very bad cold — I went up to Mrs. Burbidges this Evg a little while and took my silk waist up — She is going to fix it for me — Now I must go to bed — Good Night.

Mon. Jan 7th.
I did not write any in this last night as it was late when I got home, and did not feel like it but Manning and I went down to Sabbath School and Meeting, Mr. Morse a returned missionary preached very acceptably. I went up to Rob's to tea as did Mr. Martell, and went to the Endeavor** meeting in the Evg. Our Pastor led and we had a beautiful meeting. It closed all to soon — Manning went over to Wolf[ville] in Evg and called for me... on his way back. To day has been quite mild and snowed some this afternoon and Evg. Manning went down to Port this morning and got both horses sharpened for the ice hauling to-morrow. He and Lee both helped Mr. C.C. Cogswell fill his ice house this afternoon. I went down this Evg. to see little Fred Cogswell — Dear little fellow he is so sick. I do so hope he will be better soon. It makes my heart ache to see the little boys sick. I live it

---

*   A copy of Rebecca Ells Diary can be found in the Acadia Archives, Vaughan Memorial Library, Acadia University. We are indebted to Mary Corkum, Wolfville, for bringing this diary to our attention and for her assistance in sorting out the Ells family genealogy.
** The United Society of Christian Endeavor (after 1927 the International Society of Christian Endeavor) was founded in Maine in 1881 by Congregational Minister Francis Edward Clark to train young people in Christian and social service. Soon after its founding, Christian Endeavor expanded its mandate to include all denominations and age groups.

all over again what I have gone through in my own home. I pray
that his bright young life may be spared. I got a letter from Cyde
today written the 1st and 7 of Dec. He says he is well and seems
in excellent spirits. I hope to hear of his digging out the nuggets
soon. He will get it if it is for the best I feel sure.

Tues. Jan. 8th.
Manning filled the ice house to-day. Put in 15 large loads — I
cooked dinner (baked meat and beans and steamed pudding)
for four extra men and do you believe not one of them stayed to
dinner. It made me a lot of extra bother all for nothing. This afternoon John Cogswell took me up to Kent[ville] on an errand
for his Father. I got a frame to put my Hubby's picture in so it
will not fade all out. The snow that fell last night made fine
sleighing to-day and it looks to-night as though we might have
some more — Fred Cogswell is quite a lot better to-night.

Mon. Jan 14th
And my cold seems worse than ever to-night I thought it was
better all day, but to-night I feel pretty well stewed up so to speak
— I swept and cleaned good all the bedrooms up stairs to-day.
Also the hall and stairs, and they look much better. They
bothered me all last week they were so dirty, but I could not
seem to get to them. The men have been breaking roads to-day
— though they are not drifted very much on this street just
heavy. Manning went down and shovelled snow for his Aunt
May. Found her all right. He has gone to Wolfville to-night to
try the roads that way. I gave him money to get the Book of
poems by Rudyard Kipling — The dear Boy! he is so fond of
reading — I only wish my purse were long enough to gratify his
desires in that respect for he reads only good books.

Thurs. Jan. 17
We have had a regular Jan. thaw to-day. My cold was not well
enough for me to take advantage of such a mild day so I had to
stay in. Manning churned for me this morn 11 1/4 lbs. and this
afternoon I ironed, Mailed a letter to Cyde this afternoon, also
sent payment for Co operative Farmer $3.50 and stopped it.

Wed. Jan 23

This has been a lovely day. Capt came up and got the little bossy — Fannie Burbidge came in and sat most of the afternoon. This Evg. I went down to Mrs. Bordens and spent a very pleasant Evg — Manning called for me a little after ten. To day the news spread over the wire that our beloved Queen is dead, died yesterday Jan. 22 — Everybody mourns. Letters from Cyde to-day.

Fri. Jan 25

Mary staid all night and Manning took them home this morning — It is terribly icy, but has been a nice day not very cold — The hens have had a fine time out doors today — The Boys cut the beef down and she weighed 465 lbs. Manning took the hide down to Wolf. Got $3.18 for it. — 49 lbs. Then this afternoon he went over to Canard to get Father to come over to help him cut it up — He is coming tomorrow — I went up to Mrs. Burbidges a little while this afternoon and had my waists fitted. We got the pay for the cattle to-day and Manning paid Lee what he was owing him and some other bills.

Sat. Jan 26

This has been rather an unpleasant day — Not very cold but high wind with sleet and rain. Father came over this forenoon and helped Manning cut up the beef — We had a barrel heaping full besides a lot of fresh saved out. I rendered the tallow to-day and only wish the mince-meat was fixed up too — Manning has gone to Mrs Lawrence Eaton's tonight to a company — I do not think he will have a very pleasant drive for it is sleeting all the time.

Tues Jan 29th

And it has been a busy day for me. I cleaned mince meat this morning and cooked it, made cake etc. Just hurried all the morning — Father came in to dinner. Then this afternoon I went to Kent. with my butter and eggs, did several errands and home again. It was beautiful sleighing. After tea Lee and I went to the Port and he got a suit of clothes all through from head to foot. Then we went up to Mary's. Found her in bed but she soon got up and we staid near an hour. I got a letter from Rob. this morn

— Must answer it soon. The Charlie calf a bossy this morning
— C.V. Anthony came to-day.

Jan 30th Wed.
And pretty fine this afternoon some flurries of snow this fore-noon. Mrs. Inglis came and washed and cleaned up the kitchen and porch and ironed the most of them. She did a fine days work — The Boys were in the woods all day hauling out wood and poles.

Sat Feb. 2nd
This is the day that our beloved Queen is buried and every where throughout Canada it is observed as a day of mourning. Just 6 yrs tomorrow morning since our dear Mother died. How well I remember it. It was on Sund. too. Oh how we miss her. One by one the dear ones leave us. God grant that we may all meet again — This morning I dressed 12 lbs of butter. This afternoon made carrot pudding cleaned the halls down stairs and a little of every thing in general. It is now 11 o'clock and time I was in bed so good night dear old Diary.

Tues. Feb. 5th
It rained quite hard this morning but cleared up before noon — My company did not come to-day, expect them to morrow. I was very glad it happened so for I have been just poorly enough all day — Hope to be better to-morrow. Manning & Bess went to Canning to-day to see the big horses. We churned 11 3/4 lbs butter — I do get tired working with the butter sometimes but it brings us in quite a lot of money — Now I am going to bed early and see if I wont feel better in the morning.

Mon. Feb. 11
Churned 12 lbs butter today — It has been a cold disagreeable day, and not much stirring — I have been kind of used up to day with neuralgia or rheumatism and have not felt much good — Manning got P.O. Order to night from Will Rand for $29.20 receipts for Gravenstein Apples sent to Eng in the fall. It has been a long time coming but good when it came and very acceptable. There were 22 bbls of apples sent. So that was better than selling them here at 1.00 a bbl as he did the rest.

Mon Feb 18
You see I did not write in this yesterday as it was late when we got home was sleepy and went right to bed — We went down to meeting in the afternoon, it was a lovely day, came home did up the chores and went again in the Evg. Manning to Wolfville, I to Port to Missionary meeting. It was very interesting — Mrs Martell took charge, and I am sure we will never have her like again. We are so sorry she is going away — To day we churned 11 3/4 lbs butter, made mince pies and swept & dusted the sitting room, besides all the usual work. I have just rushed all day. Father came over to dinner and Manning has gone to spend the Evg. at Mr Martells — It is nine o'clock and I feel much like going to bed — as I have got a big days work planned out for to-morrow if all goes well. It is just two years to-day since dear Cyde went from home — Oh dear, I hope it will be so that he can come home for I do miss him so.

Thurs Feb 28
This is Father's birthday. 76 to-day and I expect he is enjoying the Evg at the Church Social at E. H. Eatons. I baked 8 pies this forenoon and ironed this afternoon. Then this Evg. Manning and I went to Wolf to hear Mr Gale — I liked him very much and only wish it were possible for me to go every meeting.

Sun. Mar 3rd
And such a lovely day it has been. We went down to Sabbath School and Meeting this afternoon. Mrs Morse filled the Pulpit very acceptably and told of some of her work in India. Manning and Lee went to Wolf. to the Men's Meeting held by Mr. Gale — while I stay home alone.

Sat. Mar 23rd
And it has been a lovely day — I swept up stairs this morning, this afternoon made doughnuts. Manning has gone to Wolf. and I am here alone again. How well I remember 16 years ago to night — the next morning at 8 o'clock my dear little boy Willie was born — and it will soon be 8 years since I lost him. I know he would of been a comfort to me had he been spared — but God knew best. I gave him to Him. Some day I hope to meet the dear sweet face once more — How many near and dear friends

that were with us then have gone too. Such a company over there — God grant we may all be found on the happy side.

Thurs Mar 28th
Yesterday it rained some and was dull all day — Lee put the ashes up for soap and wet them down — To-day he drew off some lye and got the soap started — It rained hard last night and we got a nice lot of soft water — something we have not had for weeks — Mrs Inglis came & washed — some of them got dry. We churned 12 lbs of butter Mrs O'Keys auction was to-day.

Sat Mar 30th
It snowed all the forenoon, Lee started for Boston to-day — Mr Harmon Newcomb was here to dinner. Churned 11 3/4 lbs to day and Manning has just got back from taking it to the Station. He reports A.C. More sick with small pox, and that every one is dreadfully scared. I hope that it may not prove serious. Our hall stove is going out to-night for the want of more coal — I am sorry I cant keep it going a little longer — We find by reckoning up that I have made 157 3/4 lbs butter this month and 380 this year so far — that is not too bad — The hens have done their part too all winter. Got 16 to-day.

Sun Mar 31st
This has been such a long dreary day. It has snowed and rained all day, and there have been no teams passing for the Churches in Kent were not opened on account of the small pox. I have not been well all day so did not go to Church and Manning went and got vaccinated. Altogether it has been a lonesome day.

Thurs Apr 4th
This has been an unpleasant day Cold east wind with some rain. Manning has been housed to-day with a severe cold — I do hope it will be better tomorrow — These are the times we miss Lee, though Roley does finely. Got a letter from Rob — to-night — but none from my Hubby and I am so anxious to hear from him. Just 21 years ago yesterday since we moved to Belcher St. What changes! Manning and I went to the Port last Evg — I got blue

serge for a skirt & Eton jacket — Now I must doctor up Manning and get to bed.

Fri. Apl 5th
And such a nasty day, rained all day and all night last night. Manning got up this morning and milked the cows, came in and laid on the lounge, did not get up again all day and has just gone to bed now — I think he has the measles — He has slept all day — Has a burning fever, and his face is covered pretty well with measles I should say — However tomorrow will tell better — Rob Martin came down and helped Roley milk to-night, and is coming again in the morning. It is raining out hard now — Churned 12 lbs butter to-day — Good Friday.

Sat Apl 6th
Rained hard all night, and this morning but partly cleared off later — Manning has been pretty sick all day and has kept his bed — The measles are thick enough on him now. I am doing all I can for him. A.C. More died this morning of small pox or something else — I feel very sorry, and we shall miss his pleasant face over the counter. Got a letter from Cyde to-day not a very encouraging one — I do wish he could come home.

Wed. Apl 10th
This was one of the beautiful mornings but by night was raining again — I got all ready to have washing done this morning but Mrs Inglis did not come — It made me a lot of work for nothing — Churned 11 1/4 lbs butter. After dinner went to Kent with butter and eggs. The roads were simply awful, but I got along all right. Mrs. Messinger and Minnie came over this afternoon to see Manning — It did him more good than the Dr — He got up and dressed this afternoon and has been a lot better to-day.

Mon. Apl 29th
This is Cydes birthday and a lovely day it has been — I had to go to the Station this morning with 46 lbs butter — Called to Illsley & Harveys and paid a bill of $9.10 that we owed them — Got Cretonne* for Fannie's closet, came home churned 12 1/4 lbs butter and Fannie and I cleaned Mannings room — pretty good for one day I think. Father was here to dinner.

Thurs May 2nd
And another nice day with a high East wind which feels very much like rain. We finished our washing to-day for this week curtains and white-clothes — I have just pinned down one pair of curtains and Fannie has got most of the ironing done — Manning sowed some garden seeds and planted a few potatoes this morning. He has got a nice lot of strawberry plants out and the most of his sowing done — Just eight years ago this morning our darling Willie closed his precious blue bright eyes forever — Oh how I miss him yet — That dear sweet face — but God knew best and I am sure he is better off — But O I miss him all the time — Churned 12 1/4 pounds.

Thurs May 9th.
The most beautiful Spring day — Manning & Roley have been hauling manure all day, and Fannie & I have been cleaning house or rather Fannie did the cleaning and I put to rights — Made pies too this forenoon — Mrs Bedford Chase called after tea and brought me a silver spoon that Hanna left that was my great grandmothers on my Father's side. After she went away Fannie & I went to the Port. Did not have long to stay. Bought a white counterpane for spare bed, and some groceries — Got home 1/2 past nine o'clock and it is time I was in bed now — Manning sowed some garden seeds to night, and we put them on some screens to-day.

Wed May 15th
We have got our dining room all cleaned and put to rights — and it does look so much better even though I had nothing new

---

*   A heavy unglazed cotton or linen cloth used for curtains, chair covers, etc.

to put in it, but it is clean. Manning has been hauling out manure to-day west of the house. They have worked hard.

Sat. May 18th
This has been a beautiful day — I have had head ache all day and all the week too till it is beginning to be an old story. We cleaned the pantry to-day and moved out to the shop ready for warm weather.* I have been so tired the past two nights, I have not felt like writing much in this. It does not take much to make me tired — Thurs. night Manning went down to Roberts and brought home the wagon so we have quite a pretty turn out now. Otis Jess was here Thurs. night and stayed all night. Yesterday we churned again 12 3/4 lbs butter. Have got another one ready for Mon — Manning has gone to try the new wagon and harness this Evg — He has worked hard this week and he will enjoy his outing — Every thing is looking beautiful out doors now — Cherry trees are in bloom and other kinds all budded ready to bloom. — The grass is looking finely — Vegetation is a fortnight earlier than last year so authorities say.

Sun May 26th
And a perfect Sabbath day — A great many apple trees, and all the pear, plum and cherry trees are in full bloom and every thing is so beautiful on earth now — The day has been so cool too. This morning Manning got all ready to go to Wolf — to Church but found Maud had a swelled shoulder so had to turn her out and go to doctoring her — I hope it is not any thing serious — This afternoon we went to Port to meeting. Mr. Atherton preached of Acadia — I expect we will have our new minister next Sunday.

Thurs June 6th
This has been a very warm day. Manning harrowed the land for the potatoes and planted some — hoed the strawberries, etc — I washed the carriage this morning, and it looks finely now but it took me quite a while. I have not felt very brisk all day. This would have been Sister Annie's birthday had she of lived. She

---

* Many Nova Scotia homes had a summer kitchen which was a room attached to the house used in the summer and closed in the winter. See entry for 19 October.

would be 47 — Aunt Marcy Prior is 86 to-day, quite an old Lady — and I always liked her so much too.

Wed June 19th
Had Mother lived till to-day she would of been 77 years old — How I have thought of her to-day — 7 years ago to-day she spent with me the last birthday on earth. To day has been another beautiful day I have been patching Manning's coat all day — It was quite a job but it looks better now — Manning took Roley up to night to the Dr to see his arm as it is not doing very well — He does not anticipate any thing serious, and I do hope it will come all right. I run in to see Mrs Otis a little while to-night — Now I must to bed.

Tues June 25th
Dull all day but we put the clothes out and got them dry and Fannie ironed some — I went to Kent after dinner with butter and eggs. Churned this morning 12 1/4 lbs. Laura Michener is to be married tomorrow morning in the Methodist Church to Spurgeon Cross — Fred Wickwire was married last Wed — and Lina Burgess of Wolf is to be married to-morrow too — quite a time for weddings — To day I am 45 crawling along towards 50.

Thurs June 26th
This has been a very hot day. Some cooler tonight — It clouded up last night and rained some but looks as though it would not be much — It was hot yesterday too — I commenced to paper the water closet yesterday morn, but when I had got two rolls on found that I had not near enough so left off and went to the Port at night and got some more — This morning I finished it, and it looks pretty good now. Fannie says good enough to sleep in. Last night I got a photograph from Minnie Fletcher. It is a very nice one and looks so like her as I saw her last. To morrow I am invited over to Mrs Messingers to tea, and Fannie is expecting to go home too for a couple of days — I preserved four lbs of wild strawberries this morn — Churned 12 1/4.

Mon July 1st
It has still been hot — Fannie churned this morning 12 1/2 lbs — then washed and got them most all out before dinner. I

thought her pretty smart. I went down to Bedfords and engaged 20 boxes strawberries then went to Kent with my butter, came home and did them all up before tea; they look so nice. They were beautiful berries — Then after tea Fannie and I went to the Port with Marys butter — So on the whole we have had a busy day.

Mon July 15th

And so hot with a very high wind — it is a great hay day and the boys are at it hard as they can — Father came over this morning and is raking for them this afternoon. Manning mowed for Otis this forenoon. He got Dick all harnessed with Bess to go to mowing but found Dick was sick. It seems the three horses got to the meal barrels yesterday and ate to their sorrow — Bess & Maud seem all right but Dick is dumpy enough — I hope it will learn Manning a lesson to be more careful. We churned 12 lbs butter this morning and Fannie washed. Pretty hot for it too!

Tues July 16th

And another very hot day but is just lovely and cool to-night. I have been so worried all day about the horses — Bess is having a serious time too — and Manning went over to-night to see Mr. Brown. He gave him directions what to do for them and thinks they will come around all right. But both Bess and Dick are so weak they can hardly stand on their feet — We got word last night that Clarence would be here to-day but got another card today saying he could not be here till tomorrow — Manning also got a letter from Minnie saying they would be over tomorrow to spend the afternoon — so I hope I feel pretty good — I went down the street this afternoon and called at Mrs Claytons to see her mother and sister Bessie. Also called to see Mrs Len a while. Annie & Max Herbert were in a little while this evening.

Thurs July 19th

I was so sleepy last night that I felt I could not write any — My nerves are so unstrung all the time worrying about the horses that I hardly know what I am at — Manning went up yesterday noon and got Dr. Illsley to come down and see them — He does not seem to know much about them though — and I guess we will look for some one else tomorrow — We are afraid their days of usefulness are over and it is to sad to think about — The Messinger girls and Miss Harris were over yesterday and we had a pleasant time under the circumstances — Today before noon Clarence came and he has been busy enough ever since. He is regular Godsend to Manning just now — We picked a few cherries to-day and I did up three bottles — Otis and Roley with a little help from Manning got in three loads of hay — It is pretty tough on Manning now I can tell you.

Sun July 21
It does seem as though I have neglected this sorely of late — When night comes I feel to tired to write — Yesterday and day before were very busy days — both in the house and out — What with the haying and doctoring the horses has made a busy time, but the horses are ever so much better and we feel very hopeful now that they may come around all right in time. I do feel so thankful to my Heavenly Father for all his goodness — I have taken this to him and asked him to heal them — It has been lovely hay weather but looks some like rain to-night. Clarence & I went up to Kent last night and got his trunk — To day we all went to Church this afternoon. Had a good sermon from Mr Martell or Mr Hatt I should say — Went up to see the colts to-night — They are doing nicely.

Wed Aug 7th
And no rain yet, but feels more like it tonight. This morning I baked two sheets of cake and made brown bread — I expect the W.M.A.S.* to meet with me to-morrow and want them to stop to tea. Clarence left this morning for Kingsport on his way to Pictou, from that home. Manning went to Wolf on Hardis wheel to-night but has got home now — Fannie and I went to Port. Have just got home and got the horse out. Now it is time I was in bed.

Wed. Aug 28th
This has been a busy day though I have not accomplished much — This morning churned and dressed butter 11 3/4 lbs. Did up the other work, baked lamb for dinner, then went down to Mrs

* Women's Missionary Aid Society.

Len Cogswells to help her some as she had an "At Home" to night — came home just 12 made up the fire and sat down to dinner quarter to one — thought I was pretty smart — after washing the dishes went down again and helped some more — than came home did the night chores got the Boys supper and Manning and I went to the "At Home." Had just a delightful time, saw a lot of my friends and it is just a perfect night. Think I will have one next summer if I live.

Sat Sep 14th

The President McKinley died this morning — It is a dreadful thing — Shot down in cold blood.* Every one mourns — The United States in particular. Hardie got started for home to day — Expect he is on the boat by this time — I have missed him so even this afternoon — Manning took him to the Station came home and went again to hear the Liberal Candidates elected for Local Election — They brought out Dodge and Wickwire as of yore** — He brought home a bicycle lamp also a bell — Has got her pretty well fitted up now — Hope he will get no more troubles and that he may enjoy many good rides on it. I preserved 6 1/2 lbs of plums this afternoon - Expect to do some more first of the week — Sold my two pigs to Sanford today at .08 cts — I hope they will bring $20.00. They are not six months old yet but feed is high so thought I had better sell now.

Sat Sep 21st

Yesterday was a beautiful day but hazed up at night. Manning and I went down to the Tent to meeting, just as I got in the tent the rain began to come down, and it just poured. Held up some while we were coming home but rained about all night, I think and the wind blew a gale — Broke one of our big baldwin trees most to pieces, some of the limbs broke right off — Loaded with apples too — Manning has been packing the ribstons and blenheims*** to day — Has nearly 22 bbls — Is going to send them Monday — I preserved three bottles of plums yesterday and

---

*   A reference to the assassination of the President of the United States by Leon Czolgosz, a factory worker and anarchist, 6 September 1901.
**   Henry Hamm Wickwire was Kings County representative in the Nova Scotia Legislative Assembly 1894-1906; 1911-1922 and Brenton Halliburton Dodge, MLA for Kings County, 1894-1910.
*** Baldwins, Blenheims and Ribstons are varieties of apples.

four bottles of pears to-day. It is slow work. Have just got home from meeting to-night and must go to bed now.

Sun Sep 22nd

This has been a delightful day though rather cool. A good fire has felt comfortable all day — Manning went down to the tent meeting this morning, over to Mr. Messingers to dinner and back again to Sun-School & Church this afternoon — He feels pretty thankful that he can ride his wheels once more — I went down this afternoon, had a fine sermon on Temperance from Mr Hatt — I also went to Endeavor in the Evg — has a very nice meeting on Temperance too — Two years ago this morning our darling Olive left us — Oh how I miss her yet and always shall — She was such a dear sister.

Mon Sep 23rd

Twenty one years ago this morning my first born saw the light of day — My! My! How many sad changes in that short time. I can not help but review them — Still I know we should be thankful for our many remaining mercies and I try to be — I am thankful for my Boy, and that he is a *good* boy — He has never caused me many heart aches — and has a pure, good nature — How can I thank God for it all — He has gone to Wolfville to spend the Evg — with Minnie — God bless them both. Mrs Jess and I went to Kent this afternoon with butter and eggs — Heard there that the small pox has broken out again. Too bad. It is hard to say when it will end — Miss Lockhart died yesterday at Woodside of it. It is terrible — Manning took 20 bbls of apples to the ware house to day to go in the Steamer to Eng — Ribstons & Blenheims.

Sat Sep. 28th

This has been a pretty warm muggy day — and I have been on the jump all day — Made tomatoe pickles, cleaned up in the house — and about four o'clock went to Kent sold a bush of crab-apples for .08 cts — and got orders for more. Came home got supper, then had to go over to the Station with my butter - It is a perfect moonlight night — but I am tired and must go to bed.

Wed. Oct 2nd
Churned this morning 12 1/4 lbs butter — baked Lamb for dinner — fussed around generally, then after dinner I went to the Port. Next [went] to Dex — Collins to take the freezer home then up to Marys — to the store got a dozen pint jars, then home — This is Election day between — Dodge & Wickwire "Grits" and Peter Innis and Ryan "Tories" — We have not heard the results as yet. It has been very quiet. T. J. Borden met with quite an accident this morn. His colt he was driving ran away threw him out and hurt his shoulder very badly — I am very sorry for him. Later Dodge & Wickwire Elected Large Majority. Only two tories in the House.

Thurs Oct 3rd
This has been a warm damp day rained a little most all day and is raining now — I did up 8 pint bottles of peaches this afternoon and they look lovely — after dinner sliced my tomatoes for pickles — Then had a little nap for my head aches — Manning has gone to Canard. Hope he will get home safely — It is lonely here without him.

Mon Oct 7th
And a beautiful day, as usual I have been very busy — Mixed and baked bread preserved four bottles of peaches this afternoon, then after dinner did my large ironing — I am so thankful it is done for I was dreading it, to night I am sleepy. Capt Hibbert & wife have been here the last two hours have just gone — Mrs Hibbert from Yarmouth was also with them. Manning, Perry, Roley and a boy dug and picked up 112 bushes of potatoes today — Pretty good for boys — and I know they are tired too.

Fri Oct 11th
Another fine warm day — The Boys were picking apples again to-day — Nonpareils and some baldwins. Manning has gone to Canard to-night. A night off — I picked my quinces had a half bushel of fine ones — Hope I can sell them all — I cleaned out my bedroom this afternoon but have not got it to rights yet — Hope to do that to morrow.

Fri Oct 18th
And the first snow of the season. It rained some this morning but not much — and this afternoon is very cold with high wind and some snow squalls — I tell you it is making the farmers jump to get apples picked & potatoes dug — I hope they wont freeze up for we are not done yet — Manning is doing all he can with not much help — Has been picking apples this afternoon. Yesterday I was pretty sick, one of my bilious turns and Manning had to get his own breakfast and dinner. I have felt pretty well used up to day but a lot better than yesterday.

Sat Oct 19th
A cold rough day — I have not felt extra smart to-day either, but have got along some way — I moved from the shop to the kitchen to-day with my cooking so that is better in the cold days — I preserved some crab apples — dressed the churning of butter which Roley churned 12 1/4 and did little things in general — Manning finished picking baldwins to-day 112 bbls rough, picked and hauled 46 bbls of potatoes to Illsley & Harvie this afternoon with Dick and Bess — About the first real work he has done with Bess. I feel very thankful that she is as well as she is. We do have a lot to be thankful for.

Sat Nov 2nd
And it has been such a lovely day. Almost like summer — I went to Canning this afternoon to take Mrs Steele over — and the roads are as dry as summer only not quite so dusty. It was chilly driving though — I got home soon after six — just nine years since dear Ollie was married — How it brings up sad recollections — I do so long for her at times — I shall never get over missing her — She was such a dear good sister.

Mon Nov. 4th
Just 22 years to-night since I took the marriage vow — I know my dear husband is thinking of it too in his far off cabin. Some difference in the weather though. Then it was cold with lots of snow — good sleighing that night. The guests all came in sleighs — Then our family circle was unbroken. Now what a change — I do not like to think long about it — Too sad — We are all passing away — soon our places will be empty or filled by others.

To day has been very fine. The roads are perfect. Father came over to dinner, then we went to the Port for a little while. I baked pies this morning and roast beef for dinner. Manning has been ploughing all day — Jim England and Effie Walker married to day.

Wed. Nov 20th
This has been an unpleasant day — This forenoon or nearly noon I went over to the Station with order for T. Eatons $3.89. Went up to Marys and stopped to dinner. Got home after two. Fannie cleaned the hall stove. Now we are just waiting for Manning to put pipe up then we will have a fire.

Tues Nov 26th
Still keeps dull, snowing some out now. We brought the coloured clothes in the house and finished drying them and Fannie has got them all ironed. The white ones are still on the tub. Manning went over to Canard this morning got Minnie and took her to Wolf to see the football match between Dalhousie & Acadia — Acadia got beaten. They came back here to tea — then Manning went and took her home — Father came over to dinner brought us over some cider — so I expect I will have some mince pies some day.

Tues Dec 24th
And such a storm as we are having. The wind blows a hurricane and the rain is coming in torrents — Manning has gone to Wolf just the same to help make candy for Chris — Father came over the afternoon to stay till after Chris — He brought me from Rob's Mother a beautiful set of crocheted table mats. Something I have long wanted, and so unexpected — It is so kind of her — I have got so many friends and so much to be thankful for — last night I got a remembrance from Ida and Warren — Two nice handkerchiefs and a handsome booklet, Manning also got a nice Calender.

Christmas
This has been a very quiet day — I got up at seven o'clock — dressed the goose and put it in the oven — and then hustled as fast as I could to get my chores done up before Father got back

with Mary and Lorne — I got along finely. Had a nice dinner, but it has been a long time since our numbers were so few — Manning went to Wolf — Father has gone to take Mary home — and I am here alone. It has been a fine day but windy. Too bad the snow all went off — Mrs Campbell sent me a nice book of hymns — No#1 and 2 — Every one is so kind.

Dec. Thurs 26th
This has been a very fine day but still windy. I washed out a few things and got them dry and ironed — Father went home this morning — When Manning came home last night he brought two letters from the absent one written Oct. 20 and Nov. 17. I tell you we were glad enough to hear from him — Hope to get another one soon. He also got returns from 35 bbls of apples — and we are much pleased with them. I cant help feeling thankful all the time that we did not sell to Onderdonk — How our Heavenly Father watches over all our doings — and guides us I feel sure.

Fri. Dec 27th
This has been a very rough day and is still rough — It has snowed and blown it all into heaps all day — I have only ventured out doors once or twice this morning — It is a dreadful day — I think there will be snow to be shoveled in some places — We churned to-day the last one for this year I expect — Have just been counting up the amount of butter I have made this year and find the total is thirteen hundred and sixty three pounds and a quarter (1363 1/4) not too bad for our little dairy — We have taken from that enough for home use and sold the rest of it — most all for twenty cents.

Mon. Dec 30th
This morning found the snow about all gone — and still raining — and it has rained most all day — most of the time quietly and some of the time a down pour — Manning took 25 bbls of Baldwins to the station this morning to go to London. We are chopping mince meat to night.

Tues Dec 31st.
This has been a fine bright day with heavy winds. Manning took

37 bbls of potatoes to the Port to day for Illsley & Harvey — I went to Kent this afternoon with butter. Saw Laura Thompson there who wanted to come home with me, so I brought her along. She is going to Mrs Harveys to live — I will drive her down. *Adieu old Year*

EPILOGUE: REBECCA CHASE KINSMAN ELLS

In 1911, Cyrus returned, penniless, to the farm which Manning, after some unsuccessful ventures into potato growing, had turned into fine apple orchards. He also expanded their investment in chickens and, in the 1920s, the family went heavily into the poultry business. Significantly, Rebecca's chickens, originally a sideline, became the basis of the next successful phase of the C & M Ells operations.

Manning's letters to his father, written between 1906-1911, detail his successful struggle to make the farm more productive and his attempts to persuade his father to come home. Occasionally they give us another glimpse of Rebecca. On June 20, 1909, Manning wrote: "Mother is a great help and works like an Irishman, never so happy as when she's running all outdoors and in the house too."* Rebecca died in 1928.

---

*   Manning Ells Papers, Acadia Archives, Vaughan Memorial Library, Acadia University.

MARGARET MARSHALL SAUNDERS
1861-1947

Margaret Marshall Saunders was the eldest of seven children born to Edward Manning and Maria Saunders. E. M. Saunders was a Baptist clergyman and the family followed him from his Annapolis Valley pastorate in Berwick to Halifax in 1867 when "Maggie" was six years old. In the urban environment of the Nova Scotia capital the Saunders family's commitment to personal improvement and social reform was reinforced and strengthened. E. M. Saunders took a personal interest in the education of his precocious daughter who later noted: "As a child I was steeped in Virgil, the Bible and Spurgeon's sermons. At eight I was more familiar with my Latin grammar than my English one."*

At the age of 15 Marshall left her close-knit family circle to attend school in Scotland and France. In 1878 she returned to Halifax. She participated in the family's busy social life, took courses at Dalhousie University and taught school, but longed for success as a writer, a career opening to an increasing number of women in the nineteenth century. In 1889 her novelette, *My Spanish Sailor*, an uninspired love story, was published in Britain. Had romantic novels been her only metier, Marshall would not have had a very promising literary career. However, she had a strong affinity for animals and children which served her well when the American Humane Society offered $200.00

* Karen E. Saunders, "Margaret Marshall Saunders: Children's Literature as an Expression of Early Twentieth Century Social Reform," Dalhousie University: M.A. Thesis, 1978 is the best study of Saunders' career and is the source for this biographical information.

for a dog-story sequel to Anna Sewell's *Black Beauty*. Marshall wrote *Beautiful Joe*, won the prize and embarked on a literary career which resulted in 25 more novels directed at a juvenile audience. None of her later books gained the popularity of *Beautiful Joe*, which sold over a million copies and was translated into 18 languages, including Japanese and Esperanto.

At her father's urging, Marshall began keeping a diary when she went to Scotland.* As well as chronicling daily events, her diaries in later years served as notebooks for her highly autobiographical novels. The excerpts from her 1906/7 diary abundantly document Marshall's passionate devotion to birds and other animals. By this time the Saunders' Carleton Street house was virtually an aviary and Marshall's diary entries contain far more information about her feathered family than her human one. Though it is tempting to argue that her birds were a substitute for the children she never had, Marshall would have been quick to point out that love for animals and humans was not in contradiction but ran in one grand continuum. Those who were cruel to animals were also likely to be lacking in compassion at other levels. Marshall's compassion manifested itself in a myriad of reform causes so popular among those of the 'social gospel'** persuasion at the turn of the century. She belonged to as many as 20 volunteer organizations, including the Humane Society, the WCTU, the National Council of Women, and as this portion of her diary indicates, she was deeply involved in the Playground Movement.

Her "progressive" interests notwithstanding, Marshall's white, Anglo-Saxon, Protestant perspective on the world produced prejudices that are clearly revealed in the following

---

*   Margaret Marshall Saunders' diaries are housed in Acadia University Archives. Her 1876 diary has been published in *Atlantis*, Vol. 6, No. 1 (Fall 1980), pp. 68-82.

**   For a treatment of the Canadian manifestation of this phenomenon see Richard Allen, *The Social Passion: Religion and Social Reform in Canada, 1914-28*, Toronto, 1973; and his "The Social Gospel and the Reform Tradition in Canada, 1890 - 1928," *Canadian Historical Review*, Vol. XLIX (1968), pp. 381-399. For a discussion of the social gospel in the context of the Maritime region, see E. R. Forbes, "Prohibition and the Social Gospel in Nova Scotia," *Acadiensis*, Vol. 1, No. 1 (Autumn 1971), pp. 11-36.

account. Discussions of Acadians, Blacks, Jews, and the poor are all infused with a supercilious condescension which makes much of what she says unacceptable to the modern reader. Of course, the contradictions of middle class reformers have been widely explored in recent years and Marshall was typical in her inability to transcend a world view so widely held at the time.* Instead, she increasingly retreated into the world of her animals, who, as she noted in her diary, were not "socialists" and never talked back to her when she clipped their wings.

---

* See, for example, Linda Kealey, ed., *A Not Unreasonable Claim: Women and Reform in Canada, 1880-1920* (Toronto, 1979).

MARGARET MARSHALL SAUNDERS
DIARY
1906-1907*

May 29, 1906

Few days ago children bro't young sparrow to door. Season has opened for me — I sighed and took it upstairs. Its little tail just budding — Cd not feed itself. I always tell age of young bird by size of tail. Made pills of his food and put down throat ....

Mrs. Freeman told me that she is waked up at night by Ruby's low singing on the veranda. I put him down in lower aviary clipped a wing so as to keep him from chasing other birds — bye and bye I will let them all up in upper aviary daytimes — keep them down at night. Robin has made 3rd nest this spring and is sitting on eggs.

July 10

... Let 1 young sparrow go the other day. First kept it in pigeon trap half a day where street sparrows fed it. As soon as released they flew off without feeding it whenever it fluttered wings. Any female sparrows will feed any young one. Don't see males coming to feed captives tho they fly about it. One young sparrow in Andy's cage persisted in getting in nest with canary. She picked a little but he persisted in sitting beneath her.

July 24

4 days ago was shocked to find 1 of the Brazil Cardinal babies on veranda floor. Cold & gasping. Ran for hot water bag put it on and fed it. Don't know long it has been out of nest. Kept it warm and gave it bread and milk ....

Went to Barnum Bailey circus last night with Miss Ford and some other girls. Mr Dennis** gave his tickets for a box he had.

---

*   Margaret Marshall Saunders Papers, Acadia University Archives, Vaughan Memorial Library, Acadia University.

**   Mr. Dennis refers to W. H. Dennis, publisher of the *Halifax Herald* and *Halifax Mail*, two newspapers with a decidedly Conservative Party leaning. Both W. H. and his wife, Dr. Agnes Dennis, were "progressive" in their thinking and shared many of Marshall's enthusiasms and prejudices.

A fine circus. Spent afternoon with Miss Lallemore and Miss Burke who are here .... Took them out in Harbour up to playground and to Mitchell's for tea.

July 25
... Paid carpenter's bill yesterday and went up to playground— met Mrs Dennis and Ser-Maj Gill, physical director YMCA who measured off place for basketball. Telephone Mrs McKay and carpenter and arranged to have Albro St. playground opened at one. Fed Brazil cardinals egg food last night. Doesn't agree with them, causes diarrhoea. Will go back to bran and milk. They are lively. Gave them white cloth to sit on — did not like it. No hold for feet. Put in straw and their claws curl round it. Streets in a fearful condition, all torn up for paving street car service. Disorganized. You go a little way & have to get out & walk. Muggy warm weather and lots of rain.

July 28
... Mrs. Dennis called for me and we went up to Albro St. playground which carpenters are fitting up for children. Then on to Bloomfield St. Teachers here having classes.

Aug. 6
Went up to playground this p.m. Saw little Manuel girl in Street with baby carriage. She said the baby belonged to woman who lived in upper part of their house & she was giving it an airing & allowing her little friend to have lend of it — that is wheeling the carriage — Asked her how her little sister Kathleen was — the one who sang Jesus Sends us Sunshine .... She says she is pretty well — Does she go to the playground? No, why — because you don't go. I shocked to hear that the child has been missing so much pleasure. Said tell her I want her to go to the playground. There are such nice teachers there. She said she would tell her.

Bloomfield boys were having a baseball match with Albro St. B. won. Great excitement. Teachers sitting in chairs keeping score ....

Aug. 8

Went to police court yesterday when I came home clever little Brazil peeped excitedly. He knows me. I stuffed him before I went out. He seemed lively. I put oil all over him knowing he w'd absorb some through his skin. Toward even he got weaker. At last I found him lying on his back. Then I soaked wool in chloroform & held to his beak. He gave one start and died. Chloroformed robin. He threw up food I gave him. Only way I c'd feed him was by holding him on his back. That was painful for him and me too. His eyes were sore & I thot it best to put him out of misery. Put young cardinal under his wing & buried them in common grave. Miss little cardinal peeping to me ....

In court room yesterday was a new lawyer. Clever muddle after bullying, frightening witnesses til they terrified. To Mrs Egan who said child's throat was bruised where it had been clutched — Are you an expert on bruises [?] She said first she was then that she was not ....

Aug. 10

Had telegram from Father fr. St John Aug. 8. Said he wd be home next morn. bring robin wood fr. Boston. He spent yesterday and last night with us. So glad to see him.

Mr. Dennis calls police court dog & cat court such snarling bet. lawyers & magistrates.

Spent Aug. 8 afternoon in court room. Lawyer for the defence worse than ever. He doubles in his fists, leans in their noses, his heel on seat of his chair lifts upper leg shows teeth set slightly apart — tries to look as much like a dog as possible then "bull-dogs" witness — speak out can't you — you don't look in deli-cate health. In summing up he said — Yr honor we shd not convict a man on such slight evidence. A razor strap was hang-ing in his house — that is not a proof that he beat his client with it. If it is it will become a dangerous thing to shave. Bruises were found on the child but that is not proof that they were inflicted by the accused. The stipendiary — Yes but suppose the child had been found dead with those bruises on him. Mr [lawyer] taken slightly aback. Everyone in court felt that if a child had been found with those bruises on him there was enough circum-stantial evidence to hang the man. Stip. made another wise remark — We want to get at the truth of this affair. Mr Mitchell left saying — In all my experience I never heard anyone interrupt so much referring to Rob. Murray ....

Aug. 13

Yesterday morn. Dr & Mrs Fraser & Miss Hunter & I drove to Preston abt 6 miles fr Dartmouth.* Lovely day — warm overcast no [dust] — woods lovely .... Small houses, land stony not good for farming. Passed Walker's Hotel — told them wd be back for dinner. On the Dartmouth boat & the road to Preston saw single & double carriages loaded with blacks & white sitting 3 or 4 in a seat.

When there is a baptizing** at Preston all who can get anything in the shape of a horse will go to it, dressed in their best — some extraordinary costumes. Passed several pretty ladies with yellow and white water lilies & purple flowers. The Church was an inn left by some disreputable white people .... Church on hill, little bridge with people waiting for baptism. We drove up to Church. Carriages arrive, see parents getting out black & white — only saw 1 case of 2 races mingling — a jet black man drove up in a buggy with a white woman — a slim looking woman whose waist was half dropping off her — she put her jacket on to hide line of separation between waist & skirt — one old black woman led her husband aside, took a collar & necktie fr. her pocket & put them on him. Pretty to see the old blackie dressing her mate. The middle aged woman in a big hat with violets was in a carriage behind us on way out. Saw her part of way holding hand over bowl pipe. I heard her swearing. Little Church had seats outside. Fr. gallery windows we cd see black heads protruding. Not much noise among coloured people. They greet each other in a lively rollicking way. Busily slapping on shoulders or backs but no rowdyism. We went in Church and

---

*   Preston has been a centre of Black settlement in Nova Scotia since the
     period after the War of American Independence when free Blacks
     began migrating to British North America. The majority are
     descendants from the influx of Blacks who fought in the British army
     during the War of 1812 and as a result were granted their freedom and
     free land — though as Marshall Saunders notes, not very good land.
**   Many Blacks were Baptists and therefore practiced adult baptism by
     full immersion.

were given seats to ourselves. Pulpit high up, row of black ministers behind it. Below deacons, white men among them. Candidates sit on 2 benches lengthwise in isles …. 5 girls 2 boys 1 young man. Girls in white, light hats; young men in white with darker coats. While minister preached — the rest they sang — very badly no organ — was surprised they had such poor voices c'd not keep tune well — interrupted themselves — old minister read acc't of Peter and the Fleet being let down …. Preacher announced first that it was 5 minutes to 12 & the sermon must be brief. Poor old fellow uneducated, evidently did not want to …. At close of sermon collection taken up. Long pause while it was being counted … it was done by white deacon. Don't want to be suspicious but know the coloured in church in City has had great trouble with monies. Can't trust anyone not even Pastor therefore … they count money in presence of all …. The benediction was pronounced and we went down to Partridge River. Fearing some disturbance I asked 2 or three colored women. They said was Constable there — also colored. Deacons who would preserve order. Minister in gown & white lapels & collar … went into water with 2 Deacons. Candidates went out one by one after singing and address by minister. Men and girls had white napkins bound round heads; girls had white napkins tied round legs below knees to keep dresses from floating … followed in water by a man who carried a shawl over his shoulder. First the minister took his hand & wiped water off her face — sometimes he rubbed a handkerchief over it; sometimes not ….

During baptism 1 colored woman exclaimed won't old Sarah be glad looking down fr. glory to see her daughter gettin' baptized — a mother and baptized also ….

Some black women in transparent waists cd see black necks & arms thru white. Purple silk, green silk, white dresses, all colours of dresses. Such queer effects.

After baptizing went to hotel where Miss Elliott gave us dinner in private room ….

Aug. 18
…Had a fine time at closing of playground Aug. 16. Fine Day. Crowd of people there. Children dressed in best; one boy called

King Edward Lesser very funny — father a junk dealer. King E. has a Sister 8 — looks as if was half fed. The King got a prize — stumbled as he came fr. platform. Such dirty face — eating chocolates which made it worse. Boys presented Miss Ford with belt pin apron etc. Little fellow in blue blouse with trembling voice read it. Football & baseball teams presented it.

Aug. 23
Tupper boys just bro't in branches covered with caterpillars & flies. My birds having a lovely time with them. Brazil cardinals & canaries stuffing themselves. Don't think they eat the large caterpillars only little ones & flies.

Sukey not well doesn't want to come to me trembles as she does with strangers. Think it must because I have forcibly been giving her bathes must stop it. She usually follows me abt — bothering me by wanting to be on my cap or shoulder. Java sparrow eating just now. Kept making runs at female Eng. sparrow who seemed to want to get acquainted with him. Java wd run at her. I wish they would mate.

Aug. 28
... Mr. Dennis asked to write letter to paper asking North End people why they did not apply to Imp. Govt. for Admiralty House & grounds for a park. I said it was strange North End people were so apathetic seem to want others to do everything for them. Mr. D. told story of Frenchman. English electors were talking to him abt a French candidate at election time in Clare.* He said there was only a Frenchman suitable; the Englishmen — only 1? but suppose he won't run? won't run! squealed the Frenchman. By George, I make him run — I his Father-in-law.

Nov. 1906
Father at a men's dinner-party at the Dennises. A number of clergymen there & the archbishop McCarthy. After the archb told this story. Had in his diocese a priest fr. Westphalia subject to sudden fits of gloom. One day told reason. Had a happy country home in Westphalia he, his father & an idolized sister who

---

* Clare is an Acadian district in Southwestern Nova Scotia.

boasted of fearlessness. Wasn't afraid of anything. Could not shock her. One night when girl was out to merry-making with friends the father who was a doctor said to his son: Let us play a trick on — mentioning the daughter's name — see if we can not frighten her. Together they dressed an image resembling a human being & put it in her bed. When she came home late they listened. Heard her laughing after she entered room. The father said to his son, you see we can not frighten her. She is only amused. Next morn. girl did not appear at breakfast. At last they burst open the door. She was setting in corner of room in the dress she had worn the eve. before. Her hair torn by handfuls from her head lay scattered on floor around her — was raving mad. Lived a few years then died. Her father died, son went into priesthood. Archbishop told story as a warning against practical jokes.

Java seems to have mated with English sparrow. Flies abt. with her.

Nov. 10

Nov. 8 met at lunch at Mrs. Dennises, Hartmann, celebrated Hungarian violinist. Young man black hair very long, parted in middle. Jewish cast. Small man came with Mr Weil who has a school of music here — airs of a star. Talked all the time — wanted to lead in conversation. Bohemian artistic talk ....

Hartmann at table sat next to me. Talked incessantly in boyish way — Little bit of braggart & rather humorous. Made us laugh often. Maid offered him ginger cream. He started back & said what is it? Mrs Dennis assured him it was nothing that would hurt him.

What amused me was to hear this man with German name German Jew physiognomy criticizing Germany and German institutions. He was just as foreign among us as he could be. He spoke English well but with a foreign manner. Told a good many stories about his long hair. Says that he is much called after in Germany to get his hair cut. If he is alone he does not pay much attention for he knows that while Germans love to fight a duel they don't go in for fisticuffs such as Mr. Hartmann seems to like.

The first time I saw Miss Cox I was attracted to her by hearing her tell some one in a matter of fact voice that she was once a calling on a very sick and tortured man in Shelburne who asked her whether she did not think he would be justified in committing suicide. She said she thought he would be, but she added that she did not think he would because it would be such a sneaky way of getting into heaven. She said further to him, You know how proud we all are of our legitimate birth in this world. Illegitimate birth is a thing to be ashamed of. Now if you were to sneak into heaven by a back door, don't you think you would be as much ashamed of that illegitimate birth into the next world as you would have been ashamed of an unlawful entrance into this. Her family doctor rebuked her for speaking so unconventionally to this man.

Dec. 4.
Yesterday Mr. Archibald, W. P. — Dominion Parole officer called. Had a nice talk about crime in the Dominion. He says our parole system is a magnificent one — ahead of all other countries. We are ahead in the management of adults, but behind with regard to children. We want a big reformatory he said. The provinces are too poor to keep up separate ones. There are agencies to protect young and tractable children but we want a place where our boys — refractory boys can be sent — You would not call it reformatory, I said. He replied Oh no. The best thing would be a big industrial school like the one that New York is having near Rochester with cottages for the boys to live in. The parole system so successful. The most of the men given liberty report regularly and do well. Whereas those men who serve out their sentences frequently return to prison life. Mr. A. visits all the penitentiaries several times a year. He believes in punishment without coddling. I asked him what he thought of the method pursued at Sherborne of giving the women pet lambs birds etc. He said he did not like it. They must understand that they are being punished. Ought to work. Thinks that in some of our jails and reformatories there is not enough intelligent work done. In one school for boys they did only cobbling. Why not teach the boy how to makes shoes. He says punishment is valuable if intelligently administered because it keeps the man's

thoughts on his crime. He gives religious addresses in the penitentiaries and afterward the men are permitted to talk to him alone without a guard. He said one day a murderer said to him, You were preaching about your God being full of compassion. Do you mean to say that he could forgive a man like me that murdered another man — Why I see his face before me a great deal of the time — when I am eating his face is right before me, and when I am alone in my cell. Your God could not forgive a murderer — Yes He can, and will Mr. A. told him — He said it was a perfect revelation to the man, and possibly saved his reason. I asked him whether he thought that we had many degenerates in Canada — Men who could feel no repentance. He said that we had very few of them. Our criminal class is a different one from that of large cities.

He said that in the States there is wretched administration of justice. From some jails when a discharged prisoner leaves with his ten dollars in his pocket the policeman is waiting outside to take it from him. We have no such thing in Canada. Universal graft prevails there. Then when prisoners are brought to a bar of justice they are in the U.S. not often convicted.

Dec. 6.
Been in the house for a week with a cold. Ruby Kentucky cardinal has been bad — beating other birds. I shut him up in the den with Dan the Mocking bird and he was so afraid of Dan that he would not eat. So I brought him out. He began his chasing and persecution of the Brazil cardinals, so I clipped his wing so short that he could not fly at all. He was as bad as ever going over the aviary in prodigious leaps and jumps, scuttling along so fast that he seems to go as quickly without wings as the other birds go with them. Then I put him in the furnace room. He did not like this, sat by the bird-room door and begged to go back. He is very tame would sit by the door begging to go in while I was close by. Last night I went down it looked so pitiful so seem him sitting close by the door where his mate was that I said Now If I let you in old fellow, will you behave yourself. He ran up in the door holding on to the wire screen with his claws and looked at me very eloquently. There I stood with the lamp close to him and he stared at me moving his head from side to side. At last I

said I will give you another chance, so I opened the door. He swung himself up to the top of it, and gazed about calmly. Then holding the lamp so that he could see I followed him as he hopped from the door to the shingles stuck in the wall then to a pole then to a spruce tree.

This morn. he seems to be behaving himself pretty well and I have suspended some food for the Brazils where he can not reach it. It is strange that they let him bully them so. The Brazils have almost as powerful beaks as he has. They could fight him but wont — Ruby who has such a heavy beak allows the mocking bird to rule him with his little slender bill. My birds are not socialists ... There is always a boss. While Ruby and Dan were shut up, did not Boy that clownish good-natured robin take to bullying and now is driving the female Kentucky all about the place — won't let her eat without darting at her.

Dec. 23

Last Thursday went to Rosebank — the Waddells for Circle at 1.30. Was the closing of Mr. W's boys school. Dr & Mrs Faulkner were there. Reminded me of Belmont to see so many boys abt & such nice things on the tables. They had great fun snapping bonbons & putting on the caps. After lunch Mr. Faulkner [gave] a speech & I was then called upon. The Echo* says I spoke very acceptably. I invited the boys to come to see my birds after Xmas.

Mar. 2 [1907]

Yesterday wrote in morn. went to a sewing or "thimble" party at Mrs. Murray's an afternoon tea at Mrs. T. Wood's & a lecture on Gov. Farr in the even. Mr. McDonald told us of the coming of the Loyalists to Halifax of the dissipation & immorality of early Halifax — the swaggering drinking & gaming. Had often distinguished guests. Townspeople to write fulsome addresses & give talks lasting till 7, 8, 9 & even to the next morn ....

---

* Halifax newspaper, an evening edition of the *Morning Chronicle*, Liberal in political persuasion.

Mar. 12
... Heard E. Ritchey's* lecture on Chas. Lamb last even.

Sunday even last took tea in Old Ladies' Home. About 25 old ladies sitting round long green table in dining-room when I went in listening to young man who was preaching in a loud tone of voice — a good sermon and I suppose he raised his voice so the old ladies cd. hear but some of them did not like it. said he was screaming at them. At table I sat next Miss Hall. She had an enormous urn and lots of cups and saucers before her. Had toast tea bread and butter and gingerbread.

After tea went into some of the old ladies' rooms and talked. Mrs. Johnson told us all her troubles, then Aunt Minnie Parker who was sitting opposite and who is very deaf leaned over and said to me "I suppose you are going to put us all in a book." We all shrieked and they had to shut the door as it was Sunday even. did not want to make too much noise.

As conversation had been started in a more cheerful vein Aunt Fannie told us that she might have been married half a dozen times over. Then she wanted to know why I did not get married.

Mrs. J. went into her closet and called out "I don't suppose you know what I am doing?"

Yes I said you are getting candy. She brought some out and the dear old ladies ate it like school-boys.

The widows up there are dreadfully discontented — not with their surroundings for they all acknowledge that the house is very nice and very comfortable, but because their own homes are broken up. The old maids do not seem to care so much for they are accustomed to living under someone have never had homes of their own ....

On Tues. went to Dartmouth to inquire after Dr. Kempton who has had a fall on the ice. Went next door to see Mr. Bishop. Has a fine collection of stuffed birds — nearly two hundred. Usually I hate to look at stuffed birds but these are so life like — he has so cleverly preserved natural attitudes that there is nothing unpleasant abt. seeing them.

*   Dr. Eliza Ritchie, Nova Scotia's first female college professor, and her sister Mary, were leaders in reform circles at the turn of the century.

EPILOGUE: MARGARET MARSHALL SAUNDERS

In 1913 the Saunders family moved to Toronto to be closer to Marshall's literary contacts. E. M. Saunders died in 1916 and thereafter Marshall lived with her sister Grace, who served as secretary, friend and travelling companion, and, of course, with her many animals. Marshall died in 1947 at the age of 86, the final years of her life characterized by dwindling financial resources and an increasing absorption with her animal friends.

B. Hall

BESSIE HALL
1890 - 1969

Bessie Hall grew up in Bridgewater, Nova Scotia. She had two brothers, the Gordon and Jim of these letters, and a sister, Em. After graduation Bessie taught school in her home town but did not enjoy the experience. In an effort to improve her employment prospects and ultimately to help the family out of an apparent financial crisis caused by her father's illness, Bessie decided to attend university.

Maritime universities had been opened to women since the 1870s but Bessie's letters indicate that American institutions offered better scholarships. In the fall of 1911 Bessie enrolled at Boston University. She found academic life a bigger challenge than she had anticipated. Much of her time was consumed with various jobs that she took to help finance her education and the course work was so demanding that she had little time to enjoy her freshman year. In 1912 Bessie returned to Nova Scotia and enrolled in Dalhousie University in Halifax. The letters written during her Dalhousie years are from a more self-possessed young woman, but one still preoccupied by the lack of financial resources. To help cover expenses, Bessie took a job working at the School for the Blind, a common posting for penniless students at Dalhousie.

Bessie graduated from Dalhousie in 1916. By this time Halifax was a fully mobilized naval base from which men and matériel were dispatched for the war effort in Europe. Bessie's brothers enlisted in the army and Bessie, herself, had ambitions to go overseas as a volunteer nurse. The terrible destruction of the war was brought home to Haligonians in December of 1917 when an explosion in the harbour levelled a significant portion of the city and caused nearly 2,000 deaths.* The Hall family experienced its own personal tragedies during the war years. Bessie's father died, Gordon was killed in battle and Jim returned with war wounds. These developments added to the family's financial embarrassment and increased Bessie's sense of responsibility for the family's economic well-being.

In the final letters published here, written in 1918, Bessie describes her career as a member of the Volunteer Army Division (VAD), an organization which drew upon the energies of many young women during the First World War. Her work, caring for the city's orphans (many of them casualties of the explosion) and returned convalescent soldiers, is a testimony to the role played by Nova Scotia women on the home front.**

Bessie's letters offer an insight into the career opportunities opening for women in the early decades of the twentieth century. Teaching, nursing and social work were extensions of women's helping role in the home and therefore sanctioned as appropriate women's professions. Even someone as bright as Bessie — a Governor General's Medal winner at Dalhousie University — could not move outside of the rigid occupational spheres established for women and men.

Young women of Bessie's generation faced two mutually exclusive options: career or family. The possibility of 'having it all,' both marriage and paid labour was sanctioned only for men. Hence, an increasing portion of Nova Scotia women remained single in the twentieth century despite the social pressures to conform to the domestic ideal incorporated in novels, movies and ribald jokes about 'old maids.' Once caught up in her professional activities, marriage became a difficult and conflicting option for Bessie. The death of so many young men of her generation in the war also made finding a suitable marriage partner less likely.

The following letters chronicle Bessie's experiences in Halifax between 1912 and 1918. They reveal a bright and bubbling personality as well as a very purposeful young woman who

*   Graham Metson, *The Halifax Explosion, December 17, 1917* (Toronto, 1978).
** Ernest Forbes, "The Ideas of Carol Bacchi and the Suffragettes of Halifax," *Atlantis*, Vol. 10, No. 2 (Spring 1985), pp. 119-26.

could make choices for herself and was prepared to make them for other members of her family too.

BESSIE HALL LETTERS
1912-1919*

School for the Blind, Halifax
Dec. 1. 1912.

... Look I have something very important to tell the family, so if anyone else is there when you read this, don't bother to read it aloud —

Mrs. Dan Owen phoned me yesterday to know if I could come out to see her before going up to the Blind School. I went and guess what she wanted — now this is not in a romance by Sir Walter Scott — She said that she and Mr. Owen had been talking things over and wanted to do something to help me through college so that I would not have to do the extra work at the "Blind School." What she wants is to pay my board at the Y.W., and for me not to do any extra work. Now what do you know about that?

I will not make any remarks as to what I think about it because I don't know yet what I do think. Write and tell me, at once your opinion and papa's.

You may know of course that I would never *think* of accepting it as a gift, that's definite at least ....

The truth about the blind school work is that I have become interested in it, and don't want to give it up. The only trouble is that 5 hours or more a day is — er — rather strenuous. I had a little talk with Mrs. F. last night, in regard to obtaining easier hours, and I have an appointment with *his* imperial highness tomorrow to discuss the matter. Wish me joy! ....

I was pleasantly surprised last night, to be informed by Mrs. Fraser that I was "doing splendid work with the boys, and that a great improvement could be seen in them." It was the first I had heard of it but I did not argue the matter with her! ....

Consult papa about the Owen matter. I may as well tell you that I would rather fight it out without assistance. Well we shall see — what we shall see! ....

*   Public Archives of Nova Scotia, McGregor-Miller Collection, MG 1, Vol. 661.

You want to know about the walking Party, I was at. Well we all assembled at our hostess's residence, and set out from there. The walk was divided in 8 parts at each pre-arranged stopping place we would change partners. We returned to the house about 11 o'clock. Then we played games. It was great fun...

Y.W.C.A. Halifax
Dec. 8, 1912.
... I had an interview with the "Great Mogul" — Dr. Fraser on Tuesday, as a result of which my hours are shortened so that I only have to go at about 5 o'clock each day — instead of 2.30. That is, of course until after Xmas, but then some other arrangement is to be made. At all events I am not going back to the long hours again. That's settled.

I was out to the "Dan Owens'" on Thursday. I told Mrs. Owen the result of my conference with Dr. Fraser, and I also told her that I wanted to stick to my work at the "Blind School" just as long as I could. After a while she went out and told Mr. Owen I was there; and he came in.

They were certainly just as nice as they could be, and I told them that I hoped they would not think me ungracious for refusing their offered help.

They suggested that I should go on with the work then for a while, if I was so determined to, and that I should be sure to let them know at once if I find it too trying at any time.

So that is how the matter stands now. I really feel much better to be working my way independently. However if the "worst comes to the worst" it is nice to feel that I have something to fall back on. Isn't it?

I certainly think that it was "white" of them to think of it ....

I have had a lovely lazy time today. Both Hattie and I stayed in Bed until 11.30. Then I got up and had a bath, *did my week's mending*, and got dressed for dinner at 1 o'clock. Then we scratched some of the dirt up in our room, fished my umbrella and raincoat out of the empty apple barrel, covered it over with the "white elephant," removed my books from the waste basket and sat down to compose this effusion. Bed for mine at 9 o'clock tonight!

Look here, I have not said anything about Jim and Em in my 1st letters but what *is* the matter? I expect to hear from Jim with Em's report tomorrow.

Bess Love to Papa!

Wed. evening.
... I received your letter today. I am sorry to hear that you are not feeling well. For Heaven's sake mama don't let yourself get sick now.

I think you should go out more. It would do you good. Why don't you get Dr. Marshall to give you something for your heart?

It is rather annoying that money is in papa's name in the Bank. However I suppose it *really* doesn't make a difference. Sometime why don't you both go out & have it changed, or could he do it alone?

Aunt Annie is back in town. She came on Saturday, and is staying with the Taylors now, I believe. I haven't seen her, but Hattie met her on the street.

What is this amazing talk I hear about a "new pair of rubbers" and "Emmies' new skirt." Dear me, it sounds queer to think that we can actually buy a few things now.

I would like to get home to really realize the effect. Did I tell you I got a letter from Gordon? He said he was going to send you a check. Well, I am just in from rink, and have some work to do now, so Bye Bye Bessie.

If you can manage it, you might send me a little money to effectually square up my account here. You know my Blind School salary doesn't nearly pay my board now and then I was a little behind hand from before Xmas. You can "charge it to my account."

66 Hollis St., Halifax.
Friday. [1913]
I have been waiting to write to you at home until I knew the results of all my exams. I have heard from all now except German, which comes off this afternoon. I have done *fairly* well in my work. From 40-55 is considered a "pass," from 55-70 is a second class, and from 70-85 is a first class, above that is a high first, and

I can assure you is very rarely attained. Last previous years the limit was always 82, but now they have raised it to 85.

I have made three "firsts" and a "second" so far, which is considered good. Just think I made 84 in *math*. And led the class, in chemistry I made 82, in English 70 (and let me tell you it is no cinch making a high mark in English). In Latin I did fairly well. I was glad to come off with a "second." I was mortally afraid that I wouldn't get through with it. I don't know just what my mark was — somewhere between 55 and 70.

I am beginning to get back into the routine again, but we all find it hard to settle down to study.

I have had a talk with Dr. Fraser, and my hours are permanently shortened to three hours a day, and Wed. evenings off, if I want them. *But* also my "salary" is cut down to 12 per. However, for the time I spend there that is approximately higher than what I have been getting. And if that picture firm in Toronto amounts to anything I can more than make up the difference by only working an hour a day at it, or often not that long. And so I don't have to go until 1/4 to 5 to the Blind School. It makes a big difference I can tell you — over two hours more time.

I suppose you have heard that poor Mrs. (Dr.) Mack had to go to the hospital, didn't you? She had cancer in the breast or something like that, and had to have an operation. It is too bad isn't it? They are all dreadfully cut up about it.

Did Aunt B. tell you about me meeting Kate Mack at the station? I sat with her part of the way coming up. She is very agreeable and pretty. I met her next day again coming home from work. She is coming to see me. I am glad I have met her. I haven't written to Mr. Chesley yet. I may do so on Sunday.

Lots of Love

From Bess.

The apples have come and been received into the bosom (and other organs) of the "family."

Later. Just heard from German. I did all right.

Forrest Hall, Halifax
Thursday.[1915]

I received your letter, and am glad to hear that you are all well. Yes I suppose the exhibition would naturally upset things for a while. It was a success, was it? I suppose everybody in B'water is making it their especial business to discuss Jessies' taking part in the horse parade. I don't think, myself, that she should have done it.

This evening two of the girls, who room together, held a "reception" in the drawing room at 9 o'clock. They came around to all the rooms just before dinner, knocked and solemnly handed in a little written invitation to attend. We all did so and had great fun. The girls have a chaffing dish which they brought down into the parlour, and made candy in it. Then we had sandwiches and olives and brown bread for the eats. We sang a lot of the college songs, and played intellectual games such as "Winkim" and "Blind Mans Buff." There is one "girl" here, a Miss McGrath, who is about 35 years old I guess. She taught school for ages and ages. She is a Roman Catholic. You should have seen her flying around. I guess she never had such fun before.

The girls are doing great work now, "boosting" the Athletic Club. We are going to have a class every week in the city Y.W.C.A. building. We have no gym. in the college you know. I am the Athletic executive from our class, and wont we make things hum! I'm awfully glad I have my gym. suit all made, lots of the girls have to bustle and get them now.

My roommate is too funny for anything. She is quite verdant. She said, "Oh my, do you really play in those pants thing!" (meaning bloomers). "Why I should think it would be awful." She is most woefully thin, and has had a cold in her nose ever since she came here. The other night, she heard the girls talking, and asked them "what does it mean, to have a *crush* on anyone." Oh My! She is one of the main stays of the church at home.

But then she's quite flexible and so makes a very satisfactory roommate.

On Monday evening if you please, Brent Sabean and his cousin, Jean Sabean's brother, called to see me. The girls were all much interested!

Forrest Hall, Halifax
[November 1915]

How have things been going this week? I have had a busy time as usual. We have been making Xmas things to send over to the Dal. boys at the front and in England. We each made a box of fudge and embroidered the initials of each one on a handkerchief (Khaki). Nita and I used up 5 lbs. of sugar. I managed to slip in a box for Gordon too. I had to send it to his old address. Hope he will get it. We were able to send all these things for nothing — the government is sending out a special Xmas ship.

The '64th' is in town now. They are a fine looking body of men. They are stationed down at No. 2 pier. The 85th are getting their new uniforms. They have little caps with a wing at the side ... and Tipperary tails.

I have been thinking over money matters, and I believe that if you don't mind we had better not get any more stock just now, but keep the money on hand — especially if I come down home quite often, and that will cost quite a bit.

I would rather have a little extra money this year anyway, and wait to invest until I get earning again. Then we will be rich!

Sir Charles Tupper's funeral* is to take place next Tuesday — full regimental honors etc. The service is to take place from St. Pauls. I hope we have a holiday. I should like to go see all the soldiers march.

Our gowns are here now, and we are to appear out in them next week. Won't we be something grand? We shall soon be getting our pictures taken, in our gowns and graduating hoods. Is Jim in uniform yet?

Forest Hall.
Sunday.[1916]

On Weds. afternoon I was summoned into "Stan's" sanction and told that the enlisting authorities in B'water wanted to know if the college would grant my degree now, with exams, so that I could take the school at once. Stan. said that it was just up to me, the college wld. give my degree now, if I wanted to accept the

---

* Sir Charles Tupper, Nova Scotia's pre-eminent "Father of Confederation" and briefly Prime Minister of Canada in 1896, died in November 1915 at the age of 94.

position — but of course I could not have "distinction." Well I turned it down decisively. Peg had the same offer, and did likewise! Queer isn't it? They are just playing us against each other! I wouldn't give up these last few weeks of college for anything — especially convocation day, if I "make good."

If I don't do well on these exams., I think I'll cut my neck off!

187 S. Park St.
Halifax.[1916]

... Jim didn't phone last night. It was just as well, for I couldn't give him any marks. All we know is that we are going to graduate. The list came out yesterday. We shall not know anything about "distinction" etc. till Weds. or Thursday. I am dreadfully afraid when I think of it for I fear I did not do very well. Oh well its a sure thing now that I graduate, that's one good thing anyway, isn't it? ...

This is the last night we really have in old Forrest Hall. Tomorrow Miss Wamers, the cook and the house-maid all leave, and we six girls then rent our rooms from the woman who is taking charge for the summer. We will get our own breakfasts on our alcohol lamps, and go out to lunch and dinner. We all have so many engagements that will be no difficulty.

On Weds. night we have 'class-day' — that is, the valedictory address is given and the class prophecy etc. is read. Then on Thursday comes the grand culmination point in our career. After we are 'knighted' we all go down to Pres. MacKenzie's to afternoon tea, so you see I will not be able to see an awful lot of anyone if they do come up.

I don't know just when I will come home — Friday or Saturday I suppose. How is papa? You haven't told me lately, and how is Emmie's reading getting on, and what do you want me to get before I come home? Oh by the way you will think me terribly extravagant, but we had to pay $5.00 for our 'sheepskin' and $4.00 for a class pin and so many other things beside board etc. — not to mention travelling expenses that I cannot make out without some more money. I know papa will be glad to send me some if he has his yet, if not can't Jim help me out. I must get a new hat, and shoes. I do want to look decent.

Write *soon*, Bessie.

$15.00 will do, but — send G's cheque please. This will be last to spend on my college career!

187 S. Park St.
Tuesday noon.[1916]
I am the happiest girl in ten kingdoms. I have got *Great Distinction* and the *Graduation prize*! One of the professors just phoned. Miss Fraser has great distinction too, and so has another of our girls — and just think, I have the prize! I'm scared every minute I'll wake up and find it isn't true. Ask papa what he thinks of me now!

Now, to come to earth, Mrs. Creed asks me to tell Jim to go over and stay with them. If Aunt B. and Jim come up Thursday morning they had better come right here to the house and if I'm not in, wait till I come — I may have to go out to college, but I'll be in as soon as possible. Then I can give them their tickets and put Jim en route for Mrs. Creeds. Mrs. C. will be coming out in the afternoon to the "big performance" and Jim can come with her. Aunt B. can arrange what to do at the same time. Jim *must* come now.

I got papa's mayflowers this morning also your $15.00. Thanks for the money. Tell papa the flowers are beauties — the loveliest I ever saw.

I am working on my Graduation dress now. I got the material yesterday — 'Crepe do Chene' (is that spelled right?)

Isn't this glorious? I can 'die happy' now!

Hooray Bessie

Halifax. Weds. Evening
[1918]
... Here I am at the V.G.* & haven't had a minute to write before.

When the train got in last night I went into the telephone booth to phone Mrs. Bligh & couldn't get her. When I stepped outside I met conductor Allan, who said that a lady had been madly hunting for me. Well I pursued her to her lair, about to mount a streetcar, to report my "falling away", and found it was

---

*   Victoria General Hospital

Miss Sweet the V.A.D. secretary here. She hailed me with joy — took me down & 'fed' me at the Tally-Ho and then up to the office where behold you she fitted me like the lilies of the field, in uniform. I have a thick grey coat, (a beauty) and two hats and a lot of nursing clothes, aprons etc. You should see me in my cap! Wow!

Then after that (10.30) we came right up to the V.G. where my room was waiting, and so I slept here. At 6 this a.m. the rising bell rang, breakfast at 6.30. Report for duty 1/4 to 7 — how's that Emmie, for a time-table? From then to 1/4 to 1, steady, we worked, then lunched, and right back again till now. I'm lucky — off at 6 tonight, I am in the children's ward, and like it. I don't find the work hard. The kids are cute, but you'd laugh to see me taking temperatures & looking wise. It will be dandy experience for me. The nurse I am under is particularly nice ....

Later.

... You would have laughed to see me getting into my uniform this morning. One of the V.A.D.'s (there are 5 others — one an older woman, knows Myrtle Morgan well) kindly came in & helped me with the mysterious cap etc. We wear a grey dress, white apron with bib, stiff linen collar, stiff cuffs, white belt, *and* the cap, mecca of my existence! Wait till I come home! I do hope they will let me take the rig down with me, altho when you go over-seas, you get an entire new fit-out, boots and all. I am going to definitely tell them I *must* be home for Thanksgiving, so we will plan on that, if not before. As my services are perfectly voluntary I have the privilege of leaving when I like. But really this is dandy experience for me, and will make things even so much easier for me if I ever do get over. It will be great knowing something of hospital life, and I'll come home quite content to rest on my oars until my call comes.

I wish I could send a picture of myself in all my "glory." As it is I guess you'll have to wait till I 'burst' on you. I feel terribly complacent, & really think the outfit quite becoming especially under conditions such that the 'ruby' bane of my life is not distressingly prominent ....

Sunday, A.M.

At present I am engaged in watch of 11 young reptiles. I get them quiet every now & then & will try to write a letter in between their howls. They are about 2 or 3 years old, and some are really quite cute …. Most of them are foundlings for adoption. They all call me "mama" now! Wherever they learned the word at all is a wonder. It must come by intuition. There is one kid here who when he howls has a mouth as big as the "froghole," and he opens that cavity and bellows "ma-a-a-a-a-ma." Oh I feel quite flattered! Well I've been interrupted at least a dozen times since beginning to write this, so never mind if my epistle is somewhat disjointed.

Let me see, when did I write last? I have been out every night since I came up. On Friday evening the other "V.A.D." who is here — Miss Brownell, — and I were invited by Mrs. Bligh among a lot of other V.A.D.'s to a dance aboard the Man of War "Alsatian" which has just come into Port. We were delighted, of course, but had no dresses to wear. The other nurses were much interested, however, and came to the rescue nobly, lending us each a pretty dress. Mine was brown with a lovely lot of fluffy stuff around it, and an old rose girdle & collar. They all said we looked nice. The crowd met at the corner of Barrington & Inglis, & an escort arrived from the "Alsatian" for us. The boat was down at the new Terminals. They had everything trimmed up nicely — the place where we danced was all hung with flags. They had a platform where in the intervals of the programme, special performers would sing. This platform was carpeted with a German flag — thus very appropriately the performers stood on it, & wiped their feet on it.

We went home shortly after 12 — Miss Brownell who is 5 ft. 2" had a great tall officer and I had a little short one to escort us home.

Thru the evening I had met one of the engineers and so we were accordingly shown over the whole boat — way down into the engine rooms, and where they make ice for their provisions & the electric light plant. Last evening one of the nurses here — Miss Robb — and I went down town, & were at the 'Tally Ho' having an ice cream, when who should arrive at the very next table but two naval officers — one of them my engineer. Of course then they walked home with us and as the boat is going out tomorrow they think I have permission to go off duty for a while this afternoon, to go for the inevitable English walk with him. All the other nurses are doing the best they can to fan things along because they scent invitations for parties to dine etc. on board.

When I was down town last night I went to get a tube of tooth paste and found to my immense satisfaction that being in uniform, as a 'V.A.D.' I got 20% disct. Isn't that great? I see where I do all my shopping after this in uniform ....

I am going to have a change in my work now. I go on night duty tonight, to help out Mrs. Falcons. Things are getting much better here now, and she & I have rigged up a little plan (quite between ourselves) as to how we may have alternate naps — the other one remaining on guard ....

Halifax, Sunday.
[1918]
... Well today is Sunday and I have been on night duty for nearly a week. Tonight is last however. The little nurse I've been on with is English and perfectly dandy. She is just my age. Her parents live in London and they are related to Sir somebody or other. She was only married a few weeks when her husband went overseas. She intends going to England to visit her people as soon as the embargo on passengers is lifted, and we are laying great plans for when I *go overseas*!

For awhile her people used to live in the house that Nelson used to own. She has invited me to visit her in London! What do you know. One of her brothers was killed at Ypres, one is in the Flying Corps and she has first cousins, one with a shattered arm, one shell shocked, and one blinded.

I am certainly awfully glad I met her. She studied art for two years, knows French, and is awfully nice.

We V.A.D.'s here had a pleasant surprise the other day. The committee of the Infants Home presented us each with gold brooches set with pearls, and a card of appreciation for our services. I'll bring it home with me of course. It is very delicate and pretty. I know you will like it. I am certainly pleased ....

Weds. Evening
[1918]
Just a line in a big hurry. I'm sorry but I won't be down Thurs. I sent a little box tonight to partially compensate. Hope you receive it all O.K.

Now as to why I can't come — first of all let me relieve your apprehensions by announcing something which will be a great relief to you & a terrible disappointment to me — there is no chance of going overseas now. Orders came last night to that effect. Heavens I'm sorry, but to "continue on" — there is to be a Hospital ship in on Friday also a troop ship & Mum! there is need of nurses & "V.A.D.'s" to take charge of the train load for the west — right out to the coast! Mum just imagine! But *keep this dark* till you hear from me again. Remember it's not to be known.

Of course, mum, remember its only a *chance*, but anyway there it is, and "oh boy"! we have our names down for the first choice. We will probably know by Friday. We would go out, stay a few days, & come back. My word!

I shall certainly let you know. In that case of course I'd be away for Xmas, but would be home right afterwards, and my what a "blow-in" we'll have to celebrate. Imagine a trip like that Mum! And drawing money for it!

But there I must not debate on it too much. Perhaps it will come to nothing this time. In that case I'll be home for a day or so anyway. There is a possibility of course that Jim *might* come home on these ships, but tell Em to keep her hair on anyway! He may not come till June.

I'm not going west till the next load comes over.
Halifax, Sunday.
[1918]
Well, what do you think of the world now? I suppose you know the "glad tidings of great joy." I was called to the phone yester-

day afternoon and heard a bass voice announce itself as *Jim*! my word!

He had intended to descend upon Bridgewater unannounced, but relented & so found out about me being here. Wasn't it good! Now they are giving a Xmas party here at the house for the "V.A.D.'s" on Monday night & would feel hurt if I didn't stay, so I am going to get Jim to come to it and then I shouldn't wonder if there might be some arrivals in B'water on Tuesday morning! In other words, we are coming home together then! Say, isn't it like a book? So opportune too — just the day before Xmas! Heaven's I can scarcely believe it. Jim looks dandy. Is not lame at all, and buttons up his eyes when he laughs, same as ever. He is about 6 ft. 2 ins. I should think. And his kilts! — Wow!

Now Em, keep your hair on! Look here people, we must plan things. Now listen we want everything to look nice in the house, for Jim. Have clean napkins & a nice fresh tablecloth. Sweep upstairs, and clean particularly his room (the spare room). Dust it and get some green stuff in a vase for his bureau, also clean all the rooms, *mine too*, and mum you dust your own, and have your big new mat down. Clean the bathroom Em, so it shines — tub & seat & shelf & door & everything. Then downstairs see that all the stoves are shining — particularly the base burner, & sitting room stove. Take the sitting room carpet out on the line & clean up thoroughly, and take *all* the newspapers, except Monday's Chronicle off the table, and also take them out of the wall pocket so it doesn't look ugly. Put the Chronicles on that pile in the back room, and mum you sew the Family Heralds, Monday night, and put them upstairs on the book case in the hall. Put the leaves of the table down and have some nice apples out on a plate, and some green stuff in a vase.

Clean up all the pictures on the mantel piece etc. Em, you clean up the parlor, & Mum, you dust it — now carefully, *please*. Put Silver centerpiece out on the little table. On Tuesday morning get up a good heat in the baseburner, & then open the doors right through the two rooms. You had better sweep upstairs Monday afternoon and finish my room & Jims. Then Tues. A.M. get up early fix up your room Em, and yours, Mum, and clean the bathroom, then when breakfast is out of the way clean the sitting room & parlor altho, it would be a good plan to clean the sitting room carpet & floor Monday afternoon after you've swept upstairs. Scrub up the kitchen & dining room then too. Then all you need to do to them on Tuesday is dust a bit. Mum, clean the closets!

Now about dinner. I'll see to cooking it on Xmas day. Can't you get some sort of a "biped"? Surely we can kill the fatted calf this once! Get a goose or a turkey or something! Don't bother much about the Tuesday dinner. Some nice steak or something with lots of gravy, turnips, etc. Then please be dressed up nicely — you & Em, Mum! I guess that's all. Now Em do your darndest! And Mum, its up to you! ....

Sunday Evening
[1919]

I am working up at Camp Hill* now. Was called there on Thursday. But I don't think we will be there permanently as yet. For the first few days we were in the diet kitchen, now we are in the dining room helping to wait on the crippled boys. Those who are able to, get their own trays & load them up with the meals at a counter. There are hundreds of them in a long line waiting for their turn, at every meal. They have it arranged so that first each one gets a bowl of soup, he moves on a step or two & receives a helping of meat, vegetable etc., next he gets the dessert, finally the tea & carries off his tray to a table where he "sets" & eats. The cripples of course can't stand in line, so we take their things to them.

202 Tower Rd, Halifax.
[1919]

Well to begin with your questions —

(1) Did I get the $20 Bill? Yes. Perfectly O.K. and disappeared the way of "all flesh" now!

(2) Can Aunt A. have my coat? Now just a minute! If I were quite sure I'd be "in the soldiers" indefinitely it would be quite alright, but we had a "fight" about Camp Hill the other day, at

---

* Camp Hill was a convalescent hospital built in 1917 to take care of veteran casualties of the First World War.

least we V.A.D.'s got on our dignity about our position there, and walked out until they make it better for us ....

Now about the Camp Hill matter. You see its this way. Mrs. Bligh thought we ought to be willing to do any old sort of work there. Well we didn't see it that way. We had not been doing any nursing at all, so we told them they'd better hire maids and *pay* them! Then we quit. Well now we hear rumors that we are to be requested to come back for the proper work. All right. We'll do it ....

EPILOGUE: BESSIE HALL

Bessie satisfied her wanderlust by taking a teaching post in Tripola, Alberta, in the fall of 1919. In the following year she enrolled at the University ot Toronto, receiving her M.A. in 1921. She continued her academic career at Bryn Mawr which awarded her a PhD in 1929. Her doctoral dissertation was an analysis of mothers' pensions,* a controversial policy much advocated by reformers in the 1920s, and one of particular interest to a young woman trapped by the financial constraints of her own family circumstances. Although Dr. Hall planned to work in Canada she found opportunities in the United States much more lucrative. She pursued her social work career south of the Canadian border, and returned to Bridgewater for her summer vacations until her death in 1969.

---

* Bessie Louisa Hall, "Mother's Assistance in Philadelphia: Actual and Potential Costs," PhD, Bryn Mawr, 1929.

ELLA MURIEL LISCOMBE 1902-1969

Ella Muriel Liscombe, known to her family and friends as Ellie, was born in Sydney, Cape Breton, 26 July 1902. A prolific recorder of day-to-day events, Ellie kept a diary from the age of thirteen until she was thirty-six. By 1935, the year from which this extract is taken, work in the Bank of Montreal had replaced school as the focus of her daily routine and the spirited sense of humour typical of the earlier diaries had given way to witty sarcasm. But little else had changed in Ellie's life. She still lived with her mother and sister Ollie and her private life continued to resemble that of her adolescent years when she was preoccupied by books, movies and the latest fashions. Cats — Tom and Trailer — Grace, the hired help, and a friend, Doris, round out Ellie's domestic scene in 1935.

Unlike Rebecca Ells who reckoned time by the sun and seasons, Ellie Liscombe measured labour according to the hands of a clock.* Even weekends were a time for recuperation for work the following week, rather than a period of creative activity. However, in small ways, women brought their traditional sense of timing to the workplace. On April 16, when women in the domestic sphere were engaged in spring housecleaning, Ellie comments: "Great housecleaning going on in the office. Drawers ransacked with great shaking of head on the part of Davidson. Things will be more satisfactory when it is finished." Ellie remembered the boss's birthday because it was the same

---

* Graham Lowe, "Women, Work and the Office: The Feminization of Clerical Occupations in Canada, 1901-1931," *Canadian Journal of Sociology*, Vol.5 (1980), pp.361-81

day as her own. He did not return the courtesy. Industrial time and family time, for him, belonged to strictly separate spheres.

Ellie particularly resented the lack of recognition accorded to women's work. After receiving a paltry raise of $25.00 she noted ruefully that "they seem to expect the women to work harder than the men." Instead of acting to change her absurd working conditions, she "became brave and proceeded to have her desk moved." A retreat into domestic routine offered the only defiance she could muster against discrimination on the job. At times Ellie was capable of perceiving her oppression and articulating her anger — at least in her diary. Yet she did not seek the solace and support of her female colleagues. Perhaps she recognized that in the paid work world it was male approval that was valued and must be sought. At other times she turned the anger inward and blamed herself for "getting nowhere." She reasoned, "The fault may be all my own at that. I brood so over little things. How I wish I knew what to do with myself to make me happier. Ollie is in the same box. The only thing to be thankful for is that we have jobs." Ellie's response was not untypical. Conditions in the 1930s forced many people to become fatalistic about their lives and security conscious about their work.[*]

Movies and novels helped Ellie to escape her real world. Whereas novels taught the new middle class of the late eighteenth and nineteenth century appropriate forms of behaviour, movies and the radio now supplement the print medium. The contradiction between the myths of the movies and the reality of her working class status was difficult for Ellie to reconcile. Part of the attraction of the movies was that the women in them, whether they were 'socialites' or 'career girls,' usually wore glamorous clothes and were displayed in exciting settings.[**] Ellie attended fashion shows, had her hair 'done,' and dreamed of trips to exotic places. Yet, in contrast to the movies, her life seemed neither glamorous nor romantic.

[*]   Veronica Strong-Boag, *The New Day Recalled:Lives of Girls and Women in English Canada, 1919-1939* (Toronto, 1988).

[**]   Molly Haskell, *From Reverence to Rape: The Treatment of Women in the Movies* (New York, 1974).

ELLA LISCOMBE DIARY
1935*

Thursday, 3 Jan. 1935
A very disgruntled, rather unhappy morning. Felt discouraged
and peeved. Some little thing that Basil said upset me for the entire day. It's the little things that take the toll. I really seem to be
getting nowhere at the Bank of Montreal though and if I try to
do my work well and speedily nobody seems to notice. Pride!
Pride! Why should I worry whether anybody notices as long as
my work is done to my own satisfaction. But that's just the
trouble. I really have no fondness at heart for my work and it
has become merely a matter of routine day after day. But when
I think of all the good things I do enjoy come from that self-same
Bank I try not to think of it as tedious. Eric is doing much better
lately — as far as his work is concerned. And he is much more
helpful. Although at times he is silly and spoiled I like him and
it would be a dreary place without him. Doris was in to see me
today. She is like a stranger to me now. I can understand now
what she sees in Smitty, she feels sorry for him & he seems a
lonely sort. I wonder if there is anything in the saying that "Pity
is akin to love." I have started taking Russian Mineral Oil. I hope
it will lubricate my joints as well as my insides. It is not hard to
take, like swallowing a bubble ....

Friday, 4 Jan. 1935
The mineral oil is alright at night but I gagged over it this morning. Just a state of mind as Mrs. Moore says. I have disliked Basil
intensely the last two days and feel that I can never like him
again. How I wish I could get another job or even do something
noteworthy to see his eyes stick out. Miss McDermott says we
do more harm in our thoughts than in our actions so I must try
and dispel my gloomy thoughts. One more fling before I stop.
Fourth of the month and all did not keep him from presenting
me with sundry St. George's church statements and it took me
the best part of the morning finishing them. Now I am going to

* Beaton Institute, University College of Cape Breton.

stop. Am glad tomorrow is Saturday. Ollie and I are sitting in front of the grate fire and mamma is at the table reading ....

Saturday, 5 Jan. 1935

Thought I would be writing more cheerfully tonight but I felt so discouraged when I left the Bank of Montreal this afternoon I felt as though I never wanted to see the place again. Davidson, who started out so nice is just as big a bully as the rest of them and I only wish I had a tongue in my head so I could rage out at them even if I felt sorry for it afterwards. The fault may be all my own at that. I brood so over little things. How I wish I knew what to do with myself to make me happier. Ollie is in the same box. The only thing to be thankful for is that we have jobs. Think I will stay in bed all day tomorrow as I don't have to go to Sunday School as far as I know. I think today was the coldest day this winter and not very cold at that. Came home from work at two thirty and found a letter from Gertrude. She does not sound very happy and says it is bad enough not to be the mistress of your own home but to have a lack of spending money is worse. She even says she would like to be back in the Bank again. I'd like to write and tell her she can have my job if she wants it ....

Saturday, 12 Jan. 1935

Morning pleasant. Not much like last Saturday. Out at about one-thirty which was more pleasant. Mamma had goose for dinner a thing she has been threatening for a long time. It tasted good but not so good as turkey — stronger meat. Mamma was tired after her morning's work so departed for bed — but not to sleep — to read the Geographic about the Grand Canyon. I departed to bed too for the purpose of getting ahead with my trip* but I fell asleep and did not wake up until six. Tom reclined at my feet. Mary called up and asked me to go for a walk but I declined. Then Aunt Clara called and wanted us to go up there and read — which we did. Now Ollie and I are home again. She is sitting on the Chesterfield reading a "Harper's Bazaar" which Grace brought in for Mamma's edification. Grace worked at her mat all evening. She and Ollie took the bed out of the back room and put it in Grace's as Ollie thought the cot was too small for

* Ellie is writing an account of her trip to New York in 1934.

such a big girl to sleep on …. Ollie was out with Cyril and Grace tonight for a wonderful drive away out King's Road as far as Stewart MacDonald's bungalow — rather wonderful for the twelfth of January. There is no snow on the ground and frogs and caterpillars have been reported by various parties. There is a lot of sickness however, and measles are very prevalent. Mary called for me at eight o'clock and we went first to the Groceteria to buy peas. Aunt Clara and Aunt Nettie have a lovely new radio — a Stewart-Warner — short and long wave. They were listening to a Soconyland Sketch when we arrived and were enjoying it hugely. They are wonderful women — they get such a kick out of the little things of life — a lesson to us all. Poor Doris had the last of her teeth out. I called up and her father said she felt none too good. Read Les Miserables and worked on Mary's sampler. Aunt Clara upset the kettle of boiling water all over the fender. We had crackers and cheese and marmalade and tea and chocolate brownies. Mamma cross because we are not coming to bed. Must go.

Tuesday, 15 Jan. 1935
… When I awoke the wind was still howling and snow still drifting down the hill. Mamma did not think it was fit for us to go to work but the Bank of Montreal must go on so I pulled on my over-stockings and started off. I walked out on the middle of the street where the going was not so bad and wind in my back. I couldn't beat Miss Rigby because she was there when I arrived. Eric said he left his window open last night and the cold cream was frozen on his face …. Doris in to see me. I think her new teeth will look very nice but she doesn't look very well herself. No wonder after that ordeal. Although a quiet day as far as customers were concerned it was a busy day for me and I did not cover my typewriter until nearly six. I went home for my dinner but Miss Rigby and Miss McDermott ate their lunch in the upper room — both nearly frozen to death.

Wednesday, 16 Jan. 1935
Mamma is sleeping in my bed tonight and I am sleeping in hers. With a great deal of diplomacy I got her in there claiming that I wanted to sleep in her bed — it was so comfortable. Mamma

had the minister in to see her this afternoon. He told her that she must be the most popular woman around as everybody seemed to be inquiring about her. That's what comes of being good and kind to everybody. Another busy day at the office. When are they going to stop? Eric is to go on the Ledger for the next three weeks. He is rather tickled than otherwise and says if people learn by mistakes he will certainly learn a lot. Miss McDermott is quite pleased that he is the one chosen to go on her post. She is good friends with Eric again. Went to the teacher's supper tonight - finnan haddie, potatoes, sauce, doughnuts and cake. Doris was in to see me and said she was going to be there too but she didn't turn up. The suppers are not like they used to be. Ollie stayed to hear Mr. Campbell present the lesson and I stayed with Mrs. J. T. There was a congregational meeting after but Ollie and I did not stay. I felt tired and not much pep so we went to the show for a rest. Went over to Ollie's office to get fixed and then started off. The show was quite interesting. Una Merkel, Stuart Erwin and Jim Parker in, "Have a Heart" and Una Merkel and Charles Ruggels in "Murder in the Private Car" — the latter very exciting ….

Thursday, 17 Jan. 1935
… Home all evening. Had the radio going for awhile but later on it became punk (I must try and cultivate new words). Wanted to listen to Rudy Vallee's program but had to turn it off. Wasted the whole evening. Did not even work on my trip. All my good resolutions go for naught. Ollie knitted for awhile on her mauve skirt. Mamma read "So Red the Rose." Eric excited about his coming job but I think is still hoping there is something wrong with him for he went to Dr. Roy who gave him a tonic. Miss Rigby does not think he takes enough exercise. Eric told Miss McDermott she wouldn't know her own books when she came back. The boss wrote away today for a new toilet for the women members of the staff as the present arrangements were rather objectionable separated as they were by a thin partition — not altogether tight. Brought an apple to eat but it is getting late so don't think I will eat it. Grace made a very nice butterscotch pie for supper — her crust is lovely ….

Friday, 18 Jan. 1935

Anybody reading this journal over would think I was a very melancholy person. I felt very gloomy this afternoon — feeling sorry for myself as usual. Thought I would be out early but not so, five twenty still saw me at my post doing V. O. N. work. I felt rather peeved as I wanted to go up town and buy a smock. I went at five thirty but not a smock to be had although I tried McCurdy's, Crowell's, Epstein's and Eaton's. What I wanted was a plain three quarter smock with a bow at the neck. Miss O'Callaghan showed me two, a flowered one and a dotted one but the flowered one made me look too broad and I did not like the plain one. Missed my walk today — must try to make up for it .... Mr. Stead astonished me today by telling me I figured in Dun's report — transfer of property. Mamma has put Mills house in my name in order to get the tax exemption. I can't tell why "B" spoke to me about it — was it interest or an accusation? I won't get a raise now if he thinks I am the owner of property. Tomorrow is Miss McDermott's last day for three weeks. Eric is still excited. Hope he pulls through allright. Wonder who will do the Junior's work? Smitty, I suppose.

Sunday, 20 Jan. 1935

Really nothing to write about as I stayed in bed nearly all day. It was a beautiful day, mild and sunny, and Mary called up in the afternoon but I did not arise. Got up and had my breakfast though, hearty and leisurely. Ollie went out in the afternoon. Only three in my class according to Doris — probably all sick with measles as the epidemic still rages. Ruth Davy has them now. Another blue day for me. Always blue on Sundays, I don't know why it is unless I just naturally slump after a busy week. A little disappointed I can't get a winter coat but others have to do without more and the taxes have to be attended to. Ollie can't do everything. I think it would be cheaper to board somewhere but that is not like having your own home and we are still comfortable and warm ....

Wednesday, 23 Jan. 1935

Eric very snooty today and we did not get along very well. I suppose he was nervous because it happened to be balance day. Mr.

Stead told me the plumbers were going to start work on the up-stairs room so as Miss Rigby says "We will be more comfortable." It will be nice to be able to wash your face and hands at noon time before you go home to [lunch] — make you feel as though you have more time home. The boss wrote for another typewriter for me and I hope it will turn out "O.K." Out of work at a quarter to five so went home for awhile before the teacher's supper ....

Thursday, 24 Jan. 1935
Half raining and freezing and as slippery as glass. Could have taken a header when I started out for work so I went back to warn Ollie. Turned soft later and the rain came down in earnest. Had a nasty headache and was glad to get out comparatively early. Lay down on the Chesterfield and went to sleep but when I awoke head ache was not much better and I could not eat very much supper — a nice salad that Ollie made — celery and pineapple. Grace was in to supper and went to the show with us after. Myrtle called up and wanted to come with us too. It was teeming rain and a bad night to start out afoot but I was anxious to see "Anne of Green Gables" as it was here Christmas Eve before and we could not go on that account. I was disappointed in "Anne"; it was certainly not the Anne of "Anne of Green Gables" although she was rather sweet but Gilbert and Diana were both washouts. Marilla was good and Matthew. However we enjoyed it. There was an awfully good Charlie Chan picture also. Cast seemed to be nearly all English and the girl that took the part of Pamela was rather sweet. A bowling picture ended the program .... Grace got her foot wet when it broke through at the Nepean St. crossing. Ollie and Grace never seem to walk to-gether — Grace is generally flying on ahead. They have started to work on our throne room. The plumbers have been there all day, hammering and blowing. Smitty said he thought they must be tearing down the vault. I am rather anxious to get into our new quarters but we will soon get used to it like everything else ....

Saturday, 26 Jan. 1935
Pretty cold when I started out but it did not last long. Met

Dorothy at the Bank door. She had a nice time at dancing class. They are sending me another rebuilt typewriter. Wouldn't you think they would send a new one? I am a little disappointed but will be glad of the change anyway .... No mail today so we were out at one-thirty. Didn't mind a bit. I hate Saturdays. Ollie had a cleaning fit so she went through the bureau drawers and tidied tables etc. I went down to Florrie's with some magazines. When I came home I got some thumb tacks and pinned a big map on the wall so I could examine it at leisure. I always got mixed up in the Bahamas and Cuba and Porto Rico and Jamaica and Barbados so now I have it all in a "Shell-hole" as Mrs. Ace would say. It is a very pretty map — came with mamma's Geographic. Had a little sleep and then arose and took a bath. Ollie noticed my arms were very dirty. I think the dirt seeps through the meshes in my red dress. The office is very dusty especially with the plumbing work still going on. I think the work is nearly over. I ran upstairs to peek and found that they had installed the "Aristocrat" seat. I don't think Miss Rigby would look for anything ....

Sunday, 27 Jan. 1935
After a nice breakfast of bacon and eggs I went to church with Mary and her mother. Mary was surprised to see me as I have not called for her the last two Sundays. A. R. Grant the temperance man spoke. He was quite interesting and I can see his viewpoint that liquor is a terrible thing after seeing John Scott crippling out of the Post Office and climb into a taxi to take him home. Walked home with Aunt Clara and Mary. She reminded me of the verses I promised to make about Pepsodent toothpaste in order to win $1,000 cash. Ridiculous but I promised Aunt Nettie I'd do it. Imagine me winning anything with eight million people to compete with in the city of New York alone. Ollie went to Sunday School. I did not have to go. Slept and read ....

Thursday, 31 Jan. 1935
Still slippery and still no typewriter. Am getting tired of pounding on the old red one. Eric had the pass books ready nice and early so I was able to start right in on them after work. Awfully cold in the office — everybody going around rubbing their

hands and Miss Rigby hopping over to hug the radiator every few minutes. Worked until six and then came home for my supper. Started back again about seven meeting Miss Rigby on the way. She was cold and miserable and hates the slippery walking. Was glad I went home to get warm. It is not the frost either — just a rawness. It did not seem so cold in the bank last winter. Eric balanced first shot so that worry is off his mind. Floyd did not come back and Davidson was peeved — they don't love each other. The boys are always making fun of Davidson anyway but I don't mind him as much as I did Wells. I bet Wells will be here to relieve Mr. Stead when he goes on his holidays — I hope not in a way and yet it would be almost better than having a perfect stranger. Davidson won't like it anyway. He thinks he is quite capable of running the Bank. Worked until nine helped out by Smitty. He is a new boy and is willing to help you out — something like Nausse. Smith's cheques were mountainous ....

Friday, 1 Feb. 1935
... Maitland varnished the new water closet today so we will no longer think we are in the country. I could almost imagine spiders at times. It is a lovely comfortable room to have. The sun streams in there in the morning — I almost wish I could move my typewriter upstairs. Lay down and went to sleep after work. The Chesterfield is still a comfort. Trailer is on the way again. What will we do with the little strangers? Am still working on Mary's sampler. Am going to wash my hair tomorrow afternoon. Want to finish reading about the Azores. Eric asked me today what the word debutante means and I tried to explain to him as best I could ....

Tuesday, 5 Feb. 1935
Has turned cold again. Snowed a little last night but it is still very slippery. A very, very slack day in the office. Miss McDermott's holidays are slipping away very fast. It will soon be three weeks. Mamma did not sleep at all last night. The water dripping on the bay window kept her awake so she came and told me to sleep in her bed while she slept in mine. Tom disturbed her too jumping on the window and crying so she got up, let him in and fed him. Ollie and I did not hear her at all. Ollie has

gone down to Bridge Club at Muriel's .... Called up Doris. She is home reading tonight. Got it pretty bad. Mary's eyes are tormenting her again. Too bad she can't get over that muscular trouble. Grace has started another mat. She must miss her friend Helen as she hardly ever goes out now. Must wash my hair. Must write to Miss Kimber, must write to Frances, must write to Gertrude. Must do some more on my New York trip. Mamma is reading about Sir Malcolm Campbell in the paper and is quite indignant.* What is the good of all this speeding? sez she. Aimee Semple MacPherson** is going on a four month missionary tour of the Orient. Dorothy's Aunt Marsh's husband is very sick and has been taken to Montreal. The Bankers Dance is this coming Friday. Ollie wishes I would go. It would be nice to be pretty and vivacious and full of feminine wiles but I never will be. Eric is going and Floyd. I don't know about Smitty. Mrs. Davidson is one of the chaperons. Neil himself will be there with bells on. I don't think the Steads will be going ....

Thursday, 7 Feb. 1935
Mr. Hollyer made a big stir in the office today and I am glad of it. Has moved all his banking business to Montreal. Letters had to be written to Montreal and to Mr. Hollyer and to John Hollyer and to London, England, also countless debit slips. Neil is quite good to help you out and likes to stand and tell you what to put down. The new typewriter will be getting loose — such constant service. It has been a great comfort so far though and does nice looking work and makes a nice black copy. Carbon paper lasts much longer. Eric is very much excited about the dance but more about the clothes he is going to wear than anything else. Bob Shaw is fixing him up with a tuxedo and shirt and Smitty is supplying black silk socks. All this excitement before the dance and I suppose he won't open his mouth about it afterwards. The holiday schedule is being made out. I did not know about it until

---

*	Sir Malcolm Campbell was the first man to go 5 miles a minute in his automobile. In 1935 he was preparing for this historic feat which occurred at Bonneville, 3 September 1935.
**	Aimee Semple McPherson (1890-1944), born near Ingersoll, Ontario, was a Pentecostal preacher who eventually established her own church — the International Church of the Foursquare Gospel. Using theatrical speaking tours and the radio, she became the best known female evangelist of the day.

after work when Davidson asked me when I wanted to take my vacation. I was rather peeved as everybody seemed to have a choice and I had none — except June which I certainly did not want. Makes me mad to think that Eric and Smitty get first choice. Julian was sore too. I told Davidson I did not want holidays at all if I had to take them in June. June is such an awful month in Cape Breton. Was rather sulky all evening about the matter. Davidson himself takes three weeks in August and the boss three weeks in September. I would like to wait a year and take two years in one only it is such a long time to wait. Wish I could take mamma and Ollie to Florida or somewhere. Jamaica looks like a nice restful place viewing it as I do from the bedside.

Friday, 8 Feb. 1935
… I think Davidson was holding back on me as he did not mention October last night. Floyd put his name in for November but would like to change if the hunting season is in October. However the schedule has gone in with Sept. 30 to October 12 as my time. That is better than June anyway. Eric is still all excited about the dance. Talks about it all the time. He is in a gale talking but will be cranky when it is all over. Shaking hands or rather greeting the chaperons is what he dreads the most. He practices an entrance three or four times for my benefit. The boss rather spoiled things drifting back and forth. Floyd and Davidson are going too but Smitty is not. Ollie heard that Smitty is going with one of the waitresses from the Maple Leaf Restaurant. Fully planned to wash my hair today but did not like to for fear I would catch cold. My hair is very dirty and needs cutting. Wish I had some ready money but I am flat broke ….

Thursday, 28 Feb. 1935
… The poor old decrepit Bank of Montreal condescended to give me what she could — a raise of twenty-five dollars a year. Miss Rigby, gratuity $25.00 and Miss McDermott, gratuity $20.00. Julian, raise, $25.00. It made me rather discouraged and I told Davidson there was not much encouragement to do your best — and they seem to expect the women to work harder than the men. Became very brave and started proceedings to have my desk moved. Davidson said he would move the Messenger and

put me in his place. I could hardly wait to have it done. Worked until six and then came back after tea. Finished up about nine and then walked home with Dorothy and Miss Rigby. Smitty very nice to work with.

Tuesday, 5 March 1935
Miss Rigby is not feeling well and plans to get leave of absence. She is going to see Dr. Roy tonight about it. Her eyes look very bad. Afraid she is paying up for being so faithful to the Bank for so many years. Very, very busy today. A lot of special debts letters for Head Office. Ollie still on the sick list. When she takes a cold, she takes a cold. In the evening Mary and I went to Vivian King's dance recital. It was very good and must have taken a lot of work, training those little children. Some of them were sadly out of step but you can't expect all children to be Shirley Temples ....

Wednesday, 6 March 1935
Ollie planned to go to work today but did not. Her cold is not cured yet. Teachers' supper night but I did not go. It was our turn too. Mamma made chop suey. Grace took it up. The boss asked me if I would mind working late so I thought I would rather go home than rush over to the church. Bought throat ease for Ollie. Miss Rigby applied today for two months sick leave. She looks very miserable. The Boss wrote away for a new Junior. Another young clerk who will soon become a big shot. Felt very tired and fell asleep on the Chesterfield after supper. Knitted for awhile and have my sweater well on the way to being finished. Ollie is getting along great with her skirt ....

Tuesday, 19 March 1935
Finished the Liability List so that is off my mind. Davidson was not at the office today again. Doubted whether I could go to work myself as I had a rather miserable night. Bones seem to ache all over and yet I don't seem to have a cold — only a little cough. Have been lying on the Chesterfield since tea. Mamma is going to read to me a little from Pickwick .... Funny about this ache I have in my back and legs. It hurts to put on my overshoes. Wish I could stay home with an easy conscience but my job is

such that the rest of the staff cannot get along with me. (Sarcasm)
....

Wednesday, 20 March 1935
Condition just the same. Still seem to have rheumatism all over me. Mrs. Stead is sick. I hinted to Mr. Stead to take the afternoon off but he did not take me up although he asked me if I could think of a substitute in case I got sick. Still no sign of Davidson. Stead gave me lots of work and nearing six still found me at my typewriter. Tomorrow brings Filliter the new boy. Wish I could stay in for a week.

Thursday, 21 March 1935
Filliter is a tall dark boy who seems very nice and friendly. I have developed a bad cold in my head but the ache is gone. Walked to work with Minnie MacKenzie who says she thinks she is getting the flu too. Finished up my work in the morning and stayed home in the afternoon. Left all the forms ready for Smith to do my work. Did not finish that Return for which I am sorry. Feel very miserable with my cold. Could not keep from sneezing this morning. Went to bed and stayed there but plan to go out tomorrow afternoon. Ollie and Grace to see Claudette Colbert in "The Gilded Lily" and a day in the lives of the Dionne quintuplets.* She said the babies were sweet and the Claudette picture lovely. Am sorry I missed it.

Friday, 22 March 1935
Spent the day in bed. Cold pretty bad. Thought I'd go out in the afternoon but did not feel like it. Let them get along as best they could — which is the right idea to have. No need to have illusions about your job — always somebody to take your place. Miss McDermott called up and said Filliter was taking my place. A very good typist. Finished "Pickwick Papers" and have started the "Diary of Samuel Pepys" which is too full of Parlia-

---

*   A reference to the Dionne Quintuplets who became a media sensation when they were born in 1934. See Pierre Berton, *The Dionne Years* (Toronto, 1977); Veronica Strong-Boag, "Intruders in the Nursery: Childcare Professionals Reshape the Years One to Five, 1920-1940," in Joy Parr, ed., *Childhood and Family in Canadian History* (Toronto, 1982), pp. 160-221.

ments and high sounding Lords and Ladies to please me. Mamma read for awhile from David Copperfield which I always enjoy. Mamma rather likes Sir Samuel ....

Saturday, 23 March 1935
Still in bed though I feel better. Became hard hearted even about the Saturday rush. Was a little put out with Ollie as she called up the Bank and offered to help them out, even spoke to B. Stead about it — but no harm done. It was nice to be able to eat my dinner at the correct time. Have decided to take Sir Samuel Pepys in easy doses so have started "The Mill on the Floss" which I find very engrossing. Maggie Tulliver is an interesting character. Rather dread the tragic ending but still would not like a happy one. It is not like a Dickens book which rounds out the lives of all the characters and neglects nobody. Got up and came downstairs in the evening. Mamma and I listened to a lovely quartette ....

Monday, 25 March 1935
A good day to start out after my sick spell. Grace went out early and shovelled a path to the road which saved Ollie and me from wallowing. The City is blanketed in snow just like the depths of winter .... We were nearly frozen in the office — hands, feet, noses, etc. Poor Maitland has the flu now and consequently he could not get up to look after the furnace. Every chance we got we'd run and hug a radiator. A little more bearable in the afternoon. Eric is doing collections and seems rather disgruntled. He hates the job. He and Filliter not as friendly as they were the first day. Ollie has finished her skirt and is almost ready to start her sweater.

Tuesday, 16 April 1935
Great housecleaning going on in the office. Drawers ransacked with great shaking of head on the part of Davidson. Things will be more satisfactory when it is finished however. The new cabinet smells nice and woodsy. All the boys were assisting in the campaign — Eric not so good. I heard him ask Floyd which side of the cabinet was the women's. Stayed until six o'clock typing the Liability. Confusion was going on around me but I did not

take much notice of it. Left at six o'clock. Think I will suggest to Davidson that I do the Returns after this as I did the U.S. Funds without a mistake. I don't like doing the Liability but can do it in a shorter time now. No Bridge Club for Ollie on account of its being Holy Week. Still reading "So Red the Rose" and knitting on yellow sweater. Ollie at her mauve sweater.

Thursday, 18 April 1935
With a few alterations my cupboard is put in order. Was glad to have a little time after work to do it. Floyd tells me he is not going back in the cage but is going to take over Miss Rigby's job. Miss Rigby is to go on the Cash Book. Eric will stay on collections and Smitty will stay in the cage. Miss Rigby was back today to type the reports. Am just as glad I don't have to do them - the boys would never leave me alone. Left the office at six. Cold and rather foggy. After tea Ollie and I went up town on a rampage for a hat. Went to Mrs. MacLeod's and settled on a blue hat which is very becoming. After we got home we decided to keep the red hat too as we each can wear it. Went to McCurdy's looking for a slip and then to Dave Epstein's where I managed to get what I wanted. Read Samuel Pepys when I got home. And so to bed — late.

Tuesday, 23 April 1935
Well, the Boss is back — in not too cordial a mood either. He hardly spoke to anybody and did not ask after the state of my health — as I was sick when he went away. Mrs. Stead did not come home. Maitland hinted that she stayed in New York for some kind of treatment. I still think the Boss is shy and selfish like I am ....

Friday, 26 April 1935
Typed the boy's reports. Went upstairs and paid Carrie for taking me to the Wiseman's Show. Ollie home for a change in the evening. She is still busy at her sweater. Called up Gertrude and asked her to go to the show and she said she would be delighted, as her father and mother were going out to play bridge. Emmie Frowde in all evening knitting on a white sweater. Gertrude called for me. She admired my black coat as

did also By and Wilfred whom we met. (I sound like Samuel Pepys). The show was the "Golddiggers of 1935" — not bad, but a sameness to them — Dick Powell and Gloria Stuart. Gertrude came in for awhile after and Ollie served us milk and cookies. Gertrude looks a whole lot better .... Miss Rigby is taking another week off. She is not all better yet.

Thursday, 2 May 1935
The talk now is when to go and see "David Copperfield" which is playing for four nights, starting Wednesday. Ollie and I have decided to take mamma tomorrow night. I am very much excited as I have been looking forward to seeing it for such a long time. Stayed home all evening. Ollie still working on her mauve sweater and I on my red front. Will have to save up for a wedding present for Mary and have to think about giving a little party. Miss Rigby back at work today but in a very bad humour although the boss could hardly wait to get his coat off in order to rush out to greet her. She seems sore at everybody, particularly Eric, Floyd and myself. I feel sorry for her though — it seems as though her job had been taken out from under her nose. Now she will have to do the Junior's work. I hope the boys won't hate me if I stay long in the Bank.

EPILOGUE: ELLA MURIEL LISCOMBE

Ellie eventually left the Bank of Montreal to work as a stenographer for Dominion Steel and Coal Corporation and later was employed by S. H. Stevenson Limited, a local insurance adjuster. She continued to live with her Mamma and Ollie in the same house for the rest of her life. Ella is remembered by her associates as a quiet, reserved person who got along well with people and enjoyed music and walking. She died in Sydney on 23 March 1969, survived by her sister Ollie.

Laura Slauenwhite (right) with a friend.

LAURA KAULBACK SLAUENWHITE 1880-1976

Laura Kaulback, born in 1880, grew up on a small farm in Pine Grove, Lunenburg County. When she was fourteen, her mother became seriously ill and Laura left school to "take over the hard part of the housework." Her mother died in 1900 and Laura continued to keep house for her father and two brothers, Stanley and Wesley, and a younger sister, Florence. In 1904 Laura married Harvey Slauenwhite and they moved to a farm at Falkland Ridge, Annapolis County. They raised two boys, Roy and Douglas. Harvey dealt mostly in timber until the nearby mill at Hastings closed in 1921. With their major source of income gone, the family was forced back on its own meagre farm resources.

The First World War, the post-war depression and industrial centralization had taken its toll on the Nova Scotia economy. In the 1920s, the province again experienced a vast exodus of its people whose farms, forests, fisheries and factories no longer provided a steady income. Only those farms which became large commercial enterprises, like C & M Ells in the Annapolis Valley, could maintain a middle class standard of living. The rocky soil on the South Mountain could not keep the Slauenwhites in the manner to which they had become accustomed. The slow impoverishment of the Slauenwhites was repeated in many families in Nova Scotia in the inter-war years.

In 1925, Harvey sold the livestock and took various seasonal jobs including work on the highways, lumbering and blacksmithing. Roy, Laura's older son, moved to the United States to look for work while Doug, at the age of thirteen, was employed in the same lumber camp as his father. Laura boarded with friends and relatives and, when possible, lived close to where the men were working. When conditions permitted, she returned to her home in Falkland Ridge. Throughout the 1920s, Laura complained of illnesses which were never satisfactorily diagnosed.

In 1930 Harvey died of cancer. Roy returned from the United States, married and began the difficult task of 'keeping' his own family during the Depression years. In 1932 Laura became a proud Grandmother but her new status seemed also to remind her of her advancing years and increasing vulnerability. As the unmarried son, Doug was responsible for his mother's well being but he was unable to find a steady job during the 1930s. Sporadic work in the lumber camps meant that he spent extended periods away from home. Since Laura could not manage the family homestead alone, she had to find new ways of 'keeping' herself. She easily found work as a domestic, a profession that expanded dramatically during the 'dirty thirties.'

Laura's journals written in lined scribblers consist of an overview chronology of her life and more detailed entries for the years 1936 to 1938. These latter diaries she kept as a record of her activities to exchange with her only sister Florence who lived in Sussex, New Brunswick.

The entries here begin with Laura's difficult decision to leave home to work as a housekeeper for Mr. Chesley in the nearby village of New Germany. She tried to put the best face on it — "I'm doing what is best for all of us" — but admitted also to being "a nervous wreck." Despite her busy routine, she confessed to be rather lonely. Her constant companion was the radio where she heard of the abdication of the King Edward VIII. She was moved to tears by the drama of the occasion and identified with Queen Mary: "I pity his mother." When the radio broke down, she missed its company as if it were a person. Here, we begin to see the radio network replace female networks as a source of companionship and community.

Laura eventually moved to the Penney household, where she became not only a housekeeper but also a part-time nurse and companion. Caring for the older generation in the family was difficult for Laura who was also beginning to develop a morbid sense of her own mortality. After one crisis, she commented, "Its got my nerves all gone flewy. I am all ashake again." When Mr. Penney died, Laura provided an elaborate account of the work involved in preparing for the funeral. She was similarly preoccupied with the suicide of a woman in the village who "left a letter but gave no reason except that she was afraid of going insane from the pain in her head." Laura complained about the hard work she had to do but also maintained an active social life in New Germany. She was a member of the Rebecca Lodge and Women's Institute and visited among a circle of friends. There is considerable irony in the fact that Laura's life 'working out' was fuller than it was in her own 'home.'

LAURA SLAUENWHITE DIARY
1936-1938*

Oct. 22. [1936]
Quite fine and warm. I cleaned the front room and hall. In the midst of it Mr Horton Chesley from New Germany came to hire me for a housekeeper — Mrs Penny and Eva Meisner and her sister Mrs Rhyno was with him. I couldn't give him a decided answer. I went down and talked to Stanley also wrote to Doug. Mabel was here a while in the evening. My head is going around in circles as I do not know what to do.

Oct. 26.
Dull and cold and rained in the afternoon. I made pies for Mrs Penny and helped with the work and ironed. Was talking with Mr Chesley and promised him to come with him Thursday. Mr Penny bought the cows. I was down to the Varners in the evening.

Oct. 28.
Warmer but still windy. The snow is still with us. I washed and scrubbed and dyed Doug's sweater and was invited down to Mabels to dinner. Came home and packed my trunk and packed some things away. Ironed this evening. Was alone all evening and it was a hard night as this is a sad move for me. Maybe it will look brighter bye and bye. I'm doing what I think is for the best for all of us.

Oct. 29.
It was dull in the morning. Started to rain about ten and poured all day. Bert K. came up and put on the storm doors and helped me fix up around the building and I was busy getting straightened when Mr Chesley came about nine. Then I had to tear around. Willa came up for the cat. Jean came up and I gave her the spare food I had around. We got away after a while but I was a nervous wreck. I got down about eleven. I helped Gor-

*   Laura Slauenwhite's diary is in the possession of her granddaughter, Margaret Conrad.

don get dinner. He showed me where things were kept and helped me get started. He is a great kid and as handsome as a movie star. I made some drop cookies as they were about eaten out. Had been doing their own cooking for two weeks. Listened to the radio all evening. There was a chicken supper for the Church tonight in the Parish Hall. I didn't go as it was so wet. They made over 30 dollars.

Oct. 31 [Halloween].
Dull and cold with a little sunshine. I made brown bread beans two pies and a cake and cleaned down stairs. Easy cleaning but a large house. Had several callers selling things and some kids. Had a letter from Eileen also one from Florence and her diary. All of which I surely enjoyed very much. Had just started a letter for her. Finished it this evening. Had quite a lot of kids in dressed up in queer outfits. Some I knew and some I didn't. Some of them demanded a lunch of cookies and apples.

Nov. 10.
Dull with some sunshine and a few sprinkles of rain. I washed and baked bread and did the usual work. Mrs Fred Oickle was in a hour or two this afternoon. Went up to the Womans Institute meeting in the evening. It was eleven o'clock when I got home but had a nice time about a dozen or more women there I knew them all met Cora Baker (nee Kaulback) from Maplewood. We had a nice lunch. Snowed when we came home.

Nov. 15.
A rainy Sunday with quite a bad electric storm. Heavy rain and some wind. I had a run up to Mrs Pennys this morning in the car, was home the rest of the day. Read, slept a nap talked and wrote a letter this evening. Also listened in on a Church of England service at seven. Just as if I'd been at the service. Mrs Roy Kaulback and Shirley Ann was in a while.

Nov. 17.
Colder with more snow some sunshine and snowed enough to whiten the ground in the evening. I ironed and mended and did

the usual work. Knit a mitten in the evening. Listened in on a good radio program until ten o'clock.

Nov. 19.
Very cold last night and today. High winds with snow squalls. Thero. down to 10 above zero. Freezing all day. The water pipe froze up in the barn. I was helping heat water all day to thaw it out. No success. I baked molasses cookies, made turnip kraut for dinner and potato & meat patties for supper. Do they eat. Knitting this evening. Had a nice large parcel from Eileen, over boots hat gloves muff and some worn dresses.*

Nov. 22.
Dull but warm today quite muddy. I read a book and was down to Lutheran Church this afternoon and listened in on an Anglican Church service this evening from Halifax. Heard a splendid sermon. Wrote a letter and now its bedtime. The men are both away. Rather lonely.

Nov. 28.
Colder with some snow flurries. Wesleys Birthday I sent him a card. I baked brown bread two pumpkins pies and a marble cake and did the usual work and cleaning in kitchen and pantry. Got a letter from Doug. Made macaroni & tomato for supper at Gordon's request. Flue caught fire as we were eating supper. Quite a commotion for a while. Later I went up to Alvin Wiles with Gordon and spent the evening. Had a lovely visit. Not too many young men would bother to take an old woman along with them when they go to see their girl friend. But he is different from most Boys more kind and thoughtful.

Dec. 10.
Another fine day warmer tonight. I ironed and made my fruit cakes. Got the news over the radio at noon of King Edwards abdication. Too bad I feel so sorry as we thought he would be a

---

*   Eileen as a young girl had lived with Laura in the late 1920s and now worked in Montreal. She sent packages of used clothing to help the financially strapped family.

good king. Did some mending and knit a while and wrote a letter. Lottie Barkhouse was in a while this evening.

Dec. 11.
Raining hard all forenoon and again this evening. But very warm. The ground is all thawed again. I made date cookies and cleaned upstairs this forenoon. Was up to Roys this afternoon a while. We heard the Late King Edwards farewell speech at 6 this evening. It was very touching. I had to cry. He sounded so tired and heart broken. I pity his mother. Heard it again at nine tonight from a record. We get all that is going over the radio and its a great deal.

Dec. 12.
Rained hard all day but quite warm. I made pies, a cake, beans and bread and had roast spare ribs for dinner. Did the usual cleaning in the afternoon. Listened to the radio broadcast of the proclamation of the new King George VI. It was very thrilling as it came right from London and was real clear. Did some knitting and wrote two letters in the evening.

Dec. 20.
Dull but warm and began to rain in the afternoon. Rained until eight o clock with high winds. Gales all night. I was home all day. Addressed ten Christmas Cards and wrote two letters and talked and read. Had a church service in the evening and lots of Christmas music ending up with a spelling Bee from Cincinnati. The radio was good.

Dec. 21.
Dull but cleared later with high winds. I washed and did some cleaning upstairs and then ironed and knit this evening. Am alone with the radio for company. Had a letter from Doug, 3 Xmas cards and a parcel from Eileen.

[During 1937, Laura lived and worked happily at the Chesleys, her radio a constant companion and her journal for sister Florence a regular ritual.]

1938 - Jan. 31.
Last day of January and still quite warm with rain and wind today. Did not wash, mended a pair of pants for the Boss then was fixing myself a wool suit Eileen sent me. Its a job as its to large. Sewing patchwork tonight and played cards with Laura a while. Yesterday was 8 years since Harvey passed away. It had many sad memories for me and it was hard to go to Nathan Conrads funeral in the afternoon. But it was so near. It was a large funeral as the family were all there. The widow and 9 children and lots of grandchildren. Five boys and four girls and all fine looking. The four sons and two son-in-laws were the pall bearers. He was 76 years old and had been sick for years. In the evening Mr Chesley Laura & I went up to United Church.

Feb. 14 Valentines Day.
We had a little snow storm today. But hardly enough yet for sleighing and the men here are needing snow so much to get out their pulpwood and firewood too. But its not very cold. Up in Springfield they had a snowfall of 6 in. last Thursday and down here was rain. Even in Stanburne three miles from here it was snow. Laura and I went for a walk yesterday afternoon about a mile so you see I walk quite a bit now. Was in to see Rhoda and then home for the Sunshine Hour (S[alvation] Army) which is always good (Do they get Halifax over there?) In the evening we went up to Church with Gordon and heard the best sermon I ever heard Mr Ott preach. Then we went in to Mrs Penny a while. Mailed your letter. Mr Penny is still in bed and content to stay there. I'm very much afraid its the beginning of the end for him. And he will surely be missed. Mrs Kent wanted us to come in a while with her and she gave me six lovely red tulips that she had for the table decorations at the Church tea Saturday and later on the Altar at the Church service. They are lovely. Then home and listened to a crazy program of Chase & Sanbornes Coffee. Wesley spoke of it too and wondered if it was right for a Sunday Evening. Its not bad, only funny and makes one laugh as its silly.

Mar. 3. Thursday.
Quite cold. I basted up the dress and went up and fitted it and

went up to Lodge* this evening. It was awfully cold in the Lodge room and I am toasting myself out over the register now. Laura was up to a Young Peoples meeting. I certainly enjoy the Lodge the best of anything I ever attended. We practiced for the degree work tonight. Its lovely.

Mar. 8. Tuesday evening 10:30.
Here I am just setting sponge for bread. Just got home from an Institute meeting.** It was very interesting as we had the school teachers (one a man) teaching us to do that new weaving on cardboard forms. They do caps bags belts scarfs with wools and they sure are pretty. I must get busy. Laura went back to Barss Corner on a visit today coming home tomorrow. So I rode up with Gordon to the Post Office met Mrs Jefferson & Miss Carver (our teacher) there and walk with them to Institute. Yesterday I washed and was up to Roys K. in the afternoon working at Freeloves dress and then in the evening I was up to the Oddfellows feed. Ham & corn chowders and all kinds of cake and then band music speeches & toasts. It was 12 when I got home some unholy hours for an old Grandma. But I sure enjoyed it. There was about 100 there. We had 70 at the tables at one time. Two large Birthday cakes. The Oddfellows was decorated in red & white and the Rebeccas in pink & green and the decorations were in those colors. Had 5 or 6 visitors from Bridgewater. Mr Ott was toastmaster. The weather is cold with lots of snow. Good sleighing. Some rain Sunday. But more snow came.

Mar. 14. Monday.
My Sister's Birthday. How time travels on. Quite a fine day. But cold with plenty of snow yet. I finished Freeloves dress last week took it up to her and she was pleased and gave me $1.00 for making it for her. I was up there several times last week as she is not very well but up around. Laura & I went up to Mrs Pennys Saturday evening and I saw Mr Lade. His housekeeper had left him that evening just walked out on him and his little Boy is coming on with measles. So I told him if Mr Chesley was

---

*   Rebecca Lodge was a women's auxiliary to the Independent Order of Odd Fellows, a volunteer service organization.
**   Women's Institute.

agreed I'd come with him for a few days until he could locate some one else. So he came down on Sunday and talked with the Boss and I went up in the afternoon and am here now. The measles came out on the little chap today. He is pretty sick. But easy to care for. I had lots of callers all day.

[Laura went back to the Chesley's in March and then agreed to go with the Anglican minister, Mr. Ott, who had moved from New Germany to Chester. By the fall of 1938 she had returned to the Penney household.]

Oct. 10, 1938. Thanksgiving Day.
Quite a fine day with cold winds. I have been neglecting my diary but must jot down a few happenings. No doubt we have much to be thankful for and should count our blessings often for health enough to be around and able to work and earn. For Peace when war was so near. For safety from that terrible storm and many more Blessings. We had a nice Thanksgiving service at our Church last evening. Mr Veinot spoke nicely. The Church was decorated and full of people. His Father Mother Sister and Aunt Mellinda was there I spoke a few words to them after service. We had another service at the Church last Friday which was very sad as it was the funeral of ... one of our best church members quite our best one as she had been our leading singer and had been the President of the Guild and will be greatly missed. She leaves a husband and three grown up daughters .... They had a lovely home one of the best in N.G. and plenty of money as her Uncle had died about a year ago and left them considerable of a fortune. And [her husband] owns a small box mill and she did most of his business for him. But she had been sick now for two years with some kind of nervous trouble. The doctors couldn't find any cause for it. Told her to keep going and forget about it but she just couldn't as she complained a lot about a pain in her head. Told her troubles to every one and her family did not think it was serious as she was trying to do her own work lately. But felt worse Wednesday. So her husband went to look for help. Did not get any one but was home to dinner. She did a little washing and all the house work cooked dinner was up to the Post Office before dinner and seemed like

usual. When her husband came home at dark, the house was cold and no one around. But on the table was a note saying "Look in well." He rushed up to the Hall where the Band was holding a Supper and got help and down in the cellar well they found her drounded. It was a terrible shock to everyone as she was the very last person in New Germany one would have suspected it of. She must have lost her mind all at once. She left a letter but gave no reason except she was afraid she was going insane from the pain in her head. Poor Poor Soul. I pity her so much. The funeral was a large one in our Church with lovely flowers and the full rites of the Church as Mr Veinot had to get permission from the Bishop. She had been such a good living woman and such a faithful Church Worker none better around here that we know of and a perfect lady and so sensible in every way .... They have been doing a lot of washing since then using the water from that well. Can you imagine it. I can't .... she said in her letter that her husband was good to her in every way and she had everything to live for except health and she couldn't endure the agony any longer. Mr. Penny is still with us but very low. Saturday night and Sunday he talked all the time or moaned or raved about something. But today he just moans and shakes his head. Yesterday he ate Porrage and cracker and tea and some soup. But today he only takes a bit of water. Begs so to die lately and can't help himself in any way. His daughter in law (Lois) cares for him the very best. Is always around and he gets all the care he needs or wants. She is a born nurse. Mrs Penny is very feeble some days and we are so afraid of her having a stroke or falling. But she is so nervous and can't keep quiet and bothers herself about every little thing. Yesterday Sunday Mr Kent took her for a long drive and then took her down to Church in the evening. She got too tired so today she slept quite a lot and was very shaky. We had roast deer meat for dinner. But it wasn't good. So I did not enjoy it. I was over to Mrs Silvers a few minutes and got an ice cream for my treat.

Tuesday. 11th.
Another lovely day. The leaves are beautiful. I had a strange caller. Alvin Jodrey & his wife and little girl are home on a visit from the States. Going back Friday and right by my Sisters. What

a chance to go over. But I spoke of it and they didn't bite and I can hardly leave here just now yet. But oh I'd like so much to go. We had such a busy day. Washed and ironed and cooked and cleaned and Mrs Penny is not so well. Was in bed part of the day and we must watch her so she don't fall. Mr Penny gets awful bad spells so we think he is dying. Then he revived again ate a little and talked so much. Gave Jacob good advise and talked and prayed and moans and laments. Its got my nerves all gone flewy. I'm all ashake again. I've had lots of callers Abe Varner and Mr Ott. Mrs Johnson Grace Barkhouse Archie Penny and some of his boys and Mrs Lem Silver and several others. I'm so tired tonight. About eleven we had to send for Dr. MacDonald as he was so restless and he gave him a hypo and later he fell asleep.

1938 - Oct. 12. Wednesday.
This was one glorious fine day. Real warm and the trees and woods are beautiful. Too nice a day to leave this world. But Mr Penny passed away this evening at six o'clock. He prayed and talked to Jacob and Lois all last evening and was so restless. So the doctor came at eleven and gave him a hypo. So he never awoke but went unconscious and today he just laid there and breathed shorter and shorter until it stopped. Went out so easy. Lottie and I were washing supper dishes. There was no fuss. Lottie and I cried of course. Mrs Penny was in bed all day as she is very poorly and is failing fast. She is very forgetful. So she does not mind it very much. Her mind has failed more than her body. The undertaker was here until nearly ten and then they put him in his casket that he had made to order out of oak boards just varnished in the natural color. Its quite nice and much cheaper only cost 25 dollars. Several people called and they sent telegrams to different people. Mrs Kent stayed until eleven when we all went to bed. No doubt it felt good to Lois to get a nights rest.

Thursday.
Another fine day. Quite hot (80). We did a washing and cleaned up the whole house ironed made cookies pies and nut bread & biscuits. Had lots of callers. The house was full all were coming

and going to see the body. Mrs Penny is still in bed. Feels badly. At one o'clock this morning the telephone rang and I had to come down to answer it. I was rather creepy and scared. Had to go up the front stairs to call Lois as it was her son from Boston calling. Heard him plainly. I did not sleep very well.

Friday.
Another fine day not so hot. The funeral was at one o'clock so we had to hustle around with dinner at eleven. Austin Strutters from Bridgewater an old friend of the family was here. Lots of callers all forenoon. Flowers came and we had to unpack and arrange them. Lovely ones about 10 or 12 sprays & wreaths. Besides what came later. Mr. Ott came up but they are United so Mr Palmer had the service. Just a short one in the house. Then they all marched to the Church. He had arranged it all so it was done as he wished it. His four grandsons were Pall bearers. The school children marched next. The Church was packed and its a large church too. Mr Ott & Mr Veinot were up with Mr Palmer and had part in the service. Had lovely music & singing. "Oh God our help in ages past" "Rock of Ages" "Abide with me" and "Face to Face." Senator Duff was there also J.J. Kinley the M.P. Gordon Romkey M.P.P. All Liberals and his friends — Lawyer Robertson and many others. After the service the body was taken to Northfield and buried in the Family Lot at his old home. The hearse was drawn by his own horse and the hearse was his own too. Just the family went down and a few friends by cars. They got back by six. We were alone most of the evening. Mrs Penny was in bed thro it all. Mrs Kent stayed with her. She is kept under — nerve tablets. She did not see the body or casket and did not hear any of the ceremony at her own wish but we showed her the flowers. A large pillow came tonight from Sussex. Bruce Wilson. Gorgeous, the loveliest I ever saw.

Sunday was quiet. Mrs Penny still in bed. I was down to Mrs Rassil Feindel in the afternoon and listened to the Colored Childrens Program. Did not go to Church in the evening as I felt so tired. Monday we washed and worked around all day and Tuesday we ironed. Busy all the time. Lois is a great worker we cleaned the room (parlor) where Mr Penny had died in and it was quite a job as its large and had not had a thorough cleaning for twelve years since their daughter died in it. The Boys cleaned the Flu and it made a terrible mess. Had a full day of it and I was awfully tired. I sleep in the same room as Mrs Penny and she does not rest well so I must get up often with her. We are so afraid she will fall again.

Wednesday & Thursday.
Lois was looking over old papers of Mr Pennys and I did the usual work washed some more and put up curtains. I was to Rebecca Lodge in the evening. Had a nice time. Had to fill one of the Chairs as there wasn't many there. Made plans for an afternoon tea on Halloween.

Friday.
The usual work. Mabel and her husband was here and Lois went home with them in the evening so I'm left alone. I rather like it as Mrs Penny is better. Had a busy day Saturday baking and cleaning. Several people were in and up to see Mrs Penny. Sunday was quiet. Made soup for dinner. Just Jacob and I Lois and her husband & Wilfred the oldest son who is home from Mass. on a visit was here a while. I went to Baptist Church in the evening. Was quite disappointed as I expected to hear Mr Schurman. But he had to go to the Hospital for an operation so a Mr Corey preached. He used to be in Bridgewater when I was a girl. He was very good.

Monday.
Lois came up and we washed and did a dozen different things. Kents moved away. Such a fuss they were in and out a dozen times. Finely got away about three. It will be lonely. But after all they were nothing to me but just neighbors. But were real nice to Mrs Penny and Lois. Mrs Penny sits up around but does not gain much. Wilfred and his wife were here to tea. Lois went home.

Tuesday.
I ironed and baked bread. Had a lot of callers. Six women. Mrs Fred Oickle was here all evening. We had a terrible wind and

rain storm in the night. I did not sleep much. Wrote out 20 invitations to the Rebecca Tea.

Wednesday.
Another fine day. We sure are having a lovely Oct. All fine sunshiny warm weather except the storm Monday night. Its good to be alive these days and I'd like to be out in the woods. I envy the Sports. I'm too much shut in this Fall. I ironed some washed a little more made molasses cookies and a custard pie. Cooked salt tongues to dinner. Trotted up and down stairs a dozen times or more. Had Freelove Kaulback in a while and Meda Mossman and Mrs Randall Mosher. In the evening I was down to Mrs Norman Feindel and listened in the radio a half hour. Heard the good news of the Bluenose* beating the American boat. Wasn't that good. The Cup stays here for good now. Good for Capt. Angus Walters. They will make a fuss over him. Mrs Penny is still in bed. Gets up in her room a while each day.

Saturday Evening.
More nice weather. I'm tired tonight. Mrs. Wes. Hamm called up for me to come over and help decorate the Hall for our Halloween Tea Monday. But Jacob said it was his night out. So he went and I wasn't sorry as I didn't want to go. We had lots of callers Mrs Silver & Mrs Beeswanger was in this evening. Mrs Johnson & her sister this afternoon. Also Lois and Wilfred. Lottie went down to the Parish Hall to an afternoon tea and Pantry Sale. I didn't go. But I bought a cake and sent down milk & cream. Made $15.13. Last evening I was to Hemford with a carload of Rebeccas to a meeting. Had a nice time only late when we got back (nearly twelve). There was two carloads from here and one from Bridgewater. They put on some nice work. I met Mrs Coomer a woman I had met on the Boat going to St John about 7 years ago also a Mrs Martin whose boy was killed in a car accident a few months ago. They were from Bridgewater. Thursday night the United People from here and 5 or 6 different parts of the Circuit had a cabbage supper in the Hall here. Mrs

---

* A reference to the famous Nova Scotian schooner which consistently won the Challenge cup in the Fisherman's International Race of North America.

Penny gave me my ticket so Lottie and I went over long enough to get our Supper. But I did not enjoy it much. The food wasn't very good. They only made about 75 dollars. Then I came home and went across the street to a Guild meeting. That was rather dull But I learned how to knit a nice cover for a hot water bag. I'm busy every day — but can work to suit myself so I don't mind it so much. Mrs Penny is still upstairs but plans to come down tomorrow. Had a letter from Edna at last also one from Rose Rhyno.

Monday.
Quite full and cold with a little rain these two last days. I was home all day yesterday — was reading the Rainbow Trail again. Went down to Anglican Church in the evening. Was in to the Restaurant and got my winter coat. Charlotte is gone down home on a visit. I have no desire to go to Northfield now since Martha is gone. Mrs Penny came downstairs before dinner. Feels better but missed Mr Penny a lot. Finds it lonely and hard to keep quiet. Would like to be doing her work but she just can't. Today I did the usual work and this afternoon I went over to the Hall to an Afternoon tea. Was gone about an hour. Came home and wrote a letter to Mrs Wilson for Mrs Penny. I expect her down on a visit soon. I had a letter from Doug tonight. He plans to come home in a few weeks time. So I may not be here much longer than the 12 or 13th. I'm getting along better lately as Jacob treats me better. But still I'd like to be in my own home ....

EPILOGUE: LAURA KAULBACK SLAUENWHITE

In December 1938 Laura and Doug moved back to their home in Falkland Ridge. During the Second World War Doug got a steady job in Halifax and could afford to 'keep' his mother in her home. Yet, loneliness and sickness continued to preoccupy her thoughts. In Laura's case illness served as a metaphor for the unsatisfactory situation in which she found herself.* Even after she managed to return to her home, reality failed to conform to her domestic ideal. The doctrine of separate spheres sanctioned only one acceptable role for adult women: wife and mother. With nearly 50 years of life remaining after the death of her husband, Laura seemed at a loss in developing a new 'place' for herself.

In 1944, Doug brought his city-bred wife to the Falkland Ridge homestead. Laura's diary entries for the following years were rather perfunctory and indicate that she was not particularly happy. Although back in her old place, it was, after all, another woman's home. In 1950 at the age of 70 she recorded receiving her first Old Age Pension cheque. It was her only source of independent income. Ironically, this income paid for care in a nursing 'home' where Laura spent the last 14 years of her life and where she died in 1976 at the age of 96.

---

* Carroll Smith Rosenberg, "The Hysterical Woman: Sex Roles and Role Conflict in Nineteenth-Century America," in *Disorderly Conduct: Visions of Gender in Victorian America* (New York, 1986), pp. 197-216.

AFTERWORD

In publishing these chronicles of Nova Scotia women, we were conscious of the historical context which motivated us. The women's movement which had transformed our lives also aroused our curiosity about how earlier generations of women made life choices and perceived their condition. Would their diaries and autobiographical letters reveal something we could define as women's culture? Did our foremothers themselves recognize that they lived in a separate sphere with their own ways of seeing and evaluating the world around them? If so, how did they feel about their situation? And how did their sense of identity and purpose change over time? We tried not to impose preconceived intellectual patterns upon the documents, but, of course, it was impossible not to do so. The very questions we asked betrayed our biases; and our consciousness of the transformation in women's lives over the past two hundred years enabled us find meaning both in and between the lines.

Women's private chronicles offer valuable clues to understanding women's culture in earlier times. Carroll Smith-Rosenberg, who has examined women's letters and diaries in the United States, argues that in her research she found a female world of "great emotional strength and intensity." It was, she continued:

> a world of intimacy, love, erotic passion. Uniquely female rituals drew women together during every stage in their lives, from adolescence through courtship, marriage, childbirth and child-rearing, death and mourning. Women revealed their deepest feelings to one another, helped one another with the burdens of housewifery and motherhood, nursed one another's sick, and mourned for one another's dead. It was a world in which men made only a shadowy appearance. Living in the same society, normally part of the same culture (bourgeois, farming, or working

class), certainly members of the same family, women and men experienced the world in radically different ways. Female rituals rigorously excluded male kith and kin, rituals so secret that men had little knowledge of them, so pervasive that they patterned women's lives from birth to death.*

Viewed from this perspective, tracing the contours of women's culture as it changed over time becomes central to writing women's history and to understanding our present condition. It is also a much more rewarding task than trying to assess the few women who appear in the public sphere dominated by men. It is important to note here that women's culture is not a reductionist model that explains away differences among women. Instead the concept serves as a tool to alert researchers to the unique experiences of women in various class and cultural contexts and offers a rationale for studying the specific reality of women in Nova Scotia.

It is our contention, then, that women and men in the past have occupied separate social and intellectual territories. Even if they shared geographical space, their interpretation of what happened in that space differed, sometimes profoundly. This, we argue, is especially the case in the period covered by our chroniclers. Indeed, in the eighteenth and nineteenth centuries gender roles became so self-contained that the doctrine of separate spheres was articulated to describe and preserve the distinct destinies of women and men. While men occupied the public world of politics and business, women's place, it was argued, was in the private sphere, where the virtues of purity, piety, submissiveness and domesticity prevailed.**

One of the clearest expressions of that doctrine found anywhere in the English-speaking world was delivered by the Reverend Robert Sedgewick before the Young Men's Christian Association in Halifax in November 1856.*** "Woman is the

---

* Carroll Smith-Rosenberg, *Disorderly Conduct: Visions of Gender in Victorian America* (New York, 1985), p. 28.
** Barbara Welter. "The Cult of True Womanhood, 1800-1860," *American Quarterly*, Vol. 18 (Summer 1966), pp. 151-74.
*** *The Proper Sphere and Influence of Woman in Christian Society.* A lecture delivered by Reverend Robert Sedgewick before the Young Men's Christian Association, Halifax, Nova Scotia, November 1856, reprinted in Ramsay Cook and Wendy Mitchinson, eds., *The Proper Sphere* (Toronto, 1976), pp. 8-34.

complement of man," he argued, and the "sphere of woman is home and whatever is co-relative with home in the social economy." In her role as daughter, sister, wife, mother, teacher, friend, member of the church and messenger of mercy, Sedgewick maintained, a woman found her true vocation. Most women in Nova Scotia in the 1850s would have agreed that this was an adequate description of their relational context. Sedgewick, however, was not indulging in descriptive analysis. For him, and almost certainly for the young men in his audience, this was a prescriptive injunction designed to keep women from following in the footsteps of their more radical sisters in the United States where 'women's rights' in the public sphere had become a lively topic of debate. Such a debate was also relevant in Nova Scotia and would become even more so in the changing conditions of the second half of the nineteenth century. In that period, not only were women excluded from the franchise but also from the emerging professions of medicine, law and engineering. More importantly, they were excluded from the boardrooms of corporate capitalism which defined the culture of the new industrial order.

The women's movement as it developed in nineteenth century North America was largely focused on breaking down the barriers that denied women access to the political and economic structures which increasingly governed their lives. Predictably, equal rights feminism was embraced by only a minority of middle class women who were most constrained by the 'spherical' doctrine and who usually received little more than ridicule for their efforts to secure equality for women in the public sphere. By the end of the nineteenth century, women began to turn the doctrine of separate spheres back upon men, arguing that they had a special public role to play in preserving and protecting the private sphere which was being undermined by the values of the new industrial age. Such maternal feminist arguments were more difficult to challenge than equal rights feminism, at least for those who subscribed to the doctrine of separate spheres.

A few of our diarists — most notably Mathilda Churchill — invoked maternal feminism to justify their public ambitions.

Although women like Ella Liscombe were conscious of their disadvantaged position in the work place, none of our diarists used the language of women's rights. Most women in Nova Scotia, it seems, remained outside of the public discourse about their place in society. Nevertheless, women's private writings and daily activities reflected the transformation occurring in the public world and revealed their strategies for coping with a drastically altered domestic realm. There was, of course, no place like home for any of our chroniclers but what took place in the home changed dramatically between the eighteenth and early twentieth centuries.

Tamara Hareven has brought to our attention the extent to which particular concepts of family time, nurtured in pre-industrial rural settings, were adapted and idealized in urban industrial ones; how the well worn rhythms of the household became consoling rituals in the paid work place; and how women's roles in family and community were creatively reproduced over time in vastly different circumstances.* Thus, while fathers, husbands and sons were incorporated into the wage economy, women, particularly married women, continued to work in the unpaid family economy. Although this cultural continuity may have suited patriarchal husbands and was easily exploited by greedy businessmen, it also reflected the desperate attempt by women to emerge from the trauma of social change with something that they valued still intact. That the doctrine of separate spheres and the cult of domesticity ultimately failed to serve women very well in the twentieth century does not mean that it was always an unworthy survival strategy. Nor was it imposed upon women without their active participation. It is therefore important to examine the goals that motivated women to subscribe to the doctrine of separate spheres and determine what behaviour, institutions and values characterized that sphere.

* Tamara K. Hareven, *Family Time and Industrial Time* (Cambridge, 1982).

In order to discuss women's culture, or more correctly, women's cultures, it is necessary to learn a new vocabulary and to see phenomena from different perspectives. Even such fundamental concepts as 'time' and 'space' take on new meanings in relation to women's lives.* We can understand how time and space interact for Nova Scotia women when we consider the ideal place of women in pre-industrial society: childhood and adolescence in a father's home; marriage and motherhood in a husband's home; widowhood in a son's home. In each stage of life women were assigned a space identified by the male head of household. Major turning points in women's lives were defined by the change in home ownership and often, though not always, by a change in domicile. The roles of daughter, wife/mother and widow reflect 'family time' and were perceived in relation to father, husband and son. These roles, in turn, were constrained by specific events in 'women's time,' most notably menstruation, motherhood and menopause. Such concepts, deeply rooted in social and biological reality, were profoundly altered by the values and structures of the new industrial economy. The family was replaced by the factory as the locus of production and biological rhythms were disciplined to meet new notions of time and purpose in human existence.

The extent to which nineteenth century prescriptions — taken for granted by our 'gentlewomen' — were losing their appeal for women in the twentieth century can be seen in their increasing irrelevance for our 'new women' chroniclers. While family and community relationships still dominated women's culture, they no longer sustained women's material well-being to the same degree as had been the case in the pre-industrial period. The ever-widening gap between prescription and reality helps to account for the negative tone which characterizes our later diaries. By the 1930s the possibility of living exclusively in a self-fulfilling domestic sphere had become increasingly remote.

* For a fuller discussion of women's culture in the Nova Scotia context, see Margaret Conrad, "'Sundays always make me think of home': Time and Place in Canadian Women's History," in *Not Just Pin Money: Selected Essays on the History of Women's Work in British Columbia*, ed., Barbara K. Latham and Roberta Pazdro (Victoria, 1984), pp. 1-16.

Nevertheless, Nova Scotia women strove, sometimes at enormous psychological cost, to maintain their place in the home.

The key to understanding the changing way in which women describe their circumstances can be found in the diaries of the 'comers and goers.'* In the heady atmosphere of the late nineteenth century, the opportunities for women seemed endless. New female professions of teaching, nursing and office work as well as expanding opportunities in domestic and factory work put women in the forefront of revolutionary change. Rebecca Byles had predicted in the 1780s that women — with their superior education and sensibilities — would soon surpass men — preoccupied as they were with profits and status — in their public achievements. Such a situation was not to be. Capitalist values rather than women invaded the political world and the domestic sphere was transformed from a productive economic unit to a vehicle for consuming the products of the new factories.

Nova Scotian women's attitudes were determined by the larger cultural framework in which they functioned. Whether it is the genteel Rebecca Byles and practical Louisa Collins discussing their most recent literary 'finds' from Britain and the United States or secretary Ella Liscombe and widow Laura Slauenwhite waxing enthusiastic about the latest Hollywood movie or Boston radio program, women in Nova Scotia were part of that vast bourgeois North Atlantic world which was moving toward greater uniformity in its prescriptions for both women and men. At the same time, it was difficult for Nova Scotia women to follow prescriptions laid down in more prosperous centres. As the region became increasingly marginal to the North American industrial heartland, it fell behind in opportunities and social services. Underdevelopment, in turn, led to outmigration and eventually to dependence on federal transfer payments. The impact of this process on families and communities has yet to be fully explored. Nevertheless, it is clear that economic pressures forced many Nova Scotians back on family and community while at the same time placing impossible stresses on these structures. Women in their family and community roles

* For an excellent overview of this period in the larger Canadian context see, Beth Light and Joy Parr, eds., *Canadian Women on the Move* (Toronto, 1983).

shouldered a tremendous burden in the great transformation from pre-industrial to industrial society and its peculiar manifestation in the Maritime Provinces.

Our chroniclers reflect the changing conditions for women in Nova Scotia more directly than we had anticipated. The five gentlewomen represented here, except for Anna Winslow who died at nineteen, were mistresses of their own households before they reached the age of twenty-five. They all bore children, two raising families of nine or more. While women in colonial society rarely left their domestic spheres, they did not opt for a life of idleness. For the vast majority of Nova Scotian women prior to 1850, the organic round of work, play, education, courtship, commerce and community all took place within the farm and family context. That men, women and children had their 'place' in colonial society is clearly revealed by one of our diarists."I have left them all seated round the table at ther domestic imployments," Louisa Collins wrote in 1815, "sum sowing, and others knitting, and pappa at the head reading — I must hurry to return to my work or I shall be indisgrace ...." Her father's position at the head of the table reflected the patriarchal role that he played in the family. All gentlewomen chroniclers had a male protector as well as a complex and supportive community of sisters, aunts and female friends to help them move confidently through the stages of life marked by familiar rituals and unpredictable challenges. We know, of course, that all colonial women were not as fortunate as our diarists in this regard but conditions of life were such that women outside of a sustaining domestic circle would have had difficulty even keeping a diary.

By the second half of the nineteenth century, the new values associated with railways, factories and cities had begun to undermine pre-industrial family and community structures. Our 'comers and goers' all married and all had children but at least two were thirty years old before they married and only one had more than four children. Three worked outside the home at some point in their lives. All five women travelled, some for great distances, as part of their survival strategies. These women struggled to maintain the domestic ideal passed on to them by their mothers and grandmothers but increased mobility and new ways of making a living were already beginning to transform women's sphere both in the home and outside of it.

Our twentieth century chroniclers document the extent to which conditions for women had changed. Although many women in Nova Scotia may have continued to live in happy domestic settings, not one of our twentieth century documents is written by a woman who lived in the conventional patriarchal family so idealized by the doctrine of separate spheres. None of our 'new women' had a resident husband and three of the five never married. Obviously, domesticity was becoming increasingly elusive and less attractive as a lifetime goal. Moreover, 'home' in the twentieth century bore little resemblance to its counterpart in the eighteenth century. By the interwar years, women's work in the home was largely reduced to care-giving, household management and consumerism. It was unpaid and performed in isolation from other adults. The sense of satisfaction and companionship that in earlier times had accompanied work within the home had been eroded to the point where women's self-esteem was dangerously undermined. Men's work, in contrast, was paid, social (including a subordinate rank of young women to do menial tasks) and removed from the world of children and the elderly.

Most women participated in both the public and private economies, their involvement determined by age, class and marital status. Their peripatetic movement between the two spheres, rather than being seen as a measure of their flexibility and resourcefulness, was used as an argument to deny them a full share in the wealth and power derived from the industrial order. Thus, no matter what station a woman held in society, she was denied a forum in which she could reach her full potential. And, no 'place' offered a woman the power she needed to make her traditional rituals and responsibilities relating to child-rearing, care-giving and community meaningful in the larger human context.

The disjunction between what can be and what is has been the driving force of western civilization for as long as we have a collective memory. That women's dissatisfaction was eventually focused into a movement to change their status brings us back to where we began: the urge to hear the voices of our female ancestors who have so long been considered unworthy of being heard. If we listen we can hear them express many of the concerns about home and family that still preoccupy us and still demand resolution.

PHOTO CREDITS

Anna Green Winslow, Alice Morse Earle ed., *Dairy of Anna Green Winslow: A Boston Girl of 1771* (Boston, 1894).

Rebecca Byles, oil portrait byRobert Field, courtesy of the Nova Scotia Museum.

Louisa Collins, Ferry Terminal, Cole Harbour Road, courtesy of the Dartmouth Heritage Museum.

Eliza Ann Chipman, frontispiece to the published edition of Eliza Chipman's diary, 1855.

Margaret Michener, view of Hantsport from Mount Denson, courtesy of the Public Archives of Nova Scotia.

Mathilda Faulkner Churchill, courtesy of the Acadia Archives, Vaughan Memorial Library, Acadia University.

Annie Rogers Butler, courtesy of the Yarmouth County Museum.

Hannah Richardson, Yarmouth Harbour, courtesy of the Yarmouth County Museum.

Mary MacDonald MacDougall, courtesy of Peter MacDougall.

Margaret Connell, view of Pictou from MacKenzie's Point drawn by W.O. Carlisle, engraved by E. Harberer for *Canadian Illustrated News*, 27 July, 1872.

Rebecca Ells, courtesy of Mary Corkum.

Margaret Marshall Saunders, courtesy of the Acadia Archives, Vaughan Memorial Library, Acadia University.

Elizabeth Hall, courtesy of the Dalhousie University Archives.

Ella Liscombe, courtesy of Robert Morgan, The Beaton Institute, University College of Cape Breton.

Laura Slauenwhite, courtesy of Douglas and Gladys Slauenwhite.